Russell Kolts is a licensed clinical psychologist and professor at Eastern Washington University, USA. He has many years' experience in treating anger problems and has pioneered the use of CFT in working with anger, which he has applied in private practice and in prison settings.

T0301147

Also by Russell Kolts

The Compassionate Mind Approach to Managing Your Anger

Living with an Open Heart

CFT Made Simple

THE ANGER WORKBOOK

Discover the Strength to Transform Your Anger Using Compassion Focused Therapy

RUSSELL L. KOLTS

ROBINSON

ROBINSON

First published in Great Britain in 2024 by Robinson

Copyright © Russell Kolts, 2024

Illustrations by Liane Payne

1 3 5 7 9 10 8 6 4 2

The moral right of the author has been asserted.

All rights reserved.
No part of this publication may be reproduced, stored in a retrieval system, or transmitted, in any form,
or by any means, without the prior permission in writing of the publisher, nor be otherwise circulated in any
form of binding or cover other than that in which it is published and without a similar condition including
this condition being imposed on the subsequent purchaser.

A CIP catalogue record for this book is available from the British Library.

ISBN: 978-1-47214-487-4

Typeset in Palatino by Initial Typesetting Services, Edinburgh
Printed and bound in Great Britain by Bell and Bain Ltd, Glasgow

Papers used by Robinson are from well-managed forests and other responsible sources.

Robinson
An imprint of
Little, Brown Book Group
Carmelite House
50 Victoria Embankment
London EC4Y 0DZ

An Hachette UK Company
www.hachette.co.uk

www.littlebrown.co.uk

Contents

Foreword

It is fourteen years since Dr Russell Kolts published his highly successful book *The Compassionate Mind Approach to Managing Your Anger Using Compassion Focused Therapy*. He has continued to research, help people with anger problems and travel the world presenting his influential work on anger. Here is a fresh opportunity to explore how compassion can help us with anger, in a new and updated workbook format. It brings in a number of new ideas and ways of conceptualising and working with anger that will be of immense value to readers. In addition to the workbook format designed to engage readers in a more active process of applying compassion to work with their anger, this book also explores a greater variety of the ways in which anger can play out for different people, including a focus on anger which is repressed rather than acted out, and the substantial role grief can play in anger problems.

A key question is 'Why compassion, given that there are many approaches for helping people with anger?' The simple answer is that compassion evolved from caring behaviour, and caring behaviour has a fundamental effect on how our brains, bodies and minds work. There are now many brain studies that show that when we're angry certain areas of our brain light up, whereas when we are caring very different systems in our brain light up. Compassion focusing and compassion training offer a way in which we can help our brains slow down when stressed, and give us an opportunity to behave helpfully not harmfully. This workbook guides us through these processes.

We have always understood that compassion is very important for our wellbeing. If you are stressed or upset, it's always better to have kind, helpful and supportive people around you rather than critical, rejecting or disinterested folk. However, it's not only this common sense that tells us about the value of kindness and compassion. Recent advances in the scientific study of compassion and kindness have greatly advanced our understanding of how compassionate qualities of the mind really do influence our brains, bodies and social relationships, as well as affect our health and wellbeing. Yet, despite this common sense, ancient wisdom and modern knowledge, we live in an age that can make compassion for ourselves and for others difficult. Ours is the world of seeking the competitive edge of achievement and desire, of comparison to others who may be doing better, of dissatisfaction, self-disappointment and self-criticism.

Research has now revealed that such environments actually make us unhappy and that mental ill health is on the increase, especially in younger people. As Dr Kolts helps us to understand, frustration, irritability and anger are very common symptoms of the environments we're living in today. Be it irritation with long queues, overly complex gadgets we can't work out how to use, traffic jams, whining children or what we see as incompetent politicians – the list of things that wind us up seems endless.

If *feeling* angry or irritable and stressed is not enough, we can act on these emotions and then justify our actions: 'They had it coming to them; they shouldn't have done X or Y.' And, of course, we label the people we're angry with as 'dumb', 'stupid', 'a pain', or 'thoughtless and unfeeling'. There can also be subtle messages in society that anger is about being macho – a 'no-nonsense' person. In fact, that kind of attitude can lie behind quite serious violence, in which people feel they have a need to save face, get their own back, and not be humiliated or disrespected. In some sectors of society, the fear of humiliation is so profound that explosive anger and violence are part of everyday life.

In fact, it can be easy to confuse aggressiveness with assertiveness, and when we do so, we can cause much hurt and upset to others. As Dr Kolts points out, anger is a volatile, impulsive and not very clever emotion. If we just go with its flow, we can regret acting on it in the days, weeks or years to come. Anger also has a habit of being quite 'sticky', in the sense that we tend to ruminate about the things that made us angry – we go over and over them in our minds. We don't stop to think what that process might be doing to our heads and bodies. For some people, feelings of anger can be quite frightening, so they seek to suppress these emotions in order to avoid conflict. Others can become self-critical and judge themselves for becoming angry or irritable and for not being nice or lovable people. So, we're critical of ourselves and think that by being angry with ourselves, we will stop being angry! Indeed, our society has a habit of blaming and shaming if we seem to be struggling with our emotions.

So why are we so susceptible to frustration and anger, and why are they seemingly on the increase in modern-day society? Dr Kolts uses his wealth of knowledge and experience to guide our understanding and to help us recognise that, actually, many of our emotions are the result of a very long evolutionary history. The emotions we experience today were really designed to deal with immediate threats in the jungles and savannahs of our ancestors' environment and aren't so well adapted for the modern world. Nor do our emotions do so well when our angry minds use our new brains' capacity for thinking and rumination, locking us into anger. Humans are the only animals that have the capacity to sit under a tree ruminating about how angry they are because of some event or other, planning vengeance or just keeping themselves in an angry state. We can even be angry about what we feel – angry about feeling anxious, angry because we feel depressed, angry because we feel tired all the time, angry because we're just exhausted. So the way we think about and ruminate about the stresses in our lives can really do a number on us. Understanding this and being able to stand back from our emotions allows us to see that our vulnerability to anger is not our fault at all. After all, we didn't design our brains with their capacity for emotions like anxiety and anger. Nor did we design our capacity for complex thinking, which can actually make our experience of anger and frustration all the more intense. And we didn't choose our backgrounds or our genes, both of which can make us more susceptible to anger. This is a very important message in compassionate mind training and compassion focused therapy, because compassion begins with developing a deep understanding of just how tricky our brains are and a recognition that their functions may be stuck in past ways of operating. These two realisations may seem strange at first. But once we recognise how difficult our emotions can be, we can stand back from them and feel compassion for the difficulties we experience.

So, given that our brains have been designed by evolution and shaped by the environments we grew up and live in (none of which we choose), what can we do to help ourselves when we become angry? First, we can learn to pay attention to how our minds work, and become mindful and observant of the feelings associated with anger. In this helpful book, Dr Kolts shows how people have learned to be very sensitive to the situations that can trigger our anger, such as frustrations and minor criticisms.

If we are to face anger and to really work with it, then the relationship we have with ourselves is very important. If we are critical and harsh with ourselves, then our inner worlds are not comfortable places to inhabit. Feeling ashamed and being self-critical, self-condemning or self-loathing can undermine our confidence, making us feel worse. People who generally feel confident and like themselves are much less prone to anger than those who feel unsure about themselves, are easily victimised by others and are vulnerable to rejection.

In addition, of course, anger isn't just directed outwards; it can be directed inwards, towards ourselves, and this really does cause difficulties. Sadly, many people today are self-critical, and when things go wrong or they make mistakes, rather than try to be helpful and support-ive of themselves, they react by becoming frustrated and angry with themselves. This is not a good way to deal with anger because, as Dr Kolts outlines, we are actually adding more fuel to the fire of our threat system. In contrast, self-compassion is a way of being with ourselves and all of our emotions (uncomfortable as they may be) without self-condemnation. Instead, we learn to experience them with support and encouragement. Research shows that the more compassionate we are towards ourselves, the happier we are and the more resilient we become when faced with difficult events in our lives. In addition, we are better able to reach out to others for help and feel more compassionate towards other people as well.

Compassion can sometimes be viewed as being a bit 'soft' or 'weak', as if it means letting your guard down or not trying hard enough. These notions are a major mistake because, on the contrary, compassion requires the strength to be open to and tolerate our painful feelings, to face up to our own problematic emotions and difficulties. Sometimes it's anger that hides us from more painful things and it is *compassion* that gives us the courage to face them. Compassion does not mean turning away from emotional difficulties or discomfort, or trying to get rid of them. It is *not* a soft option. Rather, compassion provides us with the courage, honesty and commitment to learn to cope with the difficulties we face, and alleviates our anger and other difficulties. It enables us to do things for ourselves that help us to flourish (however, not as a demand or requirement). Compassion enables us to live our lives more fully and contentedly.

In this book, Dr Kolts brings to bear his many years of experience as a clinical psychologist, long-time meditator and psychotherapist working with people experiencing a variety of different emotional difficulties. He has a special interest in working with people in prison for anger-related behaviours. He also brings his experience of using compassion focused therapy in the treatment of anger. In this book he outlines a model of compassion that seeks to stimulate and build your confidence so that you can engage with your anger. You will learn how to develop a supportive friendship with yourself that helps you when times are difficult. Dr Kolts guides you to develop compassionate motivations, compassionate attention, compassionate feelings, compassionate thinking and compassionate behaviour. You will learn about the potential power of developing compassionate imagery, focusing on creating a compassionate sense of yourself, and drawing on your own inner wisdom and benevolent qualities. These are the qualities you are most likely to feel when you're feeling calm or are showing concern for others. Learning breathing techniques that help you slow down and engage with these qualities can be very helpful when frustration, anger and rage wash through you like a storm. Using different compassionate images, you will discover that your compassion focus can be visual or aural (for example, imagining a compassionate voice speaking to you when you need it), and this can be especially useful in enabling you to get in touch with your internal compassionate feelings and desires at times of distress.

The approach that Dr Kolts takes is called a compassionate mind approach because, when we engage compassion, it can influence our attention, thoughts, feelings and behaviour – all the functions of the mind. The compassionate-mind approach outlined by Dr Kolts draws on many other well-developed approaches, including those of Eastern traditions such as Buddhism. In addition, compassionate-mind approaches – especially those that form part of compassion focused therapy – are rooted in a scientific understanding of how our minds work. Undoubtedly, over the years our understanding of the science will change and improve. One thing that doesn't change, however, is the fact that kindness, warmth and understanding go a long way towards helping us. In these pages you will find these qualities in abundance, so you, too, can learn to be understanding, supportive and kind, but also engaging and courageous when working with your anger.

Many suffer silently and secretly with a whole range of anger and frustration problems. Some people are ashamed of these emotions or angry about feeling them; others can be fearful that anger and frustration will get the upper hand. Sadly, shame stops many of us from reaching out for help. But by opening our hearts to compassion, we can take the first steps towards dealing with our difficulties in new ways. My compassionate wishes go with you on your journey.

Professor Paul Gilbert, PhD, FBPsS, OBE

Introduction

Welcome to *The Anger Workbook*. In this book we'll explore how to use compassion focused therapy to help you manage your anger. As a reader, I've sometimes had the tendency to skip introductions, so I sort of assume many of my readers will, too. But I hope you read this one.

Although this is a book, my goal is to make the process as interactive as possible, so you feel like you're not alone in this journey. Because you're not. We're on this journey together – and I mean this in a literal sense. I've struggled with anger and irritability myself over the course of my life (which I've talked about in a TEDx talk titled 'Anger, Compassion, and What it Means to Be Strong', available for viewing online), and since some of that struggle is rooted in how my personality works, I've learned that working with anger is a journey that never really ends. Things go smoothly for a while, and then new stressors hit (like a global pandemic!) that require me to pay more attention to managing my anger, so I can keep showing up as the sort of person I want to be. It's not a light-switch that flips on and off – it's a way of life we cultivate. And like everything we cultivate, a compassionate way of life requires attention and maintenance. This book is meant to show you how to build and maintain such a life.

People who struggle with anger often relate to it – both the feelings of anger and the behaviour we've engaged in when angry – in some common but unhelpful ways. One example is avoidance. We may find ourselves pretending nothing happened, ignoring that we have a problem at all. This avoidance can be triggered by another unhelpful way of relating to anger: shame. Shame is a sense that 'I am bad' (or 'a bad person', 'a bad parent', 'a bad partner') or that 'there's something wrong with me'. Shame sometimes follows experiences of anger, for example, when we notice we've acted in angry ways that have hurt people we care about. For some of us, even noticing angry feelings coming up can trigger shame.

When it comes to working with emotions, shame generally isn't very helpful. This sense that 'there is something wrong with me' can be so painful that we find ourselves reflexively doing anything we can to stop that feeling – so we avoid, we blame, we ignore, we rationalise. While *taking responsibility* for working with our anger is critical, shaming ourselves for struggling with it not only doesn't help us take responsibility, it often shuts us down – preventing us from doing something about it. Beating ourselves up for struggling with anger doesn't help.

Another not-so-helpful way of relating to anger can involve just acting it out or even clinging to it as a source of strength. Anger is the emotional component of the 'fight' in 'fight or flight' – it evolved to motivate us to fight off physical threats, to act quickly and decisively, our full attention locked onto the perceived danger. This means anger can feel very *powerful* in us – it's literally preparing us to fight. This can be tricky, as we may find ourselves *enjoying* feeling powerful in this way. We may find ourselves clinging to anger or failing to recognise the negative effects anger-driven behaviour is causing in our lives.

Sometimes, when we act out in anger, it feels like a *win* – the other person backs down, and we get our way. In an immediate sense, maybe we did get our way, despite the harm caused in our relationship with that person. But if we want happy lives and good relationships with our partners, friends and co-workers, anger may win us the occasional battle, but it will soon have us well on our way to losing the war. This book is about learning how to win the battle *and* the war – being able to work effectively with the challenges in our lives while building strong relationships, earning people's respect and leading the sort of lives we want to lead.

I'm assuming that, if you're reading this book, you don't want to be someone that others fear, are intimidated by and avoid. As we go through the book, I'll sometimes ask you to think about 'the sort of person you want to be'. I'll sometimes suggest you consider the roles you'd like to play in the lives of the people you care about. The answers to these questions can help provide the motivation for us to *keep going* when things get hard, because they remind us *it's worth it*. They remind us that at the end of this road is a better life – for us and for those we care about.

Compassion and compassion focused therapy

The approach we're taking in this book is based on compassion focused therapy, drawn from the work of British psychologist Paul Gilbert.[1] I think a compassion-based approach is perfect for working with anger, for lots of reasons we'll unpack as we go. But the first reason has to do with the nature of compassion itself.

In the anger management groups I've run with men in prison settings, this is when the eye-rolling starts (literally!). These men had ideas about compassion they'd picked up from the culture – that compassion was something soft, fluffy and weak. That being compassionate meant being nice all the time, always giving people what they want, or not holding yourself or others accountable. They thought having compassion meant being gullible, vulnerable and easy to take advantage of.

These ideas about compassion are common, but they're wrong. In CFT (our abbreviation for compassion focused therapy), compassion is defined as *being sensitive to suffering and being motivated to alleviate and prevent it*. Compassion is about what we do when everything goes wrong, when things get hard, when we face things that scare us – even the things that may scare us about ourselves. It's about figuring out what to do. It's about *figuring out how to help*.

The courage and wisdom of compassion

We'll be exploring different aspects of compassion as we go, but as it is core to the CFT approach, let's unpack it a bit more now. In CFT, we see compassion as a motive, and like all motives, it involves two parts: an awareness of what needs to be done and the motivation to do it, and the skills and abilities to follow through. For example, if we're going to fulfil a motive to eat, we need to have the awareness that we need to eat and the motivation to do so (hence, the experience of *hunger*), but we also need to have the skills to acquire food. In this way, compassion involves both the sensitivity to notice suffering and desire do something about it, but it also requires us to have the knowledge and ability to follow through and do what is helpful. In this book, we'll explore how to help you increase your awareness of how anger works and how it can be challenging, connect with the compassionate motivation and courage to address it, and we'll work to develop the skills to be effectively compassionate in working with anger and other challenges – to know what would be helpful to do, and how to do it.

Whether or not you consider yourself a 'compassionate person', I think you'll find you are able to connect with it somewhat naturally – tapping into what we call *intuitive wisdom* in CFT. Imagine you get a call from someone you care very much about – maybe a family member or dear friend – who is very upset about having to go to hospital for some tests regarding a potentially serious medical condition. How would you respond to them? Would you shout at them and tell them not to be stupid? Or would you listen to them, try to understand their fear? Generally, most people would be sensitive to our friend's distress, try to understand it, and perhaps even want to help them. That's the first part of compassion.

The second part is the *action* – what would we *do* if faced with this situation? There are lots of things we might do. What do you think? If you found yourself thinking, 'I'd offer to go with them', that's an example of drawing upon the *intuitive wisdom* of compassion – knowing that it's a lot easier for us (or your friend) to be courageous in facing something scary when we have someone who cares for us there to support us. This *courage* is an important part of compassion as well. Compassion is about turning towards suffering, struggle and the things that scare us. Some people may have the idea that compassion is all about being nice or pleasant, but it's about having the courage to acknowledge suffering and struggle, the wisdom to know what would be helpful in addressing it, and the commitment to do it. That's why I often use the term 'true strength' when talking about compassion. It's not about appearing nice; it's about having the strength to face suffering and to do what's necessary to address it.

The strength of compassion is a good fit for working with anger. It can help us harness its helpful qualities, such as in helping alert us to injustice and provide us with energy to fuel appropriate assertive behaviour. It can also help us have the courage to be honest with ourselves in recognising that if our anger is uncontrolled, we have the potential to behave in ways that harm ourselves and others. Acknowledging this, compassion can give us the motivation to learn to manage our anger so that we behave helpfully and not harmfully. It can also help us refrain from beating ourselves up as we do this, recognising there are lots of reasons we may struggle with anger that we didn't choose or design, and also recognising that if we want to have good lives and relationships, it's our responsibility to learn how to manage our anger. This book is designed to help you do that.

Anger

Your anger isn't who you are. I think some of us who struggle can sometimes feel like we're defined by our anger. We can feel trapped in that angry place – spending hours, days, weeks or more caught in the grips of anger and irritability, even inadvertently feeding it in ourselves. Simmering in resentment, swimming in hostility, honing an ability to immediately spot all the problems that surround us. We live in a complicated world, and if we're looking for things to be angry about, we'll almost always find them (pro tip: this is also true if we go looking for other things – things for which to be grateful, beautiful moments and experiences, opportunities to help). We can find ourselves living in a way that is steeped in frustration, irritability and anger. Like *that's just who we are.*

It's not. Anger is just one of a range of emotions our brains are designed to produce. It isn't good. It isn't bad. But it can be a good or bad *fit* with the situations we face in our lives, and can set us up to respond in more or less helpful ways. We're going to spend time unpacking anger, investigating how it plays out in us and learning how to work with it in helpful ways. Instead of avoiding our anger, seeing it as something bad about us, or trying to get rid of it, we're going to learn to understand it, explore how it makes sense that we'd struggle with it, and take responsibility for building the sort of lives we want to have.

A note on evolution

Part of a compassionate approach to anger involves *understanding* it: where it comes from, how it works and why it works that way. CFT takes a science-based approach, and part of a scientific understanding of anger involves looking through the lens of evolution. So, for example, we'll explore anger as an emotion that evolved to help early humans survive in a very different version of the world than most of us live in today.

If you're nodding along, already perhaps imagining how anger makes sense in an evolutionary context, that's great. However, I live in the United States, where not everyone is comfortable with the theory of evolution – where some people take different approaches for understanding how we got here and how we came to be the way we are, often based in religion and spirituality. While I won't apologise for taking a scientific approach (because I'm a scientist), I also don't have an agenda around challenging anyone's spiritual beliefs, and I want people of all types and perspectives to be able to benefit from this workbook. So, if you're scientifically minded and are comfortable with evolution, you'll probably find yourself in familiar waters. If you're less comfortable with evolution – or even don't accept it at all – it's not a problem. All you'll need to do is accept that I'm a scientist writing from a scientific perspective (and not get offended every time I use terms like 'evolved'), even as you take a different perspective. You may even find that how I approach evolution here isn't really a challenge to your beliefs at all. For example, I've had many people who 'don't buy into evolution' tell me they have no problem acknowledging that some of our emotions are a better fit for earlier times in the human story, and sometimes a not-so-great fit for the modern world we find ourselves in right now.

Our approach

When it comes to working with anger, it's not just about the knowing – it's about the *doing*. There are lots of books (and videos and podcasts and . . .) that contain lots of good information about how to understand and work with emotions. I've written one of them – *The*

Compassionate Mind Approach to Managing Your Anger,[2] which makes a good companion to this book for those who'd like to supplement the workbook approach taken here with something a bit more didactic. One challenge with self-help resources is that it can be easy to engage with them in passive ways – reading or listening, perhaps nodding along, and then going back to our normal lives. If we do this, it's easy to end up maybe understanding things a bit better, but never really translating that understanding into new ways of behaving or different ways of being in the world.

My hope is that going through this workbook will be an *active* process for you. I'll do my best to create an interactive experience that can be directly applied to your life. Your job is to apply it. With that in mind, it'll work much better to take the book in bite-sized chunks, reflecting on and doing the exercises, and following through with the recommended daily practices, rather than passively reading through it and skipping over parts that involve you, well, *doing stuff*.

I get it – I've sometimes been the one who skipped parts of books that asked me to do some thinking or writing, or whatever. But I'm asking you to give it a shot. Because if you do – if you dive in and let compassion work on you – well, it just might help you change your life.

A trio of companions

One obstacle that's occasionally kept me from diving in deeply when doing something new is that, sometimes, I wasn't sure *how* to apply it. I wasn't sure exactly what I should be doing or how I should do it. I'd say to myself, 'I'll think about this a bit more and then come back to it . . .', which, as you might imagine, never actually happened.

In this book, when I present you with things to do, I'll usually give you a model of what doing it might look like, based on three companion readers who are working through the book alongside you. These companions aren't actual people – they're based on combinations of individuals I've worked with over the years (with identifying information changed for privacy's sake, of course). My hope is that you may see a bit of yourself reflected in their experiences, an understanding of different ways anger can play out for different people, and that they'll provide a useful model of how one might apply the concepts we'll be exploring.

Let's meet our companions now. Their descriptions are designed to provide enough information that they're relatable, without providing details so specific as to distract from the point of the book. This is a bit tricky. Optimally, I'd like this book to be helpful to people of all races, genders, sexual orientations, etc., even as I know I don't have a hope of representing the varied experiences different people have to face – issues that are very relevant to the topic of anger. So I'm going to do my best, and in understanding that my best probably sometimes won't be good enough, I'll invite you to *take what's helpful and leave the rest*. Let's introduce our companions:

James is a forty-five-year-old married male with two children: Aiden, a thirteen-year-old boy, and Jaime, a ten-year-old girl. James has struggled with anger and irritability for much of his life – anger that was modelled by his own father as he was growing up. Over time, James has observed the impact his anger has had on those close to him – particularly his wife and children – and experiences deep shame about this, even as he's struggled unsuccessfully to change it. James approaches this programme with a combination of motivation and trepidation – he very much wants to change but feels his prior efforts haven't been successful, and is sceptical as to whether anything will help.

Antwan is a seventeen-year-old boy who lives with his mother. Antwan's father abruptly left them when he was younger. Antwan has struggled with anger-related outbursts, both in the classroom and in some of his social relationships. While Antwan doesn't like some of the consequences of his anger, he also doesn't see it as a problem and, sometimes, he likes it. He has some resistance to working with his anger, partially because it was recommended by a female teacher, and sees the suggestion as an attack on his masculinity. Antwan reluctantly agreed to go through this programme at the request of his mother, who sees his potential and doesn't want his anger to interfere with his life and relationships.

Jordan is a twenty-eight-year-old single woman working in a corporate setting. Jordan grew up with a nurturing but passive father and a critical mother. Growing up, Jordan's mother made it clear that any expression of anger was unacceptable to the adults around her – it was communicated that this was not an appropriate way for girls to behave. Jordan was shaped by these messages, to the point that, as an adult, not only does she find herself unable to express anger (or, at times, able to be appropriately assertive), she feels ashamed upon noticing that she is *feeling* anger – taking it as a sign that something is wrong with her. Jordan has experience with depression and suffers from stress-related physical symptoms such as irritable bowel syndrome. She also has a strong tendency to criticise herself – blaming herself for things that aren't her fault and running herself down for perceived failures or flaws. Jordan found her way to this programme at the encouragement of a therapist she's seeing for depression, who felt that part of her healing process needed to involve learning to accept, work with and express her anger.

Using this book

This book is organised in relatively brief modules, each of which will present you with a bit of information or a practice and then invite you to relate this information to *your lived experience* through reflective questions and guided experiences. It's my hope that moving through the book will be a *co-created experience*, based on the meeting of two experts: I'm the expert on compassion focused therapy and you're the expert on you and your life. No one on earth is better qualified to explore how this material will apply best to *you*. My goal is to present the material in a way that sets you up to apply it to your life as seamlessly as possible. From personal experience, I know this is tough stuff. And because I know that, I want you to know I respect the step you're taking in deciding to actively work to manage your anger. It's worth it, I promise.

In the service of creating an active process, the book is peppered with reflective questions and practices. As I've mentioned, it's better to move through the book slowly, giving yourself space to pause, reflect and write in response to these prompts than to skip over them and keep reading. I've included space for you to write, but you may prefer to get a notebook or journal to write in so you aren't limited by space (this will be particularly important if you've purchased or borrowed the book for use on an e-reader).

Some readers may also find writing a struggle (or may just not enjoy writing very much). I don't want the writing to become an obstacle that keeps you from using the book, so if that's the case for you, you might consider some other way of organising and recording your thoughts – for example, by installing a free voice-recording app on your phone and speaking (and recording) your responses rather than writing them. The writing or other form of recording your responses has a purpose, by the way. Writing or communicating our responses requires us to *organise* the thoughts we're having about the material, helping us relate those thoughts to our lives, and making it more likely we'll remember and apply what we're learning. It also creates a record of our work we can return to, reminding ourselves what we've learned and providing an opportunity to lock back into step if something has disrupted our progress . . . we can always come back to the work we've done and continue from there. For those who are all-in, I've also provided a suggested practice schedule for engaging with the material on an organised, daily basis, beginning after you've finished working through Section I.

This book has been designed with the assumption that most readers will move through it in order, so there's a progression designed to gradually build your understanding of the CFT approach, of anger and how it can be tricky, and of how to apply CFT in working with your anger. Interspersed in this progression will be modules focused on things like motivation. Compassion is rooted in motivation and, as with anything that requires effort, our success will be anchored in our ability to keep our motivation engaged enough to *keep going*. There are also specific modules which present skills such as mindfulness that develop and deepen over time. While it's fine to dip into different modules on topics you find particularly interesting (or to revisit those you've found helpful), I think most readers will be best served by moving through the book in order, as our companions will do.

Conclusion

As I've mentioned, compassion is about having the courage to turn towards the challenges in our lives, and the commitment to work with those challenges, even – and *especially* – when the going gets tough. I'll somewhat cheekily point out that, even if you're someone who's thought compassion isn't for you or – like many of the people I've worked with – thought it was something you just couldn't do, by reading this Introduction, *you're already compassionately working with your anger*. You're not ignoring or avoiding it – you're facing it and are doing something about it. As engaging as I'm hoping this Introduction has been, I'm guessing there are other things in your life you'd probably rather have been doing with your time. But you didn't do those things. You committed this time to working with your anger – one page, one thought, one realisation at a time. You're doing it. All you need to do now is *keep going*. I'll be here with you.

Section I:

Preparing the Ground

Module 1: The Motivation to Work with Anger

We can think of motivation as a felt experience of 'wanting to do something'. In CFT, we think it's important to acknowledge that many of our basic motivations are born into us – we have them because they *motivated* our ancestors to do things that would help them survive, reproduce and pass their genes along through the flow of life, eventually giving rise to us. We're born with a range of basic motives – motives that activate us to *defend ourselves against perceived threats*, as well as motives that help us *care for and take care of those who are important to us*. Our lives tend to go better when they're more about moving *towards* the lives we want to have (building good relationships, developing helpful skills, doing things that fit with the sort of people we want to be) than if we're constantly focused on trying to minimise or avoid experiences of discomfort.

Anger is linked with *defensive* motives, which work to protect us by focusing our attention on things we generally don't like – threats, problems, obstacles. By itself, that's not a problem – we *need* to be able to notice and work with that stuff. The problem comes when that effort takes up huge amounts of space in our lives – when we're constantly surveying for things that are *wrong*, or when our reactions to perceived threats are so big that they cause problems in our lives and relationships. We can become so focused on dealing with things we don't like in our lives that we never get around to building the sort of lives and relationships *we want to have*.

The good news is that we have other sorts of motives. For humans to survive, our ancestors had to develop *caregiving* motives. Human babies are totally helpless at birth and for a long while afterwards, so we had to develop the basic motivation to *care for one another*, particularly the vulnerable. If we abandoned our babies at birth the way reptiles abandon their young as soon as they're hatched, the human story would have ended a long time ago. We're *wired to care*. Even many of the hardest hearts will soften at the sight of a baby; even some of the toughest among us find a gentle, helpful side emerging when they're met with a small child or animal who needs help.

That means compassion – the willingness to approach and help in the face of suffering – isn't something we have to manufacture from scratch. *We've already got it.* We just need to connect with it; to dust it off and harness it. And, once it's harnessed, there's a lot of juice there. Once we get this deep motivation to help and protect online and working for us, it can be a powerful source of energy and courage.

In working compassionately with our anger we're not just harnessing that caregiving motive in the service of helping others, we're also learning to use it to help *ourselves*. Let's start by considering your motivation for working with your anger.

> - Why have you chosen to work with your anger?
> - What do you have to gain from this effort? How would your life be different if you were successful?

There are lots of different reasons for learning to manage anger. You may have had a life experience that inspired you and find yourself feeling committed to change. On the other hand, you may be more tentative . . . maybe a partner or friend passed this book along to you, and you're not yet sure if it's something you want to do. *I've been in both of those places.* Wherever you find yourself in relation to wanting to better manage your anger, it's like any meaningful effort we make to improve ourselves – it's about sustained effort over time. A good way to recharge our motivation when it begins to fade is to remind ourselves of the *important reasons* we're doing this.[1] When we connect with these good reasons, they can help us keep going even when we don't feel like it, when it gets hard or when we're doubting our efforts.

Let's see how our companions approached that first question:

Why have you chosen to work with your anger?

James: *I'm working with my anger because I want things to be different in my life and for my family. I'm tired of being irritated by everything all the time. I see all these other people having fun, but most of the time, I'm not enjoying life at all. I'm tired of being upset. It also affects my family – I see them walking on eggshells, trying not to say or do something that will set me off. I don't want my family to fear and avoid me. I want them to love me and want me around! My father seemed angry all the time when I was growing up, and I see him in the way I react to things. I don't want to pass this anger on to my children – I don't want them to struggle the way I have.*

Antwan: *Truth? I'm not so sure about this. I'm doing it because my mum asked me to. She works hard taking care of us, so when she asks something of me, I try to do it. But I have lots of other stuff I could be doing with my time. I don't really think I have an anger problem. I blow up in school sometimes, but it's usually for good reasons. But I do want to show Mum that she doesn't have to worry about me.*

Jordan: *Hmmm. I don't know I see it as 'working with my anger', but here goes. I'm tired of feeling bad about myself, and I'm tired of not being able to stand up for myself. I've always dealt with stress by being a people-pleaser, trying to be the person others want me to be, and never standing up for myself. Eventually, I get resentful about that, and it hurts my relationships . . . and I feel bad about that, too! Also, I work in a setting with mostly men, and I don't appreciate how they interact with me sometimes. I've tried to ignore it, but they don't stop. I want to be able to be assertive and set some boundaries.*

How about you? Why have you chosen to work with your anger?

_____

_____

_____

_____

_____

_____

_____

Now, the second question:

What do you have to gain from this effort? How would your life be different if you were successful?

James: *If I was successful, I think I wouldn't get rattled by all the little things . . . or the big things. I want to handle things calmly, to show my kids how to handle things when things go wrong. I'd smile more, have more good times with people I care about, rather than getting upset because things didn't go exactly the way I'd planned. I'm tired of feeling like the problem – tired of always being the bad guy, you know? Also, I want my family to feel safe with me. I've never hurt them, and I hope they're not scared of me, but I remember getting scared when my father would get angry, so I'm not sure. I want them to feel safe sharing things with me, and to feel safe to come to me when they need help with something. I think they avoid doing that now because they don't know how I'll react.*

Antwan: *What do I have to gain? Honestly, I don't know. I guess things could go better at school. There are a couple classes I get hassled in, and it would be cool if that didn't happen. It would be great to get the teachers off my case, and Mum would love it if I got better grades. I've lost friends when things blew up. I can say some pretty cold stuff if you set me off.*

Jordan: *I'd feel more comfortable in my own skin! I spend so much time being anxious, worried about what people think of me, second-guessing everything I do and beating myself up all the time. I'd just like to be me, behave in ways that are true to myself, and engage people based on what I think and feel, rather than constantly trying to figure out the 'right answer'. And I'd have boundaries that are based on my own comfort level – I'd be able to speak up for myself when people do things that make me uncomfortable, rather than shrinking into myself.*

Give yourself some time to think about it. If you were successful in learning to manage your anger, what would be different about your life? Don't just stick with negative things that would go away or be easier to manage – also consider what parts of your life you'd like to grow. How might your life be more enjoyable? How might your relationships grow, expand or improve? How might the way you show up each day fit better with the person you want to be?

What do you have to gain from this effort? How would your life be different if you were successful?

_____

_____

_____

_____

_____

Final reflection

The end of each module will present you with a question or two to reflect upon, designed to deepen your connection with the material.

What was it like to consider your motivation for working with your anger? What did it feel like to consider your reasons for doing this and the outcomes that could come from it?

_____

_____

_____

_____

_____

_____

What might help you keep this motivation in mind as you go through your daily life? How might you remind yourself of the important reasons behind the choice to work with your anger? (For example, some people write a reminder of their motivation in a note on

their phone, or carry a stone in their pocket to remind them . . . the key is to find a method that works for you.)

_____

_____

_____

_____

_____

_____

_____

_____

Module 2: Our Brains and How We Change Them

CFT is rooted in an understanding of how human beings work, drawn from several different areas of science. While we'll spend a lot of time on anger, we'll also explore why we are the way we are, why life can be so tricky and how we can change. In this module, we'll look at our brains and how they work. Making changes is easier when we've got an understanding of the tools we're working with.

We can think of our brains and bodies as adaptation machines that are shaped by everything we do and experience. When we exercise, we activate different parts of our bodies and they become stronger in ways that are linked to the sorts of exercises we've engaged in. Different athletes develop very different types of bodies, specifically tailored to their sports.

It's like that with our brains, too – they are constantly shaped by our experience. Everything we do or experience is reflected in patterns of activation in our brains. If I said the word 'car', cells in your brain would light up and you'd know I was referring to an automobile – a pattern of brain cells linking the sound of the word 'car' to a host of information you've learned to associate with that word: what a car is, what cars look like, how they work . . . that sort of thing.

Whenever we listen, speak, think, feel, take action or do anything at all, patterns of cells 'light up' in the brain, which correspond to that experience or action. Every time one of these patterns is activated, the cells within that pattern and the connections between them are strengthened. This strengthening makes it easier for the pattern to activate in the future. That's what students are doing when they study for an exam – activating brain patterns corresponding to the material again and again, until the pattern is 'worn in' and the information is remembered. Once a pattern is well established it can be activated easily by triggering any part of the pattern. When I say the word 'car', you don't have to *work* to remember what a car is, what it looks like or what it's for. That pattern in your brain has been strengthened so much over time that just hearing the word 'car' triggers the whole pattern – you just *know* what it refers to, perhaps complete with visual images and associated memories ('I was really into cars as a teenager!').

This is how we learn, and when we study for an exam, practise fingering a guitar chord, wiring a circuit or knitting a particular stitch, what we're doing is lighting up these particular patterns over and over, strengthening them. Eventually, when the pattern is sufficiently entrenched, we just *know* what the term is, play the chord automatically, wire the circuit easily or effortlessly knit entire scarves during a Zoom meeting. This is also why we want to slow down and make our practice as close as possible to the result we're trying to achieve. If we're hurried or sloppy, we can strengthen patterns that aren't quite right – patterns we then must unlearn if we want to get things right. This is where bad habits come from! To make this process even more efficient, we want to activate the pattern frequently and repeatedly over time – which is why practising guitar for fifteen minutes per day, four to six times per week, will help you improve much more quickly than will a single weekly three-hour session.

Understanding this process can help us understand how and why we struggle with anger and other problems. Sometimes we learn unhelpful patterns by accident. Imagine a child who has a particularly critical caregiver or teacher. Imagine that whenever this child is learning a difficult task and struggles – as we *all* do when we're beginning to learn a difficult task – this caregiver ridicules the child: 'What's wrong with you? Can't you do anything right? You're so stupid!' Imagine this happens many times across different situations.

This child's brain will almost certainly form patterns linking the experience of struggling with being criticised, 'not being able to do anything right' or being seen as 'stupid'. These patterns can persist well after the circumstances that created them are gone – even if this caregiver has been dead for decades, the child – now an adult – may still hear the words 'You can't do anything right! You're so stupid!' reverberating in their mind whenever they find themselves struggling. Tickle one part of the pattern (struggle) and the rest of it lights up ('You're so stupid!'). We can even forget where these messages came from. Failing to recognise them as *echoes* of our previous experience, we can perceive these thoughts as *the way it is . . .* a felt experience of *knowing there's something wrong with me.* This is tough stuff. This learning process occurs even more efficiently when we feel threatened. Our brains are designed to learn about potential danger very quickly, and humans are very sensitive to social threats such as criticism.

Learning to notice the arising of messages that are linked to unhelpful patterns laid down in our pasts can help us keep from accepting them, and create opportunities to relate compassionately to our struggles: 'Ah, there I go, thinking I'm stupid for struggling again . . . thanks, Mr Hannigan. But that's not helpful. Everyone struggles sometimes, and this is important to me, so I'm going to keep going.' We'll work to develop the ability to notice these messages.

These patterns can also involve *emotions* – we can learn to feel certain ways in response to our experiences. This learning can happen in response to things that happen directly to us, but also through our interactions with other people, and even by observing how others behave (called *social learning*). As James mentioned in his reflection in the previous module, some of us who struggle with anger may have grown up with caregivers who acted out their own anger in unhelpful ways – who *modelled* unhelpful angry behaviour for their children. When this happens, particularly during childhood, we (and our brains) can learn to respond in similar ways – our brains lay down patterns linking anger and angry behaviour with situations in which our caregivers modelled anger. Later, we can find ourselves responding in the same ways, as these patterns are activated in our own lives.

By understanding a bit about how our brains work we can create powerful changes in our minds. For example, briefly checking in with our motivation to work with our anger – taking a moment every day to remind ourselves *why* we've committed to manage our anger better – can help cement these patterns in our minds, helping us carry them with us even when we're not intentionally thinking about them. Just as we've inadvertently learned angry habits, we can *build* compassionate habits. It just takes intentional practice, repeated over time. *This is how we change.* It's not up for debate – if we repeatedly practise compassionate ways of being in the world and working with challenges (versus the old, anger-driven ways), we *will change* – because we'll literally be changing our brains!

I'm noticing I've covered a lot of information so far in this module, so let's take a moment to digest it:

What do you make of the information on how our experience creates patterns in our brains? Can you relate it to any of your own experience?

James: *I've never thought about my experience in terms of what's happening in my brain, so I'm finding it interesting. At first, I was also wondering how it related to my anger. But the piece on modelling really hit home for me. Growing up, I often watched my dad blow up when the slightest thing would go wrong. He'd be working on something like fixing the toilet, and if something went wrong, he'd get upset, yell, or throw a wrench or something. As a kid, it was terrifying, but I obviously laid down that pattern – 'When things don't go just right, get angry' – because I see myself reacting in the same way he did. And when I see the same fear in my kids' eyes that I remember having, it breaks my heart. I don't want to pass that pattern on to them. The last piece was helpful, too. I get hopeless sometimes, but knowing that doing something different can change my brain makes me want to keep going.*

Antwan: *Reading this felt a little like being in school, which was kinda lame, but I expected it, I guess. That said, it definitely explained some things. Reading the part about how parents can model anger helps me understand why I've got it. Before he left, my dad used to go off all the time. He'd get pissed off and scream at us. He used to tell me stuff like in the book, too, like if he asked me to do something and I forgot or got it wrong, I got to hear about how stupid I was.*

Jordan: *I really found myself relating to the self-criticism piece. My mother was critical when I was growing up – everything had to be just so. I'm constantly doubting myself, running myself down and wondering if whatever I've done is 'good enough', even if other people seem really satisfied. It's to the point where I sometimes feel like an imposter at work; like if other people really knew me, they would see I'm not very good and don't have any business being here. I think that underlies my tendency to be a people-pleaser. It's like if I keep people happy, they won't look at me too deeply.*

What do you make of the information we've covered on how our experience creates patterns in our brains? Can you relate it to any of your own experience?

_____

_____

_____

_____

_____

_____

_____

_____

_____

Final reflection

Considering the discussion of brain patterns, can you think of any patterns or habits that you've learned and would like to change? Given your history, does it *make sense* you would have developed those patterns? (Sometimes we can't identify where we learned our reactions and behaviours, but often we can.)

_____

_____

_____

_____

_____

_____

_____

Module 3: The Person You Want to Be

Lots of people have misconceptions about what compassion is, thinking it means being nice all the time, or being weak, soft and indulgent. And as we explored in the Introduction, compassion isn't really like this at all. Compassion is defined as being sensitive to suffering and difficulty – we notice and acknowledge it, rather than avoiding it – combined with being *motivated to help* alleviate the suffering and prevent it in the future. Compassion is about having the courage to meet the difficult parts of our lives head-on. Compassion is *true strength*.

In Module 1, we explored the power of motivation and I invited you to connect with your motivation to work with anger. In this module – and in the rest of the book – we'll go beyond working with anger. Don't worry, we'll spend plenty of time on anger. But your anger isn't *who you are*. Anger is an emotion that you, like all humans, sometimes experience. But it doesn't define us – not even those of us who struggle with anger. It doesn't decide who we are or what our lives are going to be about. *We* get to do that. That's the focus of this module.

Those of us who struggle with anger may find this hard to swallow – we may have become fused with the 'angry version' of ourselves – the version of us that shows up when we're filled with anger. We who struggle with anger may spend a lot of time acting from the perspective of our 'angry selves', and others may relate to us in ways that show this is how they experience us, too. After a while, we can fall into the trap of thinking that 'this is me. This is who I am.'

But it's not. We all have many different versions of ourselves, ways of being that are rooted in our basic survival motives, the emotions that serve them, and how these experiences organise our brains and bodies. We all have 'hungry selves', which motivate us to acquire food so we don't starve. Likewise, we all have scared selves, loving selves, interested selves, sad selves, excited selves . . . each of which powerfully shapes our experience of life, setting us up to engage with the world and other people in particular sorts of ways.

As much as we sometimes might wish we could, we can't get rid of any of these 'versions of the self', even the tricky ones we may feel ashamed of. We all have these emotions and motives built into us, for good reason – they helped keep our ancestors alive! But we can decide which versions of us we want to 'send to the gym', which motivations and skills we want to develop, strengthen and manifest more often. And when we practise these qualities, we develop the patterns in our brains that help strengthen these ways of being, making them more likely to appear spontaneously in our lives – to be the version of 'us' that shows up when we're presented with a given situation.

You probably won't be surprised to learn that in CFT, one 'version of the self' we're particularly interested in cultivating is the compassionate self.[1] The compassionate self is rooted in our basic caregiving motives and helps us to act skilfully in the face of suffering and challenge. When developing the compassionate self, we cultivate specific qualities in ourselves – qualities like the courage to face things that scare us, the ability to tolerate distress, the wisdom to understand things and make good decisions, and the mindful ability to curiously notice what's happening in the present moment rather than hastily reacting in anger. In short, cultivating our compassionate selves involves developing characteristics that help us work with anger and the other challenges in our lives.

This process works better when it's rooted in a sincere motivation, based in what we want for our lives. Maybe I'm naive, but I think that when most people feel safe and have their basic needs met, they'll naturally prefer to be helpful rather than harmful. I've seen this again and again. Even when working with men in a prison setting who'd done truly terrible things in their lives, I found that when they felt seen, valued, cared about and had ways of meeting their needs that didn't involve harming others, things changed for them. When these men really considered who they wanted to be and how they wanted to be in the world, they chose goodness. They chose to help one another. They chose working to make the world a better place. I saw it in these men, again and again – and it made a believer out of me.

There's a lot we have to do to simply get through life, and a lot of things that compete for our energy. It's easy to get so lost in the 'to do' list that we forget to ask the big questions. But it's the answers to those big questions that can help us keep going when things get hard. So let's ask them now and consider how we can remind ourselves to keep asking them in the future.

What do you care most about in your life? What sort of person do you want to be? What do you want your life to be about? If you had lived the life you wanted to live, how would you like people to describe you at your funeral?

James: *I'll start with what I care most about, which is my family. I love them so much. But I haven't been the best husband to Sarah the past few years, and Aiden and Jaime deserve a better father than they've been getting from me. By 'better', I guess I mean that I want them to experience me as loving, supportive and consistent – that I'm there when they need help, and they can feel free to ask for it without worrying about how I'll react. I want to be a rock they can rely on. I guess that's the sort of thing I'd want them to say at my funeral. I also want to have more fun – with my family and in my own life. I'm not sure I'll ever be someone people would describe as 'light-hearted', but I'd like a little of that.*

Antwan: *The person I want to be? I guess I want people to see me as strong, and like I've got it together. I want to be treated with respect, and I want to deserve it. Also, I've got some little cousins. When I was younger, particularly after my dad left, lots of times I didn't have any men in my life to look up to. I want to be someone my cousins can look up to . . . like, 'I want to be like him.' I want them to know I'm there for them if they need me. Family is important.*

Jordan: *I want to be competent, caring . . . I guess you could say compassionate, and respected. The interesting thing is that in a vacuum, I think I already am some of those things. Although I feel like an imposter sometimes, I think my colleagues would say I'm good at my job. My friends and family know I'm there for them no matter what. Respect is something I could work on, though – both from those around me and for myself. I guess a part of that is wanting to be able to stand up for myself better. One thing I'm proud of is that I already stand up for others – I participate in activism for causes I care about, and I volunteer at a shelter for women escaping domestic violence. But I think I end up getting the short end of the stick sometimes because I don't stand up for myself. I also want people to experience me as kind and compassionate, which is part of what drew me to this approach.*

What do you care most about in your life and how might that reflect in the way you live? What sort of person do you want to be in the world? What do you want your life to be about? If you had lived the life you wanted to live, how would you like people to describe you at your funeral?

_____

_____

_____

_____

In approaching this question, it can be useful to come up with a list of qualities we'd like to cultivate in ourselves. I use the term 'cultivate' because it doesn't happen instantly – these qualities are things we plan for, nurture and intentionally create space for in our lives. And we do so again and again, so they can take root. With that in mind, it's also useful to consider how we can keep these aspirations in our awareness, so they don't become overwhelmed by the countless little but important questions (what to eat for dinner?) that arise in our daily lives. We want to set this motivation as our North Star – so that as we go through life, the way we live increasingly reflects the qualities we want to be defined by.

One bit of good news is that we can often attend to the big questions and the little questions at the same time. Even when the question is 'What do I need to get done today?', we can approach things in ways that reflect our most important values. It's not just about *what* we do; it's also about *how* we do it. I can teach my university courses with irritability, laziness and arrogance . . . or I can teach them with compassion, honesty and commitment. Sometimes, connecting with our deepest motivations can transform even tasks we dislike – we can wash the dishes with irritation or with the sincere motivation that our loved ones have clean dishes to eat from, so that they can be healthy and free from disease (I dislike doing the dishes . . . and this kind of helps).

I'd encourage you to be creative about bringing these values into your daily life. CFT founder Paul Gilbert talks about 'compassion under the duvet', in which we take a moment to remind ourselves of our compassionate motivation – or any quality we're working to develop in ourselves – just before getting out of bed in the morning. It can be powerful to pause and say to ourselves, 'today I want to be a better listener in my interactions with my family', or 'today I want to take a few deep breaths before responding to situations that irritate me'.

Final reflection

What was it like to consider the person you want to be? How did it feel to consider the things that are most important to you?

_____

_____

_____

_____

_____

_____

_____

_____

Can you think of any ways you might bring these motivations into your daily life, to help you keep them in mind, even as you face the many tasks life requires of us?

_____

_____

_____

_____

_____

_____

_____

Module 4: Considering Potential Obstacles

Working with challenging emotions like anger isn't easy. Lots of obstacles and challenges will come up along the way. This is particularly true in the beginning, when we're firming up our commitment to do it, recognising it's not a change that will magically happen overnight, and before the inspiring effects of seeing our own progress have kicked in. It's kind of like working out – the going is roughest in the beginning, when we're out of shape, haven't yet built the habit of exercising, and haven't yet seen our bodies begin to change and get stronger. At this point in our progress, it's easy to get demoralised – which is why it's important to have a plan for how we're going to *keep going* even when we don't feel like it.

In this module, we'll get curious about identifying potential obstacles that can appear on the path to managing your anger, and begin thinking about how to work with these obstacles. I say 'begin thinking about' because working with obstacles isn't a 'one-time-only' type of situation but a continuous process. As with many experiences in life, there are things that won't go according to plan. Instead of letting these things halt us in our tracks (or using them as an excuse to bail on the effort), we want to anticipate that obstacles and setbacks *will* occur and consider how we'll deal with them when that happens. That can also take the sting out of it when things don't go according to plan – instead of being surprised when obstacles arise, we can remind ourselves, 'Oh, I knew this was going to happen. Let's see what might be helpful in working with this.'

This also highlights the importance of compassion in working with anger. As I mentioned in the Introduction, compassion is about what we do when struggle and suffering show up – when things go wrong, when the plan breaks down. With compassion, instead of flying into a rage or giving up when things don't go as planned, we learn to take a moment (or as long as needed) to ground ourselves, consider the obstacle or problem (so that we can learn as much about it as we can), and then consider how best to proceed. Rather than getting caught up in how things 'should be', we consider what would be most *helpful*, given the way things *are*. We'll explore an approach to working with obstacles in future modules, but for now we'll focus on the potential obstacles themselves.

Obstacles come in lots of different flavours. Some obstacles are pragmatic – like *remembering* the new habits we're trying to develop, or *finding time* to practise whatever skill we're working on. These sorts of obstacles can often be addressed with boring but reliable methods: using a schedule, setting reminders on our phones and establishing a routine (like spending forty-five minutes with this book every Tuesday, Thursday and Sunday evening at 7.30 p.m.).

Exploring fears, blocks and resistances

At this point, I'll invite you to consider potential obstacles – things that might get in the way of working with your anger. In addition to the pragmatic bits we touched on above, there can be other sorts of obstacles. In CFT, we call these *fears, blocks and resistances*, or FBRs for short.

- *Fears* are *things we worry might happen* as a result of working on our anger or cultivating compassion (for example, that we might fail; that we might look weak; that we'll be taken advantage of; that we might lose control).

- *Blocks* are *things that get in the way* of what we're working on (for example, anger triggers, life stressors and time pressures; feeling overwhelmed by shame or other feelings that come up as we face tricky parts of ourselves).

- *Resistances* are when we find ourselves *not wanting* to continue (for example, thinking it won't help, not feeling like doing it, telling ourselves others are to blame for making us angry instead of taking responsibility for how we act).

Let's consider what FBRs may be present in your journey to manage your anger, beginning with examples from a couple of your companions:

As you consider working with your anger, do you find yourself worried or reluctant about anything? What concerns do you have?

Antwan: *Worried about? These questions feel a little silly, but I'll play. I don't want to become a pushover or a wimp. Sometimes it feels like you're not allowed to be a man any more. They do these 'social-emotional learning' activities in school sometimes, and it's all about feelings – but the way it's done, the girls love it, but it almost feels like they're saying men are bad, talking about 'toxic masculinity' and shit like that. Like they're trying to turn us into these wimpy sensitive guys who talk about their feelings all the time. When it talked about some people thinking compassion means being weak, I gotta admit I had some of those ideas. It's not a 'fear', but I only agreed to do this because my mum asked me to, and I figured it would probably be a waste of time. It's been okay so far.*

> **As you consider working with your anger, what might get in the way or complicate things?** *That's an easy one. I've got a couple of teachers who seem like they have it in for me. They're always on my back for talking or looking at my phone, but they don't say a thing to kids they seem to like. I don't know if they think I'm stupid or what, but I hate that. I also have a friend who likes to push my buttons, and sometimes I take the bait. I need to stop that. I'm not here to be his entertainment.*
>
> **As you consider working with your anger, do you notice any resistance in yourself? How do you feel about what we've done so far, and about moving forwards?** *Like I said, I'm only doing this because Mum asked me to, and I expected it to be a load of bullshit.*

We see that, for Antwan, the biggest potential obstacle seems to be not feeling sure he wants to do it, as well as a sense that he'll be wasting his time. Another point of resistance is something I expect a number of people might identify with: the suggestion we might have an 'anger problem' can feel like an attack, and perhaps fearing that 'managing anger' means we're supposed to become wimpy, 'emotional' versions of ourselves (hint: *anger is an emotion, too* . . . and when we acknowledge that, it's very likely men are no more 'emotional' than are women; we're just socialised to feel safe feeling and expressing different emotions!). As Antwan did, I've seen lots of men react to the term 'toxic masculinity', feeling like it's an attack on all men – implying that somehow being a man is bad.

In considering these experiences, does it *make sense* that Antwan might have resistance to working with his anger? It's hard to *not* have resistance when we feel attacked or that we're being made to do something we don't want to do. It makes sense to me. In working with this in CFT, we don't try to *convince* clients about how great compassion is – our goal is to help them *discover* how this approach can be helpful as the process unfolds.

Since Antwan raised the topic of 'toxic masculinity', I'll speak to it, because I've seen a lot of men react strongly to this term (this will be the only time I'll speak to it in this book). A compassionate approach often begins with understanding, so let's start there. We can think of 'masculinity' as the collection of messages and ideas circulating in our culture about 'what it means to be a man'. 'Toxic masculinity' just suggests that *some of those messages and ideas might be unhelpful* – to men and to others. If you're a man and you've ever felt 'weak' or 'unmanly' after becoming tearful or feeling emotions like anxiety . . . well, that's an example of what we might call 'toxic masculinity' – the idea that *real* men aren't supposed to ever cry, or feel sad, or scared or anxious. This idea is unhelpful because we *all* have brains that will sometimes produce these sorts of feelings, so if we believe we *shouldn't* be feeling them, it's a set-up to deny and reject these feelings, or beat ourselves up for having them. Instead of just noticing we're feeling sadness, grief, anxiety or whatever, we can find ourselves working to bottle the feelings up, perhaps even shifting into anger (which may feel less vulnerable and more 'manly'). We'll be digging a good bit more into how our emotions work in future modules, but as I've mentioned, compassion isn't about becoming weak – it's about having the strength to work with *all* our difficult experiences, even the ones that may feel vulnerable.

Hopefully, like Antwan, you'll find yourself committed enough to keep going and see what happens. Reflecting on the motivation exercise from Module 1 – reminding ourselves that we're doing this for *good reasons* – can sometimes help with this.

Let's look at Jordan's reflection:

As you consider working with your anger, do you find yourself worried or reluctant about anything? What concerns do you have?

Jordan: *I do. I'm learning that I've been pushing my anger down for years, to the point it's been hard to be assertive at all. There's this sense that I shouldn't feel angry, that it's bad to feel that way. I think I've worried that if I let myself really connect to it, I might lose control. I want to stand up for myself, but I don't want to let loose on people or to be to be seen as an 'angry woman'. I've seen lots of women get dismissed that way. They just call you 'emotional', and then nothing you say matters. That sort of unfairness is one of the things that triggers my anger . . . which I then don't let myself feel, so I usually just get sad and cry about it, which makes me feel weak.*

As you consider working with your anger, what might get in the way or complicate things? *I criticise and run myself down a lot, which keeps me from trying new things. Although I've accomplished a lot in terms of my education, that was an area I felt confident in – I'm good at doing intellectual work when I'm left to myself. But in other areas of my life, I've shut myself down with criticism before I even got started . . . 'Don't talk to her, she won't like you anyway.' That sort of thing. It keeps me from trying new things.*

As you consider working with your anger, do you notice any resistance in yourself? How do you feel about what we've done so far, and about moving forwards? *Pushing down my anger – or turning it on myself – is just such a habit for me. I do it automatically. It's so easy for me to slip into the comfort of being quiet, fading into the background and going back to doing my stuff. It builds until I'm at home by myself, and then I break down and beat myself up about it. This is going to test me, but it's important so I'm going to do it. My therapist thought this compassion approach would be a good fit for me, and I like it so far. Hopefully, it will help me stand up for myself and stop criticising myself so much.*

Jordan's reflection presents a very different picture. While she seems interested in the CFT approach, she also recognises several obstacles: her habit of pushing her anger away; her tendency to fall into a passive stance when things get hard; and her habit of criticising herself, which has crippled her efforts to try new things. But now that she's identified these potential obstacles, she can begin thinking about how to work with them.

Considering fears, blocks and resistances

As you consider working with your anger, do you find yourself worried or reluctant about anything? What concerns do you have?

_____

_____

_____

_____

_____

_____

As you consider working with your anger, what might get in the way or complicate things?

_____

_____

_____

_____

_____

_____

As you consider working with your anger, do you notice any resistance in yourself? How do you feel about what we've done so far and about moving forwards?

_____

_____

_____

_____

_____

_____

_____

Becoming familiar with potential obstacles doesn't mean we won't have to face them. We almost certainly will. But it will help us be prepared when they show up. As we'll do later with anger triggers, it can be useful to game-plan potentially helpful ways to work with obstacles that we know are likely to show up.

Final reflection

What was it like to consider the potential obstacles that might arise as you work with your anger? Did anything surprise you? Did you learn anything you feel might be useful?

_____

_____

_____

_____

_____

_____

_____

If you did discover some potential obstacles, do you have any ideas about what might be helpful to address them? What might help you keep going in working with your anger even when things don't go smoothly?

_____

_____

_____

_____

_____

_____

_____

_____

_____

Module 5: Introducing Mindfulness

When talking with people about anger, one of the most frequent questions I get is, 'What can I do when I'm caught up in a rage?' There seems to be hope that I can provide some fancy technique to use when our anger is burning full-strength that will instantly dissolve it and bring us back to a calm state of mind. I suspect my answer sometimes leaves people less than satisfied: 'Not much.' Of course, I say more than that – when our anger is at its peak, there *are* things we can do – but at those times, the *first* thing to focus on is *creating some space* between ourselves and the focus of our anger, so *we don't make things worse*. As we'll explore later, anger organises our minds in powerful ways and, when it's at full strength, it's almost impossible for us to think clearly, gain a helpful perspective and act skilfully. In those cases, the best thing is to step back – go for a walk or run, listen to some music, watch a show or anything else that helps the arousal of our anger settle a bit, so we can return to the situation when we're a bit more centred.

Sometimes it can feel like we've been swept away by anger – finding ourselves triggered and, before long, we've said or done things that have made the situation worse or hurt people we care about. Mindfulness can help us avoid losing ourselves in the momentum of anger by helping us *notice it arising in us*. Mindfulness involves a particular kind of noticing – the ability to observe, 'I'm starting to get angry right now.' This can create some space between us and the anger, putting us in a sort of observer stance, a bit like we're outside the angry feelings and thoughts, watching them. This space can give us the opportunity to *consider what would be helpful for us to do*, rather than just acting out angry habits. Mindfulness can also help us learn to notice signs of anger building *before* we're enraged, so we've got the chance to turn things around before we reach that point.

Mindfulness has been defined in different ways, but probably the most common definition comes from Jon Kabat-Zinn, who defined it as *paying attention, in the present moment, non-judgementally, on purpose*.[1] I find the term *kind curiosity* to be particularly helpful. Think of a time you noticed something curious happening – nothing particularly good or bad, just sort of interesting – and you just looked at it, trying to figure out what it was: 'Huh, I wonder what those squirrels are doing over there?', 'Look at the interesting shape those clouds have taken', 'Hmmm . . . that's an interesting sound. I wonder what that instrument is?'

That's the sort of open, non-judgemental attention we see with mindfulness. We're directing the spotlight of our attention towards whatever is showing up – the external world, our bodies, mental experiences such as thoughts and feelings. Once we notice whatever is there, although we might label the experience ('Huh, I'm feeling a bit anxious right now'), we refrain from judging it as good or bad, right or wrong, etc. We're just noticing, with *kind curiosity*, as meditation teacher Tara Brach sometimes says, 'this is what it's like right now'.[2]

This ability to curiously notice our experience is *powerful*. As I mentioned above, it can shift us slightly out of the experience, so we don't feel as trapped in it. It can also help us recognise our experiences for what they are – thoughts, feelings or bodily sensations (*'I notice I'm feeling angry right now – I keep playing what he said over and over in my mind like a movie. My jaw is tense, and I really want to tell him off'*). Noticing that stuff, we can then decide what to do with it – will we continue to play the situation over in our minds, or would it be more helpful to direct our thoughts towards something else? Is *now* the time to send that email? Maybe it would be helpful to take a moment to slow down our breath, to calm some of the bodily arousal that's fuelling our anger?

Recognising our feelings, thoughts and bodily experiences can be helpful for working with anger as we can sometimes experience anger not as a temporary mental experience, but as *the way we are*. This is even reflected in how we talk about emotions – saying, 'I'm angry' (as if me and my anger are the same thing), not 'I'm experiencing anger.' Once we recognise anger as a temporary mental experience that involves different parts we can work with – feelings, thoughts and imagery, physical arousal, behaviours – it becomes a lot easier to figure out helpful ways to manage it.

Mindfulness also fits well with a compassionate approach to working with anger. Compassion involves *sensitivity* to suffering, and *motivation* to act to alleviate or prevent it. Mindfulness can help with the *sensitivity* of compassion. We non-judgementally notice the struggle ('Look, I'm getting really angry', 'I'm having a hard time with this'), which sets us up to consider what would be helpful in addressing it. The curious, non-judgemental quality of mindfulness can also help prevent secondary responses that can fuel our anger, shut us down or keep us from taking responsibility for it – like criticising ourselves (*'Damn it, there I go again!'*), or blaming people in the situation (*'How am I supposed to not be angry with what these idiots are doing?!?'*). Instead, we notice what's happening, refrain from condemning and maybe label the experience in an objective sense: 'I'm going over the situation again and again in my mind. That seems to be keeping me angry',

'She seems to be pretty angry, too – it doesn't seem like the meaning of what I'm saying is getting through.'

Let's consider some examples of how this can work, using thoughts that can represent potential obstacles to working with our anger:

Thought: *'Well, I screwed it up again. This is hopeless. I give up.'*

- **Without mindfulness:** <Gives up, followed by increased self-criticism.>
- **With mindfulness:** 'I'm feeling bad about what I did and feeling hopeless. I wonder what would help me get back on track? What might I say to a friend I wanted to help who was feeling similarly?'

Thought: *'Compassion . . . right! This guy's trying to turn me into a wimp.'*

- **Without mindfulness:** <Donates book to thrift shop.>
- **With mindfulness:** 'I notice this is pushing some of my buttons . . . I wonder what that's about? Even so, I wonder if it might be worth continuing, to see if something here might be helpful?'

Thought: *'My problem isn't anger, it's that I'm surrounded by jerks. Screw them!'*

- **Without mindfulness:** <Avoids taking responsibility for angry behaviour.>
- **With mindfulness:** 'I notice I'm getting defensive and blaming the people around me. They are certainly doing things I find frustrating. I wonder how I might handle that in a way that fits with the sort of person I want to be?'

You may *notice* that the mindful responses above begin with a judgement-free observation of what is happening – 'I notice that . . .', 'I'm feeling . . .' – followed by a compassionate response – a response considering *what might be helpful* in relation to the experience.

Mindfulness carries with it the *courage* of compassion – the courage to turn towards difficult emotions and experiences and look deeply into them, without avoiding or attacking ourselves when things get uncomfortable. When we open our awareness to our emotional experience, we'll sometimes encounter feelings we're not entirely comfortable with. This can be particularly relevant to those of us who use anger to avoid other, more vulnerable-feeling emotions like sadness, anxiety or shame. If we can approach such uncomfortable feelings with compassion ('knowing my history, it makes sense that I'd feel _____') vs. avoiding them or criticising ourselves for having them, it can make it easier to manage them.

Opening our awareness to emotions and experiences in this way can also sometimes bring up painful stuff we've been avoiding, sometimes even related to traumatic experiences in our pasts. While we'll explore compassionate approaches that can help in relating to such difficult experiences, sometimes when we look behind our anger and find trauma, it can be helpful to find a therapist to help us. For people who aren't used to asking for help, that's one of the most courageous steps of all.

Although there are lots of formal mindfulness practices (and some we'll introduce later in the book), we don't have to meditate to be mindful, and the point of mindfulness isn't doing practices – it's curious, non-judgemental, intentional awareness. We want to *build the habit* of noticing our experience in this way. We can begin to develop this habit by creating space in our daily lives to pause, notice what's happening in our lives and bring awareness to our experience. This can start by just pausing to ask ourselves some questions:

- What am I feeling in my body right now? What physical sensations are showing up for me?

- Where is my attention being drawn? Is it wide or narrow? Is it flexible and moving around, or rigid and fixed to one thing?

- What thoughts – words and images – are moving through my mind?

- What emotions do I notice? What feelings are coming up in me?

The point in asking ourselves these questions isn't necessarily to come up with answers, but to build the habit of *noticing* these aspects of our experience. Once we've noticed the different parts of our experience, we can feel free to label them, but in a non-judgemental way: 'I'm really hungry (or hangry!)', 'Wow – my attention is completely focused on how scared I am about that meeting – it's hard to think of anything else', 'I'm thinking about what I've got to do later this afternoon', 'I'm feeling a bit bored', 'I keep playing what he said over and over again, and every time I do it, I feel upset.'

Notice the wording of the thought question: 'What thoughts – words and images – are moving through my mind?' This emphasises the ephemeral nature of thoughts – not as solid, real things we *must* accept or respond to, but words and images in our minds that we can choose to engage with *or* allow to pass back out of our minds as we choose to bring our attention to *something else* (like considering what might be helpful to do about the situation). Of course, it's sometimes not that easy – some thoughts, like those we have when we feel angry – can be 'sticky', returning again and again even after we've let them go. But that doesn't mean we have to buy into them – what if we just notice this as well, again bringing our attention to what might be helpful: 'I'm having trouble letting go of what he said to me. That makes sense, I guess. This interaction was painful, given my history. I wonder what might help me shift gears? It's nice outside – maybe I'll go for a walk and call Kate. She'd understand.' This response includes a refusal to 'take the bait' and engage with the resentment, and models a compassionate response – acknowledging that, given this person's history, it makes sense that this situation would be tricky, and considering actions that might be helpful (going for a walk, calling a friend).

In building mindfulness as a habit, it can be useful to create reminders to 'check in' with our experience a few times per day. We can set phone alarms to remind us, or consider times in the day when we typically have a few moments to pause and bring our awareness to our bodily experience, emotions and thoughts – perhaps during the first commercial break of television programmes, when we're walking to our next meeting or on the tube ride home. After some time practising directing your attention in these ways, you may find yourself spontaneously noticing bodily experiences, emotions or thoughts as they arise in you.

Let's practise checking in with our experience right now:

What's going on with your body right now? What bodily sensations do you notice?

James: *I'm hungry. It's late morning now and I skipped breakfast, and I can feel my stomach starting to churn, reminding me that I need to eat.*

Antwan: *I'm feeling restless. Though I didn't notice it until just now, I've been moving my legs and feet.*

Jordan: *My body is feeling kind of tired. I've started exercising, and I went for a run right before doing this. Between that and being at work all day, I'm feeling kind of worn out. Thinking it may be time for a cup of tea to wake me up a bit.*

How about you? What's going on with your body right now? What bodily sensations do you notice?

_____

_____

_____

_____

_____

_____

_____

Now let's expand our curiosity to our attention and thinking:

> **Where is your attention being drawn? Is it wide or narrow? Is it moving around or fixed to one thing? What thoughts and images are moving through your mind?**
>
> **James:** *My attention is narrowly focused, but it's moving back and forth between the material we're covering and the fact I'm now very aware that I'm hungry – and it's another hour or so until lunchtime. I'm thinking about grabbing a snack to tide me over, and imagining the biscuits in my kitchen cupboard.*
>
> **Antwan:** *I'm kind of distracted – I'm trying to focus on what we're doing, but now I'm also thinking about what I want to do once this module is finished up. Thinking I'll call my friend Julian to see if he wants to kick a ball around.*
>
> **Jordan:** *After noticing I'm feeling a bit tired and sleepy, my attention started jumping around a bit – thinking of getting some tea, checking the time to see if it's too late to have caffeine because I don't want it to keep me up. Now that I've seen it's not, I'm planning to get some as soon as I'm done.*

As your companions' responses demonstrate, noticing our bodily sensations can sometimes alert us to needs (hunger, tiredness) and point us towards helpful actions we can take to address them. Later, we'll explore a breathing exercise (soothing rhythm breathing) we can use when we notice bodily signs that we're angry or anxious.

Where is your attention being drawn? Is it wide or narrow? Is it moving around or fixed to one thing? What thoughts and images are moving through your mind?

Let's finish up by bringing our mindful curiosity to our emotional experience:

What emotions do I notice? What feelings are coming up in me?

James: *I'm chuckling because after the last question I went into my kitchen and grabbed myself a couple of biscuits – which I really enjoyed, and now I'm not distracted by hunger. I guess I'm feeling pleased, all things considered.*

Antwan: *Right now, I'm kind of bored, and looking forward to getting together with Julian once I'm done here. We haven't played footie in a while, and it's a lot of fun.*

Jordan: *Is 'interested' an emotion? I'll assume it is. It's been interesting to slow down and bring attention to my body, my thoughts and now my feelings. I can see how it could be helpful. It would really help to notice my feelings when anger comes up and decide how I want to respond rather than automatically getting anxious and self-critical.*

What emotions do you notice? What feelings are coming up in you?

_____

_____

_____

_____

_____

_____

_____

With a bit of practice, we can learn to mindfully 'check in' with our bodies, thoughts and emotions in just a few minutes. There are also online resources to help support us in doing this, such as this YouTube video which guides us through a brief mindful check-in practice:[3] It is easy to find online by searching 'Goldstein mindful check-in'.

Final reflection

What was it like to curiously bring your attention to your body, thoughts and feelings? Can you imagine how this might be helpful in working with anger? If so, how?

_____

_____

_____

_____

_____

_____

_____

Mindfully 'checking in', asking ourselves these questions a few times per day – taking a moment to bring our attention to our bodily sensations, thoughts and feelings – can help build the habit of noticing these experiences (which is good, because the sooner we notice our anger beginning to arise, the easier it tends to be to work with it). What might help you remember to ask yourself these questions a few times per day over the next week (for example, 'When I really want to remember to do something, I'll schedule reminders in my phone')?

Module 6: Three Flows of Compassion

In working compassionately with anger, it's useful to consider that compassion has three *flows*. There is compassion that flows from us to others – our sensitivity to suffering in others, and motivation to alleviate and prevent that suffering. Another flow is our ability to receive compassion from other people – to accept help from others when we're suffering or struggling (or even . . . gasp . . . when we *ask* for it), and relate to others in ways that don't interfere with their being able or willing to help us. The third flow is our ability to relate compassionately towards our *own* struggles and suffering. Self-compassion is about giving ourselves the same understanding, validation and support we'd offer anyone we cared about and wanted to help.

Building on our earlier discussion of obstacles, with each flow there can be what CFT therapists call 'fears of compassion'[1] – concerns or obstacles that keep us from connecting with that flow. As we approach using compassion to work with anger, we'll start by considering these potential obstacles. In the next module, we'll consider ways to connect with the flows.

Let's start by exploring fears of compassion for the self:

Do you have any fears or reluctance around relating compassionately to yourself? What might keep you from giving yourself compassion when you're struggling?

James: *I guess it kind of feels like letting myself off the hook. I can't believe I'm quoting a Taylor Swift song here, but it's like that song 'Anti-hero'. All I know is the chorus: 'It's me, hi, I'm the problem, it's me.' At the end of the day, although I do a lot of blaming, I feel like I'm the one causing a lot of problems for me and my family.*

Antwan: *It seems kind of weak, you know? I think you just need to man up and take responsibility for your shit. I don't have time for 'poor me' stuff. Last module, there was the quote 'he's trying to turn me into a wimp'. I'm starting to get that's not what compassion means, but that was definitely there for me in the beginning.*

Jordan: *I have some fears. Although therapy has helped me with this, self-compassion means I won't be able to avoid the scary stuff and things I don't like about myself. But I guess I'm already experiencing it, only now I use it as a basis for criticising myself. I guess this would be looking at it in a different way.*

Do you have any fears or reluctance around relating compassionately to yourself? What might keep you from relating compassionately to yourself when you're struggling?

_____

_____

_____

_____

_____

_____

The companions' responses above highlight some common obstacles around self-compassion. James and Antwan shared concerns that self-compassion is about letting ourselves off the hook, self-coddling or avoiding responsibility. However, I think you'll find that relating compassionately towards our struggles (rather than, say, beating ourselves up for having them, blaming them on other people or avoiding them) can *help* us take responsibility for doing better. As Jordan rightly observed, compassion *does mean* we'll encounter uncomfortable feelings and experiences. But it gives us a framework for relating to these difficult experiences with understanding and a focus on figuring out how to engage with them effectively – recognising that although they're uncomfortable, they are normal human experiences we can learn to handle.

Now let's explore fears and reluctance around relating compassionately to others:

Do you have any fears or reluctance around relating compassionately to others? What might keep you from acknowledging others' suffering and struggle, or making efforts to help them?

James: *My first response is to say, 'No, I'm good at this!' I feel like I care a lot about others and help when I can. But if I'm honest, it's more complicated than that. Like I wrote before, I sometimes cause problems for the people I care most about, and I think I'm scared that if I really looked at their suffering, that would be confirmed. I want to change that, but it's painful to admit. The other part is that – at least to the extent I am the problem – I'm not sure how to fix it. At least I haven't been able to so far. I feel terrible about that. I think shame is a big barrier for me.*

Antwan: *I never really thought about it. I think I've always taken an 'every man for himself' perspective. Like, you're responsible for solving your own problems, right? But I've been thinking about that 'What kind of man do I want to be?' piece from a few modules back. I want to be the kind of man who helps people I care about. I guess I need to find some balance.*

Jordan: *I naturally tend to have compassion for others, but I think sometimes I struggle to translate that into action. One challenge is social anxiety. I have a hard time finding the words to say to others when they're struggling. With close friends, I've figured it out sometimes – just letting them know I care about them and am there for them helps a lot – but it still provokes a lot of anxiety. I think I'm also worried about being taken advantage of. At work, I've sometimes 'helped out a colleague' and ended up doing lots of work that they then took credit for. I think I've got lingering resentment from those experiences that holds me back sometimes.*

Do you have any fears or reluctance around relating compassionately to others? What might keep you from acknowledging others' suffering and struggle, or making efforts to help them?

The companions' responses above highlight common obstacles for relating compassionately with others – shame, attitudes about personal responsibility (Antwan's 'every man for himself'), anxiety about what to do, and fears of being taken advantage of. For those of us who struggle with anger in ways that have caused pain or problems for people we care about, shame can be an obstacle. It's hard to see those we care about suffer, particularly if we feel partially responsible for their pain. This is where self-compassion and compassion for others can intersect. We can have compassion for ourselves, recognising our behaviour was driven by powerful emotions we didn't choose and didn't know how to handle. We can manifest compassion for them (and us) by taking responsibility for our behaviour, acknowledging the pain we've caused, committing to do better in the future by learning to manage our anger and making efforts to follow through on that commitment (which you're doing in part by working through this book). Antwan's response highlights that a compassionate approach may require us to look at attitudes we've held for a long time to see if they're still a good fit for us. His response – as well as Jordan's – also reminds us that having compassion for others doesn't mean taking over responsibility for them. We can care for others and help them when they need it while maintaining appropriate boundaries and acknowledging their responsibility for their own lives, just as we're responsible for our own. Finally, Jordan's comment about anxiety demonstrates the *courage* compassion often requires – engaging with suffering can bring up tricky emotions, and accepting this discomfort is part of the cost of showing up for those we care about. It also provides an opportunity to practise self-compassion, as we learn to work with those feelings rather than letting them shut us down.

Next let's explore fears of receiving compassion *from* others:

Do you have any fears or reluctance around receiving compassion from others? What might keep you from accepting or being able to rely upon help from others when you're suffering or struggling?

James: *This may be the biggest challenge for me. I often think it would be really nice if I had someone on my side, but I have a hard time asking for help. I think my anger causes a lot of irritation for others – at least for my family – and I don't want to be more of a burden than I already am. I also think I engage others in ways that make it so they don't want to help me. It's like I push them away when I need them the most.*

Antwan: *I've always tried to handle everything on my own, and it felt weak to ask for help. You never know when that help is gonna be there, and when it's gonna disappear. When my father left, I was like, 'I guess I'm the man of the house now.' I think that's when I stopped asking for help. It hurts to think about that.*

Jordan: *It feels sad to say this, but I don't think I've ever felt comfortable relying on others. I've talked about this a lot with my therapist, and it goes way back. My mother was so harsh and critical that I don't remember ever feeling loved by her. I knew my father loved me, but he seemed inept and unable to stand up to Mum. I don't want to be like either one of them, really. I particularly don't want people to see me as weak . . . as a 'damsel in distress'. But I need supports in my life. I've had enough good experiences with my therapist and a few friends to know it can be helpful to have someone there when you're struggling. I need to work on this.*

Do you have any fears or reluctance around receiving compassion from others? What might keep you from accepting or being able to rely upon help from others when you're suffering or struggling?

_____

_____

_____

_____

_____

_____

For some people, this can be the trickiest flow of compassion. I think many people naturally tend to feel compassion for others but struggle to ask for help (or feel uncomfortable relying upon it) when they need it. There are several potential obstacles: fears of feeling like a burden, fears of feeling or being seen as weak, or not having had experiences of others being helpful when we've struggled in the past. Luckily, these flows of compassion involve skills that _can be learned and practised_, and _all_ of them can be helpful in working with our anger.

We'll continue to explore these flows of compassion in the next module, but for now I'd like to invite you to consider the three flows of compassion: self-to-self, self-to-other and other-to-self. Which flows do you feel come most easily for you? And which are your growth-edges, the ones you find most challenging?

Circle the number below that best corresponds to your experience with each flow:

'I am comfortable relating to my own struggles with compassion, and good at finding ways to help myself.'

'I tend to be sensitive to the struggling and suffering of others, and am motivated to find ways to help them.'

1   2   3   4   5   6   7

Not at all   Somewhat   Very much
like me   like me   like me

'I am comfortable receiving help from others when I'm struggling or suffering, and am able to ask for help when I need it.'

1   2   3   4   5   6   7

Not at all   Somewhat   Very much
like me   like me   like me

Final reflection

Considering the numbers you circled above, which of the compassion flows do you feel most comfortable with and able to utilise? Which are more of a struggle for you and have room for growth?

_____

_____

_____

_____

_____

_____

_____

Given what you know about yourself and your history, does it *make sense* that you might struggle with one or more of the flows? In your history, did you have experiences that taught you (or failed to teach you) things that make it hard to connect with these flows?

_____

_____

_____

_____

_____

_____

_____

Module 7: Working the Flows

Module 6 introduced the three flows of compassion, and we explored fears or reluctance that can exist around these flows. I think these flows relate intimately to working with anger. *Self-compassion* can help us be courageous in noticing when we're struggling (and having difficulties with anger *is* a struggle) and motivates us to figure out what will help us work with these challenges. *Compassion for others* can motivate us to keep going when it gets tough, so that our struggles with anger don't lead us to behave in ways that are hurtful to others. Learning to receive *compassion from others* can help us access feelings of being safe and supported, helping reduce feelings of threat that can fuel anger.

The rest of the book focuses heavily on self-compassion, so in this module we'll consider the other two flows: compassion from us to others, and compassion from others to us. If you find that you struggle with these flows, don't beat yourself up for it. These struggles present us with a perfect opportunity to practise self-compassion. Our ability (or struggle) to connect with these flows has a lot to do with our histories – with basic attachment patterns laid down very early in our lives. So if you struggle with one or more flow, *it's not your fault*. We can't control our histories – we didn't *choose* to struggle with giving or receiving compassion, but we can develop our ability to engage with them now.

Compassion from self to others

Compassion for others doesn't mean we do everything for others in the style of a 'helicopter parent' whose children don't learn to fend for themselves because the parent has already sorted everything. It doesn't mean we take on or take over the pain of others, trying to carry it for them. That's impossible, and it's a bit grandiose to imagine – we're not that powerful and, just like us, everyone else has a life that will sometimes involve pain and suffering. It's not our job to solve everyone else's problems, although we can often find ways to help.

Compassion for others means we are willing to *notice* and *accept* the suffering and struggle of others as something *real* and *significant* for them, and that we're motivated to try to be helpful to them to the extent it's possible and appropriate. It also means choosing to relate to others in ways that help them feel safe and refraining from engaging with them in ways that will cause them suffering. This is particularly relevant to those of us who struggle with externalised anger – I don't think most of us *want* to cause suffering in others, but we can find ourselves behaving in anger-driven ways that cause pain, irritation and even fear in those for whom we care the most.

Earlier, I invited you to consider the sort of person you want to be and the values you want to manifest in your life. Let's extend this reflection to think about compassion for others, considering the roles we want to play in their lives. I'll invite you to consider two questions:

Compassion from us to others

1.   What role do you want to play in the lives of others? How do you want your presence to impact their lives? How do you want them to feel when you're around?

2.   How do you want your presence to impact how others feel about themselves?

The first question is straightforward, asking us to consider the experiences we'd like our presence to trigger in others' lives. When we're around, do we want others to feel safe or threatened? Cared about or dismissed? Seen or invisible? Valued or ignored? The second question relates to the awareness that part of how we come to relate to ourselves is learned from how other people treat us.[1] When others treat us with respect, we learn to experience ourselves as being worthy of respect. When others care for us and nurture us, we learn that we are worthy of care and nurturing. When others relate to us in ways that are dismissive, abusive or demeaning, we can learn to experience ourselves as being unworthy of respect or deserving of poor treatment. When others only (or disproportionately) respond positively to one aspect of someone's person (for example, their physical attractiveness or what they can do for us), it's easy for them to subconsciously learn that this is the only thing about them that matters.

While we aren't *responsible* for how others feel about themselves, having compassion for others means recognising that the way we treat them *is very likely to* impact how they relate to themselves. Knowing this, what messages do we want to send them?

Let's consider these questions:

What role do you want to play in the lives of others? How would you like your presence to impact how they feel, and how they feel about themselves?

James: *This question hit hard. It brought up thoughts of my family, and feelings that I've failed them. I want them to feel safe with me, to know they're loved, and to feel able to turn to me when they need help or someone who cares about them. I want them to feel valued and respected. In thinking about this, I'm flooded with memories of treating them in ways that were the opposite to this – things like criticising them. Instead of being a safe, helpful presence, I think I've often been the one stirring things up. I want to make things work better, both at home and at work. I'm going to keep this in mind and work on it.*

Antwan: *I've never really thought about this. In terms of the role I want to play in people's lives, I guess I want to be solid – you know, someone they can trust, rely on and turn to when they need it. I want them to know my word means something, that if I say I'm going to do it, it's done. I haven't always done as well at that as I'd like, at least when my mum's asked me to put more into school. With the 'How do I want them to feel about themselves?' question, I guess I want to give respect as well as get it, and to let people I care about know it, so they don't feel taken for granted.*

Jordan: *I think I'd like people to think of me as kind, competent and reliable. In terms of the role I play in their lives, I could do a better job of expressing kindness and affection, letting people know how I feel about them. I guess that relates to the second question, too. Anxiety gets in the way of me saying what I mean. I think part of kindness also means sometimes being a mirror and letting people know when I don't appreciate what I'm getting from them, so they have the chance to do better. But I'd never want to be someone who makes people feel badly about themselves. My mother's criticism left me feeling like I was pathetic – like I couldn't do anything right. I'd never want to make people feel like that. I guess I'd like to help people feel seen and appreciated.*

What role do you want to play in the lives of others? How would you like your presence to impact how they feel, and how they feel about themselves?

_____

_____

_____

_____

_____

_____

When our companions thought about it, all three sought to be a positive force in the lives of others – to be helpful, reliable and honest. James pointed out a dynamic that can be tricky: the pain that can arise when we become aware that we've sometimes engaged with others in ways that are very different from how we *want* to be there for them. This is a potential obstacle but also a turning point. Instead of turning this pain into shame ('what a bad partner/parent/etc. I've been . . .'), we can use it to fuel our commitment to work with our anger, so we can give those around us the best of ourselves. Finally, Jordan highlighted that being helpful to others doesn't always mean being 'nice' but can also involve giving them assertive feedback when they're doing something problematic, in ways that help them improve rather than feeling attacked. We'll explore how to do this in Section VI on compassionate communication, later in the book.

Receiving compassion from others

As we considered in the previous module, many of us find it easier to *offer* help than to *receive* it. Let's explore the dynamics of this flow by reflecting on a few questions:

Compassion from others to us

- How would I like others to treat me when I'm struggling with anger?

- What might be helpful for me to experience from others when I am struggling with anger?

- What keeps me from being able to rely on or receive help from others?

- What might I need to do so they will be able to help me?

I've anchored the first two questions to anger, but they could just as easily have ended after the word 'struggling'. The first two questions relate to what that other-to-self flow of compassion might *look like* – considering how we'd like to be treated when we're struggling, then more specifically considering what would be *helpful* to receive from others in these situations. The third and fourth questions follow our pattern of considering obstacles – thinking about what gets in the way of relying upon or receiving help from others, and how we might address these obstacles so this flow of compassion can be a support for us. Spend as much time as you need to think about these questions. When you're ready, continue to the reflections below.

What would be helpful for you to receive from others when you're struggling? What gets in the way of that happening, and is there anything you might do to improve your ability to benefit from this other-to-self flow of compassion?

James: *I think it would be most helpful for me to receive patience and understanding. Working with anger is going to be a long road for me – I get that, and I'm committed to doing it. It would help if Sarah and others understood that I really am committed to doing better, that it's hard but that I'm working on it. It would feel good to have that acknowledged. I think my irritability gets in the way by naturally pushing her away. If I could get a handle on that – overreacting, coming off as critical and irritable – I think it would be easier for her to support me. She's appreciated it in the past when she saw me making an effort.*

Antwan: *What keeps me from getting help from others is me. I gotta admit there's a part of me that thinks I shouldn't need help, that a man should be able to handle everything on his own. Sometimes, I do really think that. But there's another part of me that knows, 'of course, we're all gonna need help sometimes'. My mum and a few teachers helped me over the years, but sometimes I've pushed them away. I guess the first thing I'd need to do is stop pushing.*

Jordan: *Objectively, I know my life would be better if I let people in and let them help me. Just having people to do things with would really help – to hang out with, chat about life, that sort of thing. When I've risked opening up to others, it's been helpful. My therapist is a godsend, and the time I've spent time with friends has been nice. It's my anxiety and fears of being a burden that have held me back. But I don't feel burdened when friends ask me for support, so maybe I shouldn't let that stop me.*

What thoughts did the questions prompt in you? What would be helpful for you to receive from others when you're struggling? What gets in the way of that happening, and is there anything you might do to improve your ability to benefit from this other-to-self flow of compassion?

All three companions acknowledged that it might be helpful to receive kindness and support when they're struggling. I think sometimes we can get so accustomed to 'going it on our own' that it doesn't even *occur* to *ask* for help, much less consider what we'd need to do to make it possible for others to help us. But it makes no sense to resent not receiving help if we're not asking for it (something I've occasionally been guilty of). Our companions highlighted obstacles as well – acting in ways that push others away, feeling we *should* be able to handle everything on our own, and worrying about being a burden. Rather than letting these obstacles stop us, we can bring compassion to them – recognising *how it makes sense* that we learned to cope in these tricky ways and considering how we might approach things differently to get this flow of compassion working for us.

Final reflection

What stood out to you as you considered the self-to-other and other-to-self flows of compassion? In working to manage your anger, might it be helpful to strengthen your ability to relate compassionately to others or to receive compassion from them? What might you be able to do to practise extending compassion to others or receiving it from them?

End of section check-in

How are you feeling about your progress so far? What have you noticed?

_____

_____

_____

What have you found helpful?

_____

_____

_____

What obstacles have arisen?

_____

_____

_____

What would be helpful for you to keep in mind going forwards?

_____

_____

_____

Compassion practice plan

Now we've finished the first section, let's pause and consider how you'd like to proceed as you work through the rest of the book. One option is to simply move through the book, working through the modules in order. That will probably be of some benefit, but if you're like me, you may find yourself appreciating the material as you go, then having things fade as time passes. For new learning and behaviours to stick, we need to revisit and practise them – to develop and strengthen the brain patterns that correspond to this new learning.

With that in mind, I'll invite you to put what you're learning into daily practice to translate this new learning into positive life changes – like a workout plan for working with your anger and developing your compassionate self. We'll revise the plan after each section to incorporate new material.

To prepare for our first practice plan, let's revisit the skills and learning we've explored so far, presented as practices you can do during the week:

1. **Check in with your motivation to work with anger** (Module 1): Take five minutes to reconnect with why you've committed to work with your anger. Think about the important reasons you've chosen to do this, and how your life and relationships will benefit when you succeed.

2. **Consider how you want to change your brain** (Module 2): Take five minutes to reflect that every time you do a new behaviour (including thinking about something in a different way – like connecting with compassion) you're strengthening brain patterns that will build that new behaviour into a habit. Consider what habits you want to build today (each of the other items on this list is a potential example).

3. **Reflect on the person you want to be** (Module 3): Take five minutes to revisit your ideas about the sort of person you'd like to be and become. Consider those qualities and how you might build them into today. If you wrote that you want to be kind, how might you express kindness today? If you wrote that you wanted to be patient, how might you demonstrate that patience in one of your interactions today?

4. **Consider an obstacle and how you'll work with it** (Module 4): Take five minutes to notice obstacles that have made things difficult this week, and how you might work with them. Consider obstacles and challenges that might arise in the future and how you might plan to approach them in ways that fit with the sort of person you want to be.

5. **Mindful awareness** (Module 5): Do a mindful check-in, pausing to notice your bodily experience, emotions and thoughts. Try to do this curiously and in a non-critical way: 'I'm noticing I'm a little irritable today and I'm going over and over what happened at work yesterday afternoon.'

6. **Connect with a flow of compassion** (Modules 6 and 7): Take five minutes to connect with either the self-to-other or other-to-self flow of compassion. Pick a flow from Module 7 and reflect on the questions posed. Consider how you might express compassion to another person, or how you might engage others in ways that make it possible for them to be able (and willing) to relate compassionately to you.

I've suggested a practice time of five minutes for each option. That's to keep them brief and doable. *It's much more effective to do short practices repeatedly over time than to do long but infrequent practices.* If five minutes is too long, scale it down to what feels doable. Thirty seconds? Two minutes? The key is to figure out how to practise consistently, to keep strengthening these new paths you're developing in your brain. Just like working out, you might get a little benefit from weekly sessions with a trainer to teach you lots of different exercises, but you'll grow a lot more if you work out in between appointments and *use what you've learned*.

Here's the invitation:

> **Every day, do one mindful check-in and one other practice from the list above, not repeating any one practice more than twice during the week** (to get some variety). Even at the recommended dosage, that's only ten minutes per day – but that ten minutes will go a long way in helping you build those new brain patterns and the habits that go with them. Feel free to mix up the daily mindful check-in as well – there are *lots* of different mindfulness apps and recordings of practices available online. Check them out – it will keep them from getting old and give you the chance to discover some favourites.

> On the next page I've included a form for keeping track of your daily practice (you can also find a reproducible copy in Appendix B, or you can download or print it from https://overcoming.co.uk/715/resources-to-download). If you're more high-tech than me – as most people are – you may want to come up with a way to record your practice on your phone instead. But *make sure you record it*. This will help build the habit of doing it, and provide you with a reminder of your work and progress. The practice log is laid out in the form of two tables. The first includes boxes that can be

checked to record the practices you did each day. The second is for notes and reflections about your practice, with space to indicate things you found helpful – both about the practices themselves and in figuring out how to practise regularly ('I noticed that the end of my lunch break, right after I've finished eating, is a good time to fit in my practice.'). There's also a space to note obstacles, which could either be things having to do with a practice ('I didn't really like . . .') or things that interfered with you doing the practice that might be worth considering and planning for ('I was too tired to do anything at the end of the day as I'd planned. Going forwards, I'm going to practise right after breakfast').

Daily practice log

Practice	Sun	Mon	Tues	Weds	Thurs	Fri	Sat
Mindfulness							
Checking in with motivation to work with anger							
Considering how you want to change your brain							
Reflect on the person you want to be							
Consider an obstacle and how to work with it							
Connect with a flow of compassion							

Practice notes

Day	What was helpful?	What obstacles came up?
Sunday		
Monday		
Tuesday		
Wednesday		
Thursday		
Friday		
Saturday		

Section II:

Building Blocks of a Compassionate Approach for Working with Anger

Module 8: Three Systems of Emotion

CFT understands human motivations and emotions through the lens of evolution – that we have these feelings and motives because they helped our ancestors stay alive and pass their genes along to us. This can help us make sense of things that otherwise might be quite confusing. Let's consider an example. Have you ever wondered why you don't crave broccoli (substitute any healthy vegetable here) the way you crave pizza (substitute any high-fat, high sugar or high-salt snack here)? Why would many of us tend to crave and/or feel comforted by eating the very sorts of foods that – if we eat too much of them – will compromise our health? How does that make sense?

If we consider that humans evolved to survive in a world of scarcity – not knowing when the next meal would come – it makes a lot of sense that we'd crave and find comfort in sugary, fatty, salty snacks. Sugar is energy. Fat helps us store calories we can draw upon when food is scarce. And salt is an essential nutrient that occurs relatively rarely in the natural world. Craving and consuming these foods meant survival for our ancestors, who faced a world in which regular access to food was far from certain. Fast-forward to today, in which high-sugar, high-fat and high-salt foods are mass produced, inexpensive and more readily available than healthy alternatives, and this tendency to crave and consume high quantities of such foods becomes a health risk. This isn't our fault – we didn't *choose* to have tricky brains that crave unhealthy food. But if we want to be healthy, it's our job to find ways to manage this trickiness – for example, figuring out how to eat in a relatively healthy fashion even when we'd rather have crisps. For me, that means not keeping crisps in the house most of the time!

In this way, we can see that our traits and emotions – even those that are a tricky fit for a modern world that's very different from the one faced by our ancestors – exist because they were *functional*. They helped keep our ancestors alive so they could pass along their genes to us. Rather than seeing experiences like anger as something *wrong* with us, and condemning ourselves for having them, we can *accept* them as a part of having a human life, try to *understand* them and learn to work with them. We didn't choose to have these experiences and sometimes they can be hard to manage. But if we can accept them as part of the hand we've been dealt in having a human life, we can learn to play that hand in ways that fit with our values.

In CFT, we sometimes do what's called an *evolutionary functional analysis* of emotions and experiences, which is a fancy way of saying 'Why am I like this, anyway? How does it make sense that I would have this experience?', while looking through the lens of evolution. One helpful guide in developing this understanding is the *three systems model of emotion*, pictured in Figure 8.1.

Figure 8.1: The three systems model of emotion

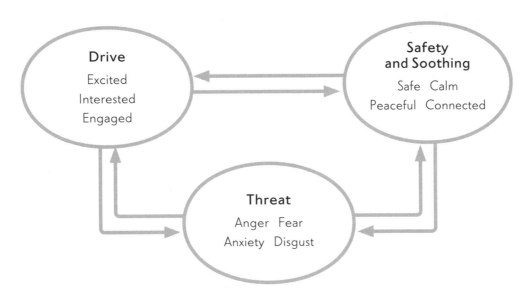

Figure 8.1 features three circles, each representing a system of emotions. These emotions are grouped according to evolutionary function[1] – by the way they contributed to our ancestors' survival. We've evolved emotions that help us identify and respond to things that threaten us; emotions that help us identify and pursue resources and goals, and reward us for attaining and completing them, and emotions that help us feel safe, balanced and content. We'll spend the rest of this module unpacking the threat system, and we'll explore the drive system and the soothing and safeness system in the next two modules.

The threat system

To survive in a world filled with real physical dangers, our ancestors needed to be very good at quickly identifying and responding to things that could harm them. That's the purpose of threat emotions, which evolved to help us anticipate threats (anxiety), respond to them – for example, by fleeing or fighting (fear and anger), and avoid things that might make us sick (disgust). While we may experience them as unpleasant, these emotions served very valuable functions for our ancestors.

They can be tricky, though, because the ways threat emotions work in us can be a better fit for earlier times in the human story. For example, threat emotions like anger or fear prepare us to fight, flee or freeze, which are relatively well suited to encountering a bear in the forest, but in modern life we're more likely to face complicated social or work situations in which we'd be better served to pause, thoughtfully consider the situation and carefully decide how to proceed.

In this way, our basic threat responses can sometimes hinder rather than help us in the face of modern challenges. As I mentioned above, *this isn't our fault* – we didn't *choose* to have these tricky brains with emotions that sometimes work in outdated ways. It's not our fault that social change happens *way faster* than does biological evolution. As my friend and CFT founder Paul Gilbert says, 'our brains were designed *for* us, not *by* us'. But if we want to have good lives and fulfilling relationships, it's our job to learn how to work with the challenges these tricky brains can create for us.

The awareness that our anger, fear, anxiety and disgust are part of a system that evolved to help our ancestors deal with threats can help us have compassionate understanding for these experiences. It's easy to get swept up by these feelings because *they are designed* to capture and hold our attention. Threat emotions are our brains' attempts to protect us when they've detected potential danger or blocks to our resource-gathering efforts. Evolution designed these emotions to grab our attention, focus our thinking and attention on the threat, and motivate us to *do something now* to address it. These emotions are powerful, so it's easy to get swept up in them. They're also uncomfortable, so it's tempting to try to get rid of them, or to interpret them as 'something that's wrong with me'. But what if instead of just acting on them, trying to avoid or push them away, or beating ourselves up for having them, we tried to notice them for what they are, and thoughtfully considered how to proceed? 'Wow, I'm angry right now. My threat system is working hard to protect me. I wonder what might be most helpful to do?'

This response begins with the mindful curiosity we explored in Module 5. Recognising what we're experiencing without rushing to react or judge opens the door to lots of helpful possibilities.

Let's bring some mindful curiosity to the threat system emotions:

What threat emotions do you commonly experience? What situations tend to trigger them?

James: *Definitely anger – as I've mentioned, it's often triggered by things not going how I'd planned, or people not responding in the way I anticipate or think they should. But I'm noticing I also get anxious pretty frequently, particularly around what other people think of me. I worry my kids are afraid of me, and don't understand how much I love them. I worry my wife must get tired of having to deal with me, and that she must wish she'd married someone else – someone easier to be with. I worry about that stuff a lot, actually.*

Antwan: *I get angry if I feel someone's disrespected me or if they talk down to me. I've got in fights over that. For the other stuff, I don't get scared a lot, but I know my mum is worried I'll turn out like my dad – sometimes I worry I'll let her down. Maybe that's anxiety, I don't know. Thinking about my father brings up a lot of feelings for me – painful stuff – but I usually end up feeling angry. I guess I kinda use anger to not have to feel that other stuff.*

Jordan: *I'm acquainted with lots of threat emotions! I get angry at social injustice – things like sexism and racism – although often that anger turns into anxiety and sadness before I do anything. I get anxious about people not seeing what I have to offer at work, and about general life stuff, like whether I'll ever find a partner, whether I want kids … that sort of thing. Sometimes it can be scary being a woman, not in a theoretical way, but in terms of real-world stuff that happens. I'm scared of being attacked when walking back to my car at night, I'm scared of being raped. And it's complicated, because then I can get anxious and angry that I have to be scared about such things – that this is the world I live in.*

The companions' responses highlight a few important points. First, although our focus is anger and how to manage it, we'll all sometimes experience other threat emotions as well. Second, we see that threat emotions can trigger one another in ways that can sometimes make it hard to know exactly *what* we're feeling. We can feel *angry* about being *scared*; we can feel *anxious* about feeling *angry*. As Antwan highlights, we can sometimes use anger to avoid feeling more vulnerable emotions, like anxiety, sadness or grief. In trying to sort all of that out, it can help to pause and get curious – considering the situation or trigger, noticing what feelings come up in our body, reflecting on our histories and how they may have set us up to be triggered by these experiences. We can even begin offering ourselves some compassion, recognising that this is difficult, and that it makes sense that we'd struggle with it.

What threat emotions do you tend to experience? What situations tend to trigger them?

_____

_____

_____

_____

_____

_____

_____

Now you've considered the way threat emotions show up in your life, let's touch base with the other important message in this module – that we didn't *choose* to have these experiences.

What was it like to consider that it's not your fault you have these threat emotions – that these emotions are your brain's efforts to protect you by helping you identify and deal with threats in your life?

James: *It's a different way of thinking about things, that's for sure. It makes sense, but I'm not entirely sure about this 'not your fault' stuff. It sure feels like it's my fault. I find myself wanting to believe it, but it does kind of seem like letting myself off the hook. I certainly didn't choose to struggle with anger, and I've always thought there was something wrong with me. I'm not sure exactly where I'm at with it, but I'm interested to learn more.*

Antwan: *It's cool to learn about how our brains work. I never really thought about where my feelings come from. It was weird to read that my emotions aren't my fault, because a lot of people in my life like to tell me all about the shit that's my fault. This feels different.*

Jordan: *I found it useful to think about threat emotions as our brains' efforts to protect us. My brain apparently is working to protect me a lot! But it does help me feel less like I'm broken, and more like maybe I've just got an overactive threat system. I want to learn more about the safeness and soothing system, because I'd like to learn how to strengthen mine.*

What was it like to consider that it's not your fault you have these threat emotions – that these emotions are your brain's efforts to protect you by helping you identify and deal with threats in your life?

_____

_____

_____

_____

_____

_____

_____

Final reflection

Is there anything you can take away from this module that might be helpful to remember when you notice yourself feeling angry?

_____

_____

_____

_____

_____

_____

_____

Module 9: The Drive System

In addition to detecting and responding to threats, our ancestors had needs to fulfil. They needed food, shelter, mating opportunities and a host of other resources to help them survive and pass their genes along to us. Pursuing such goals is the domain of the 'drive and resource acquisition' system, or 'drive system' for short. We know the drive system is active when we find ourselves excited, interested and engaged; when we feel ourselves committed to achieving that next step in whatever we're doing, and when we feel like celebrating after a success.

The drive system is all about getting things done. It alerts us when resources and goals are available, motivates us to pursue and work towards them, and rewards us when a goal has been achieved or a resource acquired. Every time you have the 'Ooh . . . I want that!' experience, it's your drive system orienting you to a potential resource or goal. And then when we achieve a goal – say, get a promotion or a raise at work, ace an exam or successfully complete any number of life tasks – there's a burst of positive feeling (reflected by a release of brain chemicals like dopamine), rewarding us for our efforts and motivating us to keep at it in the future. As we learn to manage our anger, it can be helpful to notice and allow ourselves to feel good about the progress we've made, however small – those feelings are fuel that will help us keep going, even when things get hard. So I'd encourage you to take a moment to recognise you've made it a good way into this book – well done!

The drive system is very powerful at motivating us, and in this way it can be helpful. But it can also present challenges. We can find ourselves chasing the 'rush' that comes with pursuing and attaining goals . . . sometimes through means like using drugs, pornography addiction or 'recreational shopping', finding ourselves purchasing lots of things we don't need (my wife might suggest I've fallen into this a bit with my vinyl record collecting, and she's almost certainly right!).

We also can end up unintentionally causing suffering when we become so focused on pursuing our goals that we become blind to the impacts our behaviour has on others – think of wealth-hoarding, the parent who is so motivated around their career that they neglect their family, or the individual who is so energised in their pursuit of sex that they fail to recognise their partner isn't as into things as they are. Like the threat system, the drive system tends to *narrow* the focus of our attention and thinking. With the threat system, our attention, thinking and mental imagery are focused on perceived threats – which helped our ancestors survive, as it's no good getting distracted by the beautiful flowers when one comes upon a moose with her calf when hiking (pro tip: back away slowly!). The drive system narrows our attention, thinking and imagination as well, focusing our attention, thinking and fantasies on our goal – as when we've got a new love interest, or I've noticed a vintage Martin guitar in my local music shop. This narrowing of our attention and thinking helps us move towards goals more efficiently, but it can also keep us from noticing other things that are happening in our lives, or in the lives of the people around us.

I'm convinced that a huge amount of suffering in the world isn't caused by people who *intentionally* harm others; they are just so focused on pursuing their own goals that they become blind or insensitive to the harm others experience as a result of their pursuits. I don't think most online retailers *intended* to drive out small local businesses, but when enough book lovers order their books online, bookshops close. Marriages crumble when people pursue everyone to whom they find themselves attracted. Democracies can't survive when politicians value gaining and keeping power more than they value the fairness of the voting process. And both my bank account and marriage would suffer if I snapped up every vintage Martin that found its way into my local guitar shop! While the drive system is good at helping us pursue and achieve our goals, mindful awareness is needed so we aren't swept up in ways that negatively impact our lives or those of others.

Let's take a moment to consider this system.

What thoughts do you have on the drive system? What gets your drive system going?

James: *When I'm not caught up in irritability, lots of things get me excited. I like cheering on my football team with my mates. I don't always love my job, but I want to do it well, and it's satisfying when I complete a project. These days I'm most motivated around doing things with my family. In the rare moments when we have a nice, easy day together, it feels great. The problem is that I make these plans about how I want things to go and if something doesn't work quite right, I overreact and end up ruining it for everyone.*

Antwan: *I'm a competitive guy, so I can relate. I like to prove myself. That comes out when I play sports and video games. I get locked into what I'm doing and it's like everything else disappears. When I do well, it's awesome. But I can get angry when I lose or do badly. I'm not a very good loser, particularly when other people are around.*

> **Jordan:** *I love my job, and I'm motivated to do it well. But while I love the feeling of having done a good job, I have a hard time when others recognise me for that – I tend to make a self-deprecating comment or pass the credit to someone else. It's hard to give myself credit, like I feel like an imposter or something. I also think anxiety sometimes blocks my drive system – I want to be in a relationship, but I get anxious and end up not approaching people I'm attracted to. I want to make friendships, but then that voice in my head says, 'Why would they want to spend time with you?'*

These responses highlight different life areas in which the drive system comes into play – at work, in relationships and in recreational activities like sports and video games. They also bring up an important point for understanding how anger works: *our different emotion-regulation systems can interact with one another*. Threat emotions like anger can arise quickly when we've set our sights on a goal and we're blocked (for example, when things don't go the way James has planned them, or when Antwan loses at a sport or video game). Jordan's response demonstrates how threat emotions can inhibit our drive system – we may hesitate to pursue important goals because we feel anxious or insecure.

What thoughts do you have on the drive system? What gets your drive system going?

_____

_____

_____

_____

_____

_____

_____

Let's continue our exploration of the drive system:

Have you seen any examples of how the drive system can be tricky in your own life?

James: *I can see how people get so locked into their goals that it causes problems. I think that happens with me getting frustrated with things not going the way I've planned. It's like I have this picture in my head of how things are 'supposed' to go, so I try and make that happen, which is good. But if something doesn't go according to plan, I get upset and end up ruining a situation that could have turned out okay if I'd given it a chance. My drive and threat systems definitely interact.*

Antwan: *I clicked with the part about how goals can blind us to other stuff. When I get competitive, everything else disappears. Thinking about this is tough, because it feels like my dad did that when he left us. He had things he wanted, so he chased after them. Doing that, he bailed on us. I guess he was so hooked that he didn't think about what it would do to us. A lot of the time, I hate him for that. I wish he could see the pain he caused us.*

Jordan: *I connected with this part because it seemed to explain so much of what happens in the world . . . people hurting people because they're caught up in their own goals. And my anxiety clearly interferes with pursing my own goals – it kicks in so quickly. It's like the moment after I think 'I'd like to do _____', there's a voice in my head saying, 'yeah, but . . .', telling me I can't do it and coming up with all the ways it could go wrong.*

Things can get tricky if we're completely swept up by our emotion-regulation systems, so it's helpful to learn to notice when these systems become activated in us. This noticing can help us utilise the activation of our threat and drive systems when it's helpful, while refraining from acting out our urges in ways that cause harm – to others, or in our own lives. This highlights a core message of CFT: *it's not our fault* that we inherited these tricky emotion systems that can set us up to struggle, and *it's our responsibility* to work with what we've got so we don't cause suffering for ourselves or others. What are your thoughts?

What are your thoughts about how the drive system can be tricky? Have you seen any examples of that in your own life?

_____

_____

_____

_____

Lots of challenges come with having a human life. There's a lot of pain built into it. Compassion is about acknowledging this pain and figuring out what would be helpful in addressing it. Sometimes 'what is helpful' involves taking action to change things we're unhappy with, and sometimes it means accepting there are things we don't have the power to change right now and considering what would help us be the best version of ourselves as we work with this difficult reality. In the next module, we'll explore the soothing and safeness system, which can be a great help with this.

Final reflection

This module explored the drive system, which is all about goals. As you've gone through the book, have you come up with any specific goals for yourself as you learn to manage your anger and move towards the life you want to have? Examples might be things like 'learning to communicate with my partner better in difficult situations', 'exercising regularly', 'drinking less', or 'letting the people I care about know I love them'. What do you think?

_____

_____

_____

_____

_____

_____

Module 10: The Soothing and Safeness System

The previous two modules explored the threat and drive systems, which evolved to help our ancestors *do things* to help them survive and reproduce – focusing us on threats and goals, and activating our minds and bodies to help us engage them. These systems narrow and focus our attention, thinking and mental imagery, and motivate us towards action. There's a felt sense of urgency when we feel threatened or excited – when these systems are active, we *want* to do things (or at least, we feel the urge to do so, in the case of anger or fear). This is why advertisers and political groups work so hard to trigger our threat and drive systems – often in combination. 'Your life sucks the way it is, but if you buy _____ (or vote for _____), everything will be better!' Threat and drive get us moving.

These systems are so good at focusing and energising us around threats and goals that if we become caught up in the emotions they create – anger, fear, attraction, excitement, etc. – we can end up doing things that cause problems in our lives. Ever say something out of anger or irritation that you wish you could take back? Spend too much money on something you really didn't need (and ended up not even liking that much)? Me too. Those things tend to happen when our threat and drive systems are constantly in control.

Luckily, there's a third emotion-regulation system to help us balance things out: the safeness and soothing system, or 'safeness system' for short. 'Safeness' sounds like a weird sort of made-up word, but it captures something unique – the feeling we have when we're safe, calm and balanced. In contrast to the narrow focus and 'I need to do this now!' urgency of the threat and drive systems, when the safeness system is active, we feel calm, content and balanced with flexible and open attention and thinking.

Recall a time you were hanging out with people who like and accept you, just taking it easy and having a good time. What did you talk and think about? The answer I get most often is 'All kinds of things!' When we feel safe and connected, we're not rigidly focused on threats or goals – our minds can easily shift from topic to topic, flexibly considering different perspectives. When this system is active, we're also more creative, more likely to help others and, yes, more *compassionate*.[1] It makes sense, doesn't it? When we feel safe and aren't caught up in fighting off threats or chasing after goals, we're better able to think about the kind of person we want to be, consider our most important values and act in ways that reflect them. This is important. Learning to help ourselves feel safe isn't just about feeling more *comfortable* – although it certainly helps with that – it's about *helping us be better versions of ourselves*.

If you have pets, consider how they spend their time. Sure, they spend some time pursuing goals (eating, asking for treats) and if threats appear in their lives, they'll activate to address them. But if your pets are anything like mine, they spend a *lot* of time taking it easy. Our ancestors were a lot like this as well, in contrast to the hectic lives many of us now find ourselves caught up in – in addition to feeling nice, taking it easy also helps preserve caloric resources when access to food is uncertain. A growing body of scientific research shows that one critical piece of a healthy human life is having *free time* – unallocated time in which we feel safe and aren't rushing to complete tasks.[2] This downtime gives us a chance to step back from the demands of daily life, connect with people we care about and do things that bring us positive emotions like joy. Having fun is important! This time also provides space to pause and reflect on our lives and how they're going, think openly about different courses of action we might want to take, consider adjustments we might make if things aren't going quite as we'd wish, and plan how to make these adjustments come to life in our daily routines. It's almost impossible to do this if we're constantly caught up in dealing with threats or in chasing after goals.

Let's pause to explore the safeness system:

Bring to mind a time you felt safe, calm and balanced – when your safeness and soothing system was active. What was going on in your life then? What was it like?

James: *Growing up, I didn't have much of this. My dad was always upset about something, and we'd do our best to not set him off – usually unsuccessfully. There was always tension in the house and fear you'd do something wrong. My greatest fear is that my kids will say the same thing when they're grown. But there are times that give me hope. Last year we went to a Christmas market and had a really nice day – a rare time I didn't spoil by getting upset about something. We walked up and down the street, had some bratwurst, crêpes and warm drinks, listened to singers and did a little shopping. It was so nice – no agenda, just wandering around doing whatever we felt like. It continued when we got home. After the kids broke off to do other things, Sarah and I had a drink and chatted about nothing in particular. It was wonderful. Often there's some underlying tension in our conversation, but that night we just enjoyed each other's company. It reminded me of when we were dating.*

Antwan: *I'm not sure about this one. I like downtime, but then I'm usually playing video games and sports and, like I said, I can get competitive. I guess sometimes I have this with my mum. Sometimes, at the end of the week, she'll pick up a pizza on her way home and we'll just sit and watch a movie – something funny, you know? And it just feels good. I like pizza nights.*

Jordan: *Growing up, I was anxious a lot . . . I still am. My mother was constantly critical, and it seemed like I couldn't do anything right. In secondary school I made a good friend, Abbie, who I really connected with. We had a lot in common. We were both anxious and into things like reading and playing music – neither of us fitted in with the popular crowd. We'd spend hours after school in coffee shops and then on the phone after we got home. We'd talk about everything – what we wanted to do after school, places we wanted to travel . . . We came up with plans to open a business together so we could see each other every day. Abbie is still my best friend, though we don't live near each other any more. I need to give her a call.*

Our companions' comments demonstrate an important point about the soothing and safeness system: *humans are designed to feel safe through caring connection* – through contact with those who accept us, care about us and value us. What have you noticed about how your safeness system works?

Bring to mind a time you felt safe, calm and balanced – when your safeness and soothing system was active. What was going on in your life then? What was it like?

What was it like to consider how you feel safe? Were you able to identify times like that? People who struggle with threat emotions like anger and anxiety may have a hard time feeling safe and soothed. If we've had difficult relationship histories or trauma involving other people, brain networks reflecting experiences of connection with others may link with threat, harm or betrayal rather than with experiences of feeling safe and cared for.[3]

If we have histories like this, managing emotions can be tough. We evolved not to 'regulate' emotions, but to *co-regulate* them through contact with caring others.[4] This may be particularly tricky for those of us who struggle with anger, as anger can manifest in ways that interfere with exactly the sort of connections that would help soothe us. I've sometimes described myself as a porcupine – when I'm struggling with irritability, I can desperately want to connect, but it can be hard for others to soothe me, even when they want to, because my quills – my facial expression, tone of voice, etc. – pop out and scare them away.

Part of working with anger involves becoming familiar with blocks to the safeness and soothing system, and how we can get this system online and working for us. While probably the best way to get the safeness system online is through caring interactions with others, relationships aren't entirely under our control and can take time to cultivate, so it can be helpful to have options for helping ourselves feel safe and soothed.

Let's get curious about how your safeness system works, and create a list of experiences that help you feel calm, safe, soothed and connected. We want to become familiar with such experiences and intentionally weave them into our daily lives. Safeness system emotions don't involve the urgency we see in drive and threat emotions, so it's *unlikely these activities will happen by accident* – they can get pushed off the radar by all the things we need to do. But as we notice what helps bring these feelings up in us, we can *intentionally* create space for them in our lives.

Let's get curious about your safeness and soothing system. What sorts of experiences get this system working for you? Think of experiences that involve other people but also things you can do on your own.

James: *My favourite option is spending time with my family but, as you say, that can be tricky. There are a few things I find soothing. I like going to the pub with friends to watch the football. There are also movies and shows that give me a sense of comfort. Music also helps. In the hardest moments of my life, music has been a comfort – particularly when a song captures feelings I'm struggling with. It helps me realise that other people struggle too, so I don't feel so alone. I still put those records on sometimes.*

Antwan: *Lots of times after school, I'll come home and watch YouTube streamers play games I like. Games like* Minecraft, *which I don't play much any more, but it reminds me of good times with my friends when I was younger. Especially if it's a streamer I've watched for a long time, it's almost like hanging out with friends. Sometimes I'll even talk my friends into playing* Minecraft *or another old game like that. It's fun but not competitive. It helps me calm down when I'm upset, so I guess that's soothing.*

Jordan: *Well, hanging out with Abbie or other friends helps me feel safe and soothed. But during the pandemic when we were all so disconnected, I spent so much time snuggling with my dog, Stella. It really helps! I can feel myself calming down in real time. Spending time in nature helps me, too. I love a good walk in the woods. Also, I'm a reader, and sometimes when I'm struggling, I'll reread book series I've loved in the past. If I'm reading a book with characters I really like, it's almost like spending time with friends without any social demands.*

The companions' comments emphasise that many soothing experiences involve *connection*. This can involve connection with other people (video games, hanging out at the pub, doing things with friends), but it can also involve other experiences that bring a sense of connection: contact with animals; spending time in nature; revisiting familiar movies, games, music and books . . . particularly those that help us recapture positive experiences from our pasts. Both Antwan and Jordan used the phrase 'it's almost like hanging out with friends' to capture the experience of some of their favourite soothing activities – giving them feelings of connection in the *present*.

Other experiences can activate our safeness systems as well. You might find that slowing down and taking time to focus on pleasant sensory experiences – having a cup of tea or cocoa, taking a hot bath or shower – can be helpful in bringing on feelings of soothing. Later, we'll introduce some breathing and imagery exercises that can help with this as well, but for now let's bring curiosity to how we might get your safeness system online and working for you:

What sorts of experiences get your safeness and soothing system working for you? Think of experiences that involve other people but also things you can do on your own.

_____

_____

_____

_____

_____

_____

_____

Let's begin creating a list of specific activities and experiences you find soothing. I'd recommend you begin this list now and spend the rest of your life adding to it!

Soothing activities:

1. _____

2. _____

3. _____

4. _____

5. _____

6. _____

7. _____

8. _____

Final reflection

Now that you've begun creating a list of experiences that help you feel safe, soothed and balanced, let's consider how you might weave these experiences into your daily life. Selecting at least one experience from your list above, how might you fit that activity into the next three days? When might you do it? What might help you to remember to do it?

_____

_____

_____

_____

_____

_____

_____

Module 11: Understanding Attachment Patterns

Module 10 explored the safeness and soothing system, and highlighted that *human beings evolved to feel safe and soothed through caring connection.* As we touched on, we aren't really designed to regulate our emotions in isolation, but to *co-regulate* them through connection with other people who accept, value and care about us. Even thinking about or being reminded of those who care about us can be helpful. In one of my favourite lines of psychological research, Phillip Shaver and Mario Mikulincer conducted a series of studies showing that prompting *attachment security*[1] – for example, having someone bring to mind a person who cares about them – boosted creativity, compassion and even prosocial behaviour. Caring connection is linked with the release of chemicals like oxytocin, which can literally 'turn down' areas of the brain that produce feelings of threat.[2] When we have these sorts of caring connections it's a huge help in dealing with the difficult parts of life and enhancing our happiness, and when we struggle with them, life challenges can feel much more overwhelming.

One tricky bit is that our ability to feel safe through connection with other people is powerfully shaped during the time in our lives when we're *most helpless to influence it* – during our first few years. Especially in that first year or so, we're almost completely helpless, and only survive due to the care given to us by others. When we're infants, all we can do when we're in pain – or hungry, tired, uncomfortable or struggling in any other way – is make a distress call. We can't do much, but we can *cry.*

What happens *when we cry* is of vital importance. A baby's cry is a call for help: 'Something's not right and I need you to help me with it!' Some have suggested that the way to get crying babies to stop is to ignore them. Sure enough, if you ignore a crying baby for long enough, they'll eventually stop. But – and please believe me, because this may be the single most important paragraph in this book – *this is a truly terrible parenting strategy.* When an ignored baby stops crying, *why* does it stop? What has it learned? The ignored baby stops crying – the *only behaviour* it can do when it needs help – because it has learned that *no help is coming.* It has learned that, however bad things are, there is nothing it can do, no one to help and no way to find soothing. That's a terrible thing for a baby to learn, and this learning can reverberate through their life as they grow older.

The way an infant's caregivers respond to their distress teaches them a *lot* – about relationships, other people, themselves, their emotions, and what to do when they feel emotions like fear, anxiety and anger. This is the focus of an area of psychology called *attachment theory*. Let's briefly unpack a few of the core ideas behind it.

Secure attachment

'Secure attachment' results when an infant has responsive caregivers who are consistently helpful in responding to their distress calls. Over time, this child learns a lot of good things:

- They learn there are helpful actions they can take when upset (call for help from caregivers).

- They learn that other people can be helpful when they're struggling.

- They learn to experience themselves as being worthy of love, acceptance and help.

- They learn that, although uncomfortable, threat emotions like fear can be soothed – so that the emotions don't totally overwhelm them.

Secure attachment relationships help us learn to face stressful situations and accept our own uncomfortable emotions, because we learn that there are things we can do – and people we can call on – that will help. Instead of becoming completely dysregulated when faced with difficult situations or painful emotions, we can meet this discomfort with the confident knowing that there are helpful things to be done and help available if we need it. They also give us a model for how to respond when others are in pain or need help, setting us up to engage compassionately with others.

Insecure attachment

'Insecure attachment' styles can result when an infant *doesn't have* caregivers who are able to respond in a consistently helpful manner to their distress cries. This can play out in a few ways. Attachment *anxiety* tends to result from having caregivers who are inconsistent – sometimes they respond helpfully and sometimes they don't. Sometimes they may try to help and then become overwhelmed and withdraw (for example, because they've become emotionally dysregulated themselves), and sometimes they may even respond *unhelpfully* (for example, by yelling or otherwise behaving in ways that feel scary to the infant).

If we have such experiences with caregivers, we can find ourselves craving connection but *unable to trust* it, fearing it will disappear when we need it most. We may fear that if others see what we're *really* like, they won't want us. Having learned that caring connections are unstable and can quickly be lost, people with attachment anxiety can find themselves panicking at the first sign of any relationship rupture (argument, disapproval, etc.), terrified they'll be abandoned or that the relationship has been ruined. For those who have experienced fear or even harm at the hands of caregivers or other people they were close to, close connections can be scary rather than soothing – because they have learned that closeness equals vulnerability.

In contrast, attachment *avoidance* tends to spring from experiences of neglect – having distress cries that were consistently ignored or simply not responded to; having needs that went unmet. If this is our history, we can fail to learn the value of connection at all. Secure attachment experiences help us learn to be soothed by connection and teach us that other people can be helpful when we're distressed. Without such experiences, we can learn that, however scary things get, we must go it alone. People with attachment avoidance may avoid close relationships with others because they haven't experienced them or learned how they can be helpful. They can also *not know how* to be helpful when others are distressed, as they haven't had this behaviour modelled for them. We learn how to effectively care for others through our experiences of receiving care.

Such individuals may also find themselves avoiding their own emotions – particularly vulnerable-feeling emotions like anxiety, fear, grief or sadness. We learn to tolerate and work with such feelings through contact with caregivers who soothe us, so the feelings aren't so overwhelming. Without such nurturing and the soothing to make the emotions manageable, infants can find themselves completely overwhelmed. What do we do when we're faced with overwhelming experiences we aren't equipped to handle? We develop ways to *avoid them*. We may even use other emotions – like anger or drive – to help us avoid feelings that scare us. When discussing fear, anxiety, sadness or shame with clients, I've often heard things like 'I just throw myself into my work until it goes away.' Not having had experiences that taught us how to soothe and manage difficult feelings, we can find ourselves going to great lengths to try not to feel these things . . . an impossible task, since we all possess brains that *will* produce these emotions at different times.

Which of the following statements bests captures your experience?

(a)   I feel comfortable connecting with others, sharing my experience with them, and can depend on others and receive help from them in times of need.

(b)   While I'd like to have caring connections with others, I feel uncomfortable opening up and fear they may reject me, abandon me or not care as much about me as I do about them.

(c)   I tend to avoid close connection with others and am uncomfortable sharing my experiences with them or depending on them.

These statements are just my attempt to briefly capture experiences of attachment security (a), anxiety (b) and avoidance (c). Attachment styles are interesting, as we'll tend to have a dominant style – how we generally tend to experience ourselves in relation to others – and our style of connecting can vary across different relationships. This is important, because even if we tend to have a lot of attachment anxiety, we can still develop secure relationships and learn to *feel safe* in a relationship with another person. If we're a 'go it alone' person who tends to avoid close relationships, it's still possible to develop relationships that help us learn how to have meaningful, supportive and soothing connections with others if we're willing to stretch ourselves a bit.

This is an important goal in psychotherapy – therapists work to cultivate relationships with clients in which the client can learn to feel safe in connection with another person, learn that such relationships can be helpful, and become more comfortable pursuing connection with other people outside of the therapy setting. In CFT, part of our work is to help you develop a *secure attachment relationship with yourself* – by developing a compassionate version of the self that can offer validation, support, encouragement and help when you are struggling.

Let's take a moment to reflect on attachment, considering James's example:

Growing up, who did you feel close to? When you were upset, what did you do? Did you have caregivers who were able to help you feel safe and calm down?

James: *This module has been tough for me. It's brought up a lot of painful memories. I felt alone a lot growing up. I knew my parents loved me, and sometimes when I was upset, they'd ask what was wrong. But lots of the time I kept it to myself. I wasn't sure how my father would react – his anger was unpredictable, so I never knew what I was going to get. My mother was more predictable but not very emotionally available – probably exhausted from dealing with my father's anger – so, often, I'd just go to my room and hang out on my own. I guess I had caregivers who were sometimes helpful but not consistently so.*

How about your present life? Did any of the attachment styles discussed above feel familiar? Do you have relationships in which you feel safe and accepted? Do you find it easy or difficult to feel close to others?

I definitely fall into the 'anxious attachment' category. I crave close relationships with others, and I find them terrifying. I'm scared I'll come to rely on a relationship and then lose it, scared that others will tire of me and decide it's just not worth it, that if they see what I'm really like they won't want me. I'm terrified that one day Sarah will just be done. I'll come home, and she and the kids will be gone. But some days, things are great between us, and it feels close and loving. When things are going well, we're an affectionate family. Clearly they love me because they've put up with all my crap and they're still here. I want to make it easier on them. I can feel close to others, but it's difficult for me to really relax and feel safe in relationships.

These days, what do you do when you're upset or struggling with something? Are you able to turn to others for help? Are your connections with others helpful at these times?

My default is to handle things by myself, although I often wish someone would help me. I guess I ask for help when I really need it – particularly with things at work. That stuff usually works out. With emotions, it's a lot harder. Last module, I kept reading the word 'soothe'. I struggle to soothe myself. When I'm having a hard time, what people usually see from me is anger and irritability, so they steer clear. At those times, I don't ask for help ... although I still really want it.

I'll invite you to reflect on your own attachment experiences, both in childhood and your current life. Thinking about this stuff can be tricky; we can discover unexpected pockets of pain. Give yourself some time to work through these questions, and if you find yourself connecting with painful memories or experiences, see if it's possible to give yourself some compassion. Acknowledge the pain, recognise how it makes sense that you would have it, and try to relate to yourself with the same kindness you'd offer anyone else you cared about and wanted to help. *We don't get to choose* our attachment patterns and *it's not our fault* if we've learned to feel unsafe in our relationships. But once we recognise these patterns, we can work to *heal* them.

Growing up, who did you feel close to? When you were upset, what did you do? Did you have caregivers who were able to help you feel safe and calm down?

_____

_____

_____

_____

How about your present life? Did any of the attachment styles discussed above feel familiar? Do you have relationships in which you feel safe and accepted? Do you find it easy or difficult to feel close to others?

_____

_____

_____

_____

_____

These days, what do you do when you're upset or struggling with something? Are you able to turn to others for help? Are your connections with others helpful at these times?

_____

_____

_____

_____

_____

Attachment styles have a profound effect on our lives, and much of what shapes our attachment patterns has to do with factors over which we had no control. We don't get to *choose* how our early attachment patterns will be shaped. If you're someone who generally feels safe connecting with others, sharing your experience with them and accepting help from them, feel good about that . . . and recognise that many other people have a very different experience of life. And if you're someone who struggles with these experiences, understand that this isn't your fault. This can be tough stuff – we're designed to feel safe through connection, so if we struggle with that, it can be hard for us to truly feel safe, period. Recognising these patterns in ourselves, we can work to heal them. This is also not about blaming our caregivers for our struggles with attachment – much of how we're able to care for our children is related to our own attachment patterns, so if we had caregivers who were unable to give us what we needed, it's a safe bet they were struggling themselves. If this is a significant area of difficulty for you, it might be worth finding a therapist to help you with it – therapy involves a relationship with another person who is accepting and committed to help you, so it's a perfect laboratory for restructuring these patterns of connection.

Final reflection

What was it like to consider your attachment history and patterns? Did any feelings come up for you?

_____

_____

_____

_____

_____

_____

_____

_____

In thinking about your attachment patterns and history, did you notice anything that might be related to your anger and how it plays out?

_____

_____

_____

_____

_____

_____

_____

_____

Is there anything you'd like to change about your connections with other people that might be helpful in working with your anger and other tricky emotions?

_____

_____

_____

_____

_____

_____

_____

_____

Module 12: The Social Shaping of the Self

In this section, we're introducing how to bring compassionate understanding to different areas of our lives. We all struggle sometimes, for good reasons – there are a lot of things about having a human life that are just difficult to deal with. We've got tricky brains that produce powerful emotions that can be hard to handle. Our earliest learning experiences powerfully shape whether we feel safe and competent (or unsafe and incompetent) in connecting with other people in ways over which we have absolutely no control. We're then shaped by lots of other experiences as our lives play out – many of which we don't choose, and over which we may have little or no control.

As I mentioned in the Introduction, suffering is the price of admission for having a human life. We'll all experience pain, loss, disappointment and a host of difficult experiences over the course of our lives. Sometimes I've heard people use the phrase 'We're all in the same boat.' I recently encountered a meme that felt much more accurate: 'We're all in the same *storm*, but we're in very different boats.' We'll all face the tricky, often painful, business of having a human life . . . but some of us are born into luxury liners, while others are harshly dropped onto the narrowest plank of wood, offering no shelter from the storm.

As CFT founder Paul Gilbert often says, we all just find ourselves here – born into circumstances over which we have no control but must adapt to deal with. We don't get to choose whether we're born into a family that is wealthy or poor; whether the physical aspects of our bodies allow us to easily fit in or set us apart; whether our caregivers are equipped to care for us; whether the area of the world we're born into is safe and comfortable or filled with danger. But all these factors shape how our lives will play out – and shape how we develop, in ways we don't get to choose or design.

As I've mentioned, human bodies and brains are adaptation machines. We learn, adapt to and are shaped by everything that happens to us. Evolution designed us to learn to protect ourselves, fit in and to do whatever is necessary to get our needs met. During my experience volunteering in a prison setting, it became clear that many of the men's lives had systematically trained them to perform exactly the behaviours that had landed them in prison. If, instead of being born to a stable, safe, middle-class family who valued and encouraged my education, I had been born into poverty in an unsafe environment in which I was abused and had to fight to survive, would the current version of me – the professor sitting in my recliner writing this book on my laptop – even be possible? It seems more likely I'd have ended up in one of those prison anger groups as a participant rather than the facilitator.

In CFT, instead of beating ourselves up for our struggles and things we've done that have caused problems, the goal is to understand how things came to be this way and figure out how to do better in the future. In this module, we'll explore how the angry versions of ourselves *learned* to struggle with anger and manifest it in unhelpful ways. In doing this, we'll consider different ways our experiences shape how we develop and how we can begin to take control of this process.

Shaped by our experiences

While we may think of learning as an intentional process – like the learning we did in school – our brains are learning *all the time*. Evolution designed our brains to be constantly absorbing information about the world around us and how it works, to help us survive and get our needs met. This learning can occur without effort or awareness, and how efficiently we learn (how quickly new information is stored, and how powerfully) is modified by emotional factors. For example, our brains learn very efficiently and powerfully when our threat systems are activated – working hard to store all the information they can about potential danger, to help us keep ourselves safe in the future.

While learning about threats can happen very quickly, *learning that we're safe* is a much less efficient process. Our brains are oriented to attend to threatening information in a 'better safe than sorry' sort of way. There's survival value in adapting very quickly to high-threat environments, but evolution doesn't care so much about helping us *feel* safe – it's all about keeping us alive so we can pass along our genes. This can be tricky if we've a history of being in high-threat environments like growing up in an abusive household or doing military service in a combat zone. When we've had such experiences, our brains can become tuned to the high-threat environment – we learn to be constantly vigilant for potential danger, may become wary of other people, and develop hair-trigger threat responses. These ways of being keep us safe when we're in high-threat environments, but can cause us problems once we've returned (or found our way) to a safe environment. I've seen this in many combat veterans who've returned home. They've come home, thinking everything will be better, looking forward to enjoying fun time with their families, only to discover a version of reality in which they are constantly on edge, in which affection for their families, and the peace and enjoyment they'd imagined having is overridden by constant experiences of threat. They can find their combat-ready reactiveness translated into a hair-trigger temper, fear, hypervigilance and only feeling safe when they're out shooting with their combat buddies.

I've had such veterans tell me they thought they'd 'gone crazy' or were 'broken'. In reality, they had brains that had adapted to a high-threat combat environment and *had not yet* adapted back to the relatively safe home life to which they'd returned. Learning to feel safe takes much longer than learning to feel threatened, and requires many more learning trials (being in the same situation repeatedly over time). It's literally about teaching our brains that the world is different now – no longer so dangerous – and because our brains are focused on protecting us, it takes a while for those lessons to sink in. But after going to the park with their family again and again, eventually these veterans noticed they spent less time scanning for danger and more time spontaneously enjoying the time with their loved ones.

Even if we aren't caught in high-threat environments, a lot of our learning takes place *implicitly* (without conscious awareness) in our lives, including learning about anger. As we've mentioned, we learn by *observing how others behave* – particularly parents, caregivers and others with whom we spend a lot of time. We also learn by observing *things that go together in time*, such as when we've had a painful experience with another person and then find ourselves feeling threatened when we encounter someone else who reminds us of the person who hurt us. And we learn *by what outcomes follow our actions* – if we do something and something pleasurable happens (or something aversive *stops*), we're more likely to do that behaviour again (psychologists call this *reinforcement*). On the other hand, if we do something and it's followed by a painful or unwanted outcome, we're less likely to do that behaviour again – this is called *punishment*.

Discussions about types of learning can get complicated, but we won't go into it that deeply here. We're interested in understanding how we learned our angry habits. People who struggle with anger *learned* to struggle with it, and recognising this can help us resist urges to beat ourselves up when we find ourselves struggling. We're not 'angry people'. We've had learning experiences that have taught us unhelpful ways of responding, and haven't taught us to manage this tricky emotion. This awareness can also help us *give ourselves permission to move beyond what we were taught growing up*. Sometimes I hear people refer to unhelpful parenting strategies (like any form of aggression towards a child, such as spanking) and say things like, 'Well, it happened to me, and I turned out fine.' Better to recognise that perhaps our caregivers struggled too, and we turned out as well as we did *despite* this modelling and harsh treatment. Once we recognise how it *makes sense* we'd struggle with anger, it can free us up to consider how we might manage those angry habits in ways that reflect the sort of person we want to be.

Let's consider a few questions:

What did you learn about anger growing up? What did you learn about when you should become angry and how to behave when you are angry? How did you learn this?

James: I take after my father when it comes to anger. It wasn't what he said to me but how he acted. I see myself doing things he did; things I hated as a kid. He'd get angry all the time – if something went wrong, if people didn't do what he wanted, if things didn't go as planned . . . I guess I learned that if things aren't going just as I'd hoped, it's time to get upset. For him, that meant yelling and sometimes throwing things. I'm glad it doesn't go that far with me – for me it's more being irritable, cursing, snapping at people and just stomping about. It's not fun to write about, because it feels immature – like I'm acting like a toddler who didn't get his way.

Antwan: I don't remember learning anything about anger – it's not something we talked about, you know? I remember my parents arguing a lot. Before he left, my father had a hair-trigger temper. He'd drink and get in fights sometimes. I never saw him hit my mum, but I wondered about it – he smacked me a few times when he was upset. Like I said before, he told me never to let anyone disrespect me, and when that happens I can lose it quick. Sometimes, my dad seemed to like it when I'd get angry. One time, this other kid was mouthing off and I got tired of him and hit him a few times. My mum was really upset about that, but it was one of the few times my dad stood up for me – he said something like 'That's my boy! He doesn't take shit off no one.' I was kind of proud about that. Now it seems a little sad.

Jordan: In my house, we never talked about emotions – I don't remember my parents ever saying the word 'emotion' or using any feeling-words. There certainly wasn't any discussion about how to handle them or what to do when you have them. In terms of learning about anger, my father was soft-spoken, so he didn't model it at all. My mother never looked angry, but you could tell when she was upset about something. It usually took the form of disapproval – she'd become really critical, and make you feel like dirt. That's one thing I learned about anger – she let me know it was never acceptable to express it. If I acted angrily at all – raising my voice, even making angry facial expressions – it would be a long lecture with consequences like getting grounded, being sent to my room for hours or having my things taken away. I was supposed to act pleasantly and politely all the time. If I got upset, I'd just go to my room and cry. There just wasn't any room for it in their world.

The companions' responses demonstrate several different types of learning. James and Antwan describe their fathers modelling anger. We also see this in Jordan's description of her mother's criticism, although Jordan learned to direct criticism at herself rather than towards others. We also see how anger can be shaped by consequences. Antwan described his father praising him for fighting when angry, which stood out because his father's approval was hard to come by. On the other hand, Jordan described being punished for showing any sign of anger – both through her mother's disapproval and through consequences such as being sent to her room for hours.

What did you learn about anger growing up? What did you learn about when you should become angry and how to behave when you are angry? How did you learn this?

_____

_____

_____

_____

_____

_____

_____

Often, when we look back at our lives and the different learning experiences we've had, we can see how our struggles _make sense_ – how it makes complete sense that we would struggle with _exactly this_. Sometimes it's hard to see how the dots fit together, but believe me – if you struggle with something, you can be sure this struggle _makes sense_ in relation to your learning history and the ways our tricky brains can work. This awareness is important. Instead of feeling ashamed and beating ourselves up for struggling, we can compassionately recognise that we didn't choose to struggle with this, that we _learned_ things that set us up to struggle in these ways, and that we can learn new ways of engaging with life that will work better.

Final reflection

What was it like to consider what you learned about anger growing up? Did any feelings come up for you?

_____

_____

_____

_____

_____

_____

_____

Considering your responses, can you see how it makes sense that you would struggle with anger in the ways you do? What is it like to recognise that? If not, can you imagine that, even if you can't see the connection, your life experiences may have taught you (or failed to teach you) things that shaped your experience of anger and how it plays out?

_____

_____

_____

_____

_____

_____

_____

Module 13: Factors that Maintain Our Anger

The previous module explored how our anger can be shaped by our learning history – by things we witness and which happen to us in our lives. But learning doesn't stop when we reach a certain age. If our angry habits continue, it's probably because consequences in our lives keep them in place. There are several ways this can happen, and if we can identify factors that maintain our anger, it can be helpful as we learn to manage it.

Some of us find anger or its consequences rewarding – enjoying the 'strong' feeling that comes with anger, or finding that it sometimes seems helpful as we work to meet our needs and pursue our goals. When I volunteered in a prison, one man in our group had a history of radiating anger and hostility, and a reputation for rapidly escalating into violence. This caused him problems, but also helped keep him safe in a prison environment – other men gave him a wide berth and didn't hassle him. They didn't want to face his explosiveness.

We also have psychological needs, including the need to feel a sense of agency, personal power or strength. As I touched on in the Introduction, if we don't feel powerful in other areas of our lives – like our jobs or relationships – the way anger activates our bodies can be seductive. Our interactions can even play out in ways that reinforce this feeling of power – there's a conflict, we escalate in anger, the other person backs down, and we experience feelings of dominance or 'winning'. 'Winning' in this way comes at great cost to our relationships and, ultimately, our happiness – but if our anger-driven behaviour seems to help us in pursuing goals or meeting our needs (such as helping keep this man safe in prison), it makes sense we'd have a difficult time giving it up, doesn't it? We need to find other ways to meet those needs if we're to commit to managing our anger.

As James has described in his reflections, another potential obstacle for managing anger is shame. Some of us engage in angry behaviour that causes problems or pain for people we care about. Recognising this can be deeply painful. I know from personal experience what it's like to look at a situation that's going badly and realise *the problem here is me* – or, more accurately, my angry or irritable behaviour. Seeing that, it's easy to think shame-driven thoughts like 'There's something wrong with me', 'I'm such a terrible father/mother/

partner/etc.' or 'Why do I always screw everything up?!?' I think shame is one of the most painful mental experiences we can have, setting us up to shift into patterns of avoidance that allow escape from this pain, like blaming the other person ('I only said _____ because you did _____!') or pretending that nothing happened. We can also double down on the shame, getting caught up in self-criticism about what happened. Like Jordan, if we've been taught that we should *never* be angry, even *feeling* anger can bring up feelings of shame and thoughts that something is wrong with us.

The problem with these strategies is that *they keep us from taking responsibility for our anger and finding better ways to handle situations that trigger it*. Although it can be challenging at first, working with anger means being willing to step out of our angry selves, notice and name what's happening ('I'm getting really irritated/angry right now'), resist urges to do things that will fuel the anger or make things worse, and figure out better ways to handle things. Coming modules will explore this process in greater detail.

Let's explore the consequences of your anger in your current life and see if we can figure out anything helpful:

What's it like when you have an anger episode? Think about a situation that commonly triggers your anger. How does it usually play out? What do you usually do? What happens afterwards – how do you feel after the anger episode? What do you do then?

James: *I resonated with the piece about shame. Shame plays a big role in my anger triggers. My anger tends to come up when things don't go as I'd like, and I think underneath that is the sense it's somehow my fault that things are messed up, whether that's true or not. I think sometimes my anger helps mask those feelings of shame. But then I say things that are hurtful to my family – snapping at Sarah or the kids – and then the shame lands on me full-force. I feel terrible about myself. After that, things can play out in different ways. Sometimes I double down and get blamey like the book talks about. Sometimes I argue and defend my position. And sometimes I just get overwhelmed, shut down and refuse to interact, which my wife has called 'tantrumming'. But none of it helps.*

Antwan: *Like I've said, I get angry when I feel disrespected or when something is unfair. It does seem powerful, like I'm full of energy and no one can touch me. Usually I lash out, most of the time with words, and sometimes by fighting. After, it feels fine. Like I put them in their place and let them know they couldn't disrespect me. I guess it does feel kind of strong. I also get angry sometimes when I see families out in public, particularly kids doing stuff with their fathers. All I can think about is how I don't have that. I feel cheated. There's so much anger, but nothing to do with it. I think that bleeds into school and other places sometimes. It's like I've got this anger stored up that's just looking for somewhere to go, so I end up letting it out when I shouldn't. Then I feel bad, but usually I find a way to justify it – blame the other person or whatever. It doesn't feel good to admit that.*

> **Jordan:** *Thinking about it, my 'triggers' all seem appropriate. My anger comes up when people engage me in inappropriate ways, when things seem unfair, or in response to things like sexism or racism. But as soon as I notice the anger, there's a feeling like I'm doing something wrong. Then I start doubting myself – 'Am I being too sensitive?', 'Am I making this up?' Looking at my past, I experienced a lot of gaslighting – when I'd get upset, my mother and others would always tell me there was nothing to be upset about. I think I learned that being upset meant there was something wrong with me. There was no acknowledgement that sometimes things happen that it's appropriate to be upset about. Anyway, this all circles in on itself – rather than being assertive and dealing with the situation, I shut down, cry and vacillate between criticising myself and thinking about how I hate my life (which isn't really true). My therapist thinks this plays a role in my depression.*

What's it like when you have an anger episode? Think about a situation that commonly triggers your anger. How does it usually play out? What do you usually do? What happens afterwards – how do you feel after the anger episode? What do you do then?

_____

_____

_____

_____

_____

_____

_____

Our companions shared several examples of how different experiences can shape how anger plays out in us. James highlighted shame as a precipitant of his anger, as well as noting self-attacking, blaming others and shutting down after observing the consequences of his angry behaviour. Antwan described feeling strong and dominant after 'putting them in their place' but then acknowledged that perhaps some of his reactivity around 'being disrespected' was displaced anger that may have been primed by feelings of grief and loss. His response also highlights why working compassionately with anger requires courage – when we take a close look at how things play out for us, we can figure out things that make us uncomfortable. Jordan described getting caught in a cycle of doubting herself and self-criticism, both of which function to keep her from addressing situations that trigger her anger. What did you notice as you explored how your anger plays out and the consequences that tend to follow it? Once we're aware of consequences that reward our anger, or obstacles that keep us from taking responsibility for working with it, we can look out for these things and consider how we might approach such situations in more helpful ways.

This process is another example of compassion – *noticing the obstacle/struggle* (sensitivity to suffering) and *considering what might be helpful for addressing this challenge* (motivation and action to alleviate and prevent the suffering). With that in mind, now might be a good time for a reminder that *we didn't choose to learn unhelpful ways of relating to our anger*. They represent understandable efforts to pursue our goals, deal with threats or meet our needs – and, at the point at which we learned them, these strategies *were the best we could do*. But once we become aware that the ways we've learned to cope are unhelpful, we can take responsibility for replacing these outdated strategies with more helpful ways of engaging that better reflect the sort of people we want to be.

Final reflection

What was it like to consider the way your anger plays out, and the consequences that can keep it going or keep you from dealing with it? What feelings came up as you explored this?

Did you learn anything that might be useful in understanding and working with your anger going forwards? Anything you think might be important to remember or that you'd like to curiously watch out for in the future?

_____

_____

_____

_____

_____

_____

_____

_____

End of section check-in

How are you feeling about your progress so far? What have you noticed?

_____

_____

_____

What have you found helpful?

_____

_____

_____

What obstacles have arisen that should be considered as you move forwards?

_____

_____

_____

What would be helpful for you to keep in mind going forwards?

_____

_____

_____

Compassion practice plan

Now we've completed the second section, let's update the practice plan. Here are a few practices based mainly on the modules in Section II:

1. **Check in with the three systems** (Modules 8–10): As an alternative to the mindful check-in, you can pause to check in with your three systems: threat (anger, fear, anxiety, disgust), drive (excited, interested, energised) and safeness/soothing (safe, calm, content). Here are a couple of options. First, take a moment to notice which system is most activated for you: 'Which system is in charge for me right now?' Alternatively, you could quickly assign each system a rating from 1 to 10 (where 1 is low and 10 is high) indicating how threatened, driven or safe you feel right now (as I write, my threat is about a 3 because I'm in COVID isolation right now; my drive is a 6 as I'm excited to be putting the final touches to the book; and my safeness is a 7, as I'm comfortable, with a tasty cup of coffee at hand).

2. **Validate an experience of threat** (Modules 8–13): Validation involves observing an emotional response in ourselves or another person, accepting it as real and valid, and acknowledging how it makes sense that you or the other person might feel this way. Pick an emotion you've experienced today or observed in another person, name it ('I'm feeling/felt _____', 'They're feeling/felt _____'). Then consider how *it makes sense* that you or they would feel this way, given your (or their) history, our tricky brains and the situation ('Of course they would feel attacked when this happens', 'Of course I'd struggle with this, given my history').

3. **Unpack an experience of threat, drive or safeness** (Modules 8–10): Take five minutes to pick an emotional experience of threat, drive or safeness/soothing you've had today. Notice how this experience shaped your attention, thinking, imagery, bodily feelings, motivation and behaviour. Notice how threat and drive emotions narrow your focus and activate you – notice the feelings of urgency that go with them. Notice how the safeness system opens your attention, helps you think more flexibly and creatively, and helps balance your emotions. If you chose a threat experience, remind yourself 'this *anger* is my threat system trying to protect me'.

4. **Engage in a soothing activity** (Module 10): Pick an item from your list of soothing activities and do it! Go for a walk. Have a cup of coffee or tea. Listen to some music. Take a bath. Using what you know is soothing for you, try to carve out at least fifteen to thirty minutes today to do something that has no other purpose than to bring your soothing and safeness system online. Enjoy! Savour it.

5. **Notice your attachment patterns playing out** (Module 12): Take five minutes to bring awareness to attachment patterns that played out for you today. Notice times you anticipated or feared rejection. Notice times you pulled back and withdrew from others. Notice times you connected helpfully with others. Consider how these patterns make sense given your history, how more or less helpful they were in the situations, and how you might want to approach these experiences with others in the future.

6. **Connect with a flow of compassion** (Modules 7–11): Take five minutes to connect with the self-to-self, self-to-other or other-to-self flows of compassion. Using what you've learned, recall a time you've struggled and offer yourself some compassionate understanding. Consider how it makes sense that you would struggle with this, and what this struggling version of you might need. For other flows, select a flow from Module 7 and reflect on the questions posed. Consider how you might express compassion to another person, or reflect on how you might engage with others in ways that help them relate compassionately to you.

Every day, do one mindful check-in or three systems check-in, and one other practice. Take your practices from those listed above, as well as those included in the first practice plan, on pages 64–6. Make sure to do at least two or three of the newer practices, and don't repeat any practice more than twice per week, to get some variety.

Bonus suggestion

If you like, see if you can add in a safeness/soothing system activity every day, on top of the daily check-in and practice. We want to *get into the habit* of building soothing activities into our daily lives. You might consider how you could decorate or arrange your environment in soothing ways – using pictures, art and other things to create spaces that help you feel soothed and comfortable. For example, my music room is filled with art created by friends, and posters from bands I've loved since my teens, and I find keeping it relatively free from clutter helps me relax.

As the list of practices is growing, I've left most of the entries in the practice log form blank, so you can write in the ones you've done for the week.

Daily practice log

Practice	Sun	Mon	Tues	Weds	Thurs	Fri	Sat
Mindful check-in/ three systems check-in							

Practice notes

Day	What was helpful?	What obstacles came up?
Sunday		
Monday		
Tuesday		
Wednesday		
Thursday		
Friday		
Saturday		

SECTION III:

Self-compassion and Self-care

Module 14: Introducing the Compassionate Self

This section will focus more directly on self-compassion, self-care and how we can use this to manage anger. This module explores a core concept in CFT – the compassionate self. As we explored in the previous section, different motives and emotions work within us to powerfully organise how we experience and interact with the world. They shape how we pay attention, think and reason, imagine, feel in our bodies, are motivated to behave, and how we respond to different situations.

In this way, it's like there are different versions of us – different 'versions of the self' – threat-focused versions (angry self, anxious self, scared self), drive-focused versions (excited self, interested self, competitive self, romantic self), and versions linked with feeling safe and connected (loving self, caring self, relaxed at-ease self). This 'versions of the self' piece may be a different way of talking about things than we're used to, but it can be a handy way of describing how basic motives and emotions can powerfully organise our experience. These different versions of us have their own patterns of being and relating with the world. For example, my 'competitive self' – the version of me that shows up when I'm anchored in an achievement-focused motivation to win or obtain a goal – relates very differently to other people than does my 'caring self' – the version of me that's rooted in a caregiving motivation to take care of others who are suffering or struggling.

We can't get rid of any of these 'selves', because they're based in how our brains work, but we *can* decide which ones we want to send to the gym – which ones we want to cultivate, practise and strengthen. The more we engage with and behave from the perspective of a particular version of the self, the more we strengthen the brain patterns linked with those ways of being, so that we'll increasingly embody these qualities in the everyday moments of our lives.

In CFT, the version of the self we want to cultivate, strengthen and practise is the *compassionate self*. The compassionate self is strong and courageous enough to handle whatever life throws at us. It provides a framework for everything we'll be doing from here on – tying together everything we're doing. Instead of trying out a bunch of random techniques, we'll be developing your compassionate self's repertoire of skills.

Earlier, you were invited to consider the person you would like to be – what characteristics you would have, how you would engage with the world and how you would show up in your relationships with other people if you were at your very best. The compassionate self is sort of like this. It's a version of the self that is rooted in our deepest values – designed to help us embody our best aspirations even when things get hard . . . *especially when they get hard*. Cultivating the compassionate self is about developing the strength to face suffering, struggle and difficulty head-on, and to work with these challenges in ways that are helpful – for us and for others. In this way, the compassionate self has certain qualities we'll be working to develop.

Let's explore some of those qualities:

- **Courage:** A willingness to engage with suffering, struggle and difficulty. The courage of compassion is the willingness to look deeply into suffering to discover the causes and conditions that produce and maintain it; to work with the things that scare us the most, even the things we like least about ourselves.

- **Kindness:** Sometimes called 'caring commitment', this doesn't mean 'niceness'. It's about motivation – the motivation *to help* when things get hard.

- **Wisdom:** Anger *reacts*. Compassion *responds*. The wisdom of compassion can manifest in numerous ways, including knowledge (for example, how our tricky brains work and how we're shaped by things that are out of our control), the ability to see things from different perspectives rather than getting caught up in narrowed threat- or drive-focused views, and the ability to think flexibly and creatively when addressing suffering.

- **Kind curiosity:** When faced with suffering or struggle, instead of blaming and shaming, the compassionate self is *curious*. It strives to notice and learn about suffering and struggle; to discover what will be helpful in addressing it.

- **Acknowledging acceptance:** Rather than getting upset about things not being how we *want* them to be, compassion sees things how they are – acknowledging and accepting the reality of the current suffering or struggle: 'This is tough right now.'

- **Sympathy:** Sympathy involves allowing ourselves to be *moved* – to *feel something* – when we witness suffering. The heart-sink we feel can help motivate us to do something about it.

- **Empathy:** Empathy is about understanding the experience of the person who is suffering. What is going on? What are they (or I) feeling? How does it make sense that they (or I) feel this way?

- **Non-condemnation:** Sometimes we can find ourselves criticising ourselves when we suffer, or blaming others for their own pain or struggle, implying that struggling means they (or we) are weak, flawed or not good enough. The compassionate self refrains from attaching negative labels, recognising them as unhelpful.

- **Distress tolerance:** Coming into contact with suffering and struggle is often uncomfortable and sometimes deeply painful. The compassionate self has the willingness to tolerate discomfort when it arises, and the skills to help us keep from being overwhelmed by it.

- **Confidence:** The confidence of the compassionate self isn't arrogance but a calm *knowing* that, whatever is going on in our lives and in our minds, *we will find helpful ways to work with it.*

The qualities listed above are just a sampling of the strengths we cultivate in developing our compassionate selves. As you move along, it might be helpful to consider 'What would be helpful in preparing me to deal with (*insert struggle or suffering here*)?' We're continually trying to get better, grow stronger and develop more skills for dealing with the challenges life presents, in working with anger and beyond.

Let's take a moment to consider this:

> **What do you think about this compassionate self business so far? Did any of the qualities stand out to you? Would you add any others – things you think would be helpful as you work with your anger and the other stresses in your life?**
>
> **James:** *I'm still getting a handle on this idea of having multiple 'selves', but I guess it makes sense. It does seem like there are different versions of me that show up at different times – the way I am when I'm angry is completely different from when I'm feeling safe and connected, or when I'm working on a project. I like the idea of a 'compassionate self'. Several qualities resonated with me, but the one that stands out right now is **distress tolerance**. Lots of my anger triggers involve things that most other people don't get bent out of shape about. If I were better at tolerating distress, I might be able to keep it together rather than getting angry when things don't go just how I want. I'm not sure what I'd add. Maybe **patience**, so I can wait to see what happens rather than just reacting the moment things seem like they're going sideways.*

Antwan: *When I first read the words 'compassionate self' I thought it was pretty lame. But reading about the qualities, it made more sense. I like the idea of '**courage**', and facing the stuff that's scary. If I was going to add a quality, I guess I'd add **strong**. I want to be strong, and it seems like it fits.*

Jordan: *I like the idea of the compassionate self. When I was a girl, I wanted to grow up to be Wonder Woman, and that's what came to mind as I was reading this module – someone who is strong and focused on helping. I admire people who use their power and influence to help others. In terms of qualities, **non-condemnation** really stood out to me. It was different, as the only one that was about something you don't* do *as the compassionate self, but my life would be completely different if I could stop beating myself up for everything I do. I think it would free me up. I guess I might add **encouraging**, because it's kind of the opposite of condemnation. A voice saying, 'You can do this' when I'm struggling would really help.*

What do you think about this compassionate self business so far? Did any of the qualities stand out to you? Would you add any others – things that would be helpful as you work with your anger and the other stresses in your life?

_____

_____

_____

_____

_____

_____

In CFT, we use an acting approach when developing the compassionate self. Some people might read that list of qualities and think, 'Well, that's nice, but I'm not anything like that.' Taking an acting approach, this isn't a problem. Actors play roles *all the time* that are very different to how they experience themselves in real life. Otherwise, they wouldn't get many jobs! How do they manage it? They use their imagination – imagining what it would be like if they were this character, with the character's attributes and motivation. They imagine what this character would care about; what they would pay attention to; how they would understand, experience and respond to things that happen in their lives.

We can take the same approach with the compassionate self. Relaxing our grip on our ideas about ourselves, what we're like and what we're capable of, we can *imagine what it would be like* to be a deeply compassionate person. We can imagine having qualities like the courage to face things that scare us, the deep desire to *help* in the face of suffering or struggle, the wisdom to figure out how best to engage with difficult situations, and the confidence that *we will find a way* to engage with the situation in a helpful manner. It doesn't matter if we see ourselves like this or not – like an actor, we can step into the role, imagining what it would be like if we *did* have these qualities. What would this courageous, kind, wise, confident version of us pay attention to? What would they care about? How would they feel when things get difficult? How would they engage with other people? How would we move through the world as this compassionate being? Some find it helpful to consider people in their lives (or even public figures) who embody these qualities and consider them as a model. We're stepping into the persona of this deeply compassionate figure, imagining having these qualities and how they shape our lives.

When we imagine what we would think, care about or do as a deeply compassionate being, *we're creating and strengthening new networks in our brains.* We're literally creating the neural architecture – the patterns of connections in our brains – that will help us develop these compassionate strengths and build them into habits. Just like everything else we learn, the more we activate these patterns – the more we connect with and imagine being this compassionate version of ourselves – the stronger the patterns become. Eventually, we just find ourselves reacting in compassionate ways. *This is how we change.*

Now, let's try the compassionate self practice. I've described the practice below, but several audio versions of it can be found online: www.compassionatemind.co.uk/resource/audio. I'd encourage you to try several different methods to see which works best for you.

The compassionate self practice

- Take a few moments to prepare for the practice. Sit in an upright, dignified posture. Allow your breath to slow down to a soothing, comfortable rhythm. If you notice any tension in your body, see if it's possible to relax those areas. Spend a couple of minutes just enjoying some slow, comfortable breaths.

- Imagine the qualities you would have as a compassionate person, and what it would be like to be filled with these qualities. Spend a few minutes on each of the following experiences.

- Focus on your desire to become a compassionate person, and think, act and feel compassionately, spending time on each quality:

  - Imagine being filled with a caring motivation – a deep desire to help yourself and others cope with suffering and have happy lives. If you're visual, you might imagine this caring commitment beginning as a light at the level of your heart, gradually filling you with this desire to be helpful.

  - Imagine being calm and having wisdom.

  - Imagine being empathic, aware of what you and others feel, and how these feelings make sense.

  - Imagine being filled with a sense of confidence, knowing you can tolerate difficulties and that you'll figure out a way to work with them.

  - Imagine being warm and kind, able to help yourself and others feel safe.

  - Imagine being non-condemning, but also wanting to help relieve suffering and to produce change and happiness.

- Try to create a compassionate facial expression, perhaps a kind half-smile.
- Imagine yourself becoming more powerful, mature and wise.
- Imagine the sensations you'd have in your body as this compassionate being. Imagine feeling calm, centred and strong.
- Think about your tone of voice and the kind of things you'd like to say or do.
- Think about your pleasure in being able to be kind.

Remember, it doesn't matter if you feel you have these qualities or not – just *imagine what it would feel like if you* did *have them*. See yourself having them in your mind, and work through them steadily. Notice how the qualities affect your body. It's okay if you lose focus or if it feels awkward – developing new skills often feels awkward, like learning to play an instrument or a new sport, or to speak a new language. All these activities involve learning new patterns – and with all of them, we get better with *practice*.

We'll explore many opportunities to deepen the compassionate self practice in the rest of the book, growing our ability to understand and manage anger in compassionate ways. The goal now is to begin familiarising ourselves with this compassionate version of the self and the acting approach we're using to imagine what it would be like to have these compassionate qualities.

Final reflection

What do you think about the acting approach taken to develop the compassionate self? Did you notice any resistance in yourself? If so, does it make sense that you would have some resistance? What might help you stay motivated to give it a try?

_____

_____

_____

_____

_____

_____

_____

_____

Can you identify a life situation that you could approach as your compassionate self – in which you could imagine what it would be like to have these compassionate qualities, and how you would experience, understand and engage with this situation from this place of compassion? What situation might be helpful to engage with in this way?

_____

_____

_____

_____

_____

_____

_____

_____

Module 15: Building Self-compassionate Lifestyles

In CFT, we define compassion as involving the motivation to alleviate and *prevent* suffering, acknowledging that the best way to address suffering and struggle is to prevent it happening in the first place. In this way, perhaps the purest form of self-compassion involves self-care: living in ways that meet our basic needs, prepare us to engage with life in meaningful and rewarding ways, and minimise the extent to which we'll experience unnecessary stress, discomfort and trauma. I say *unnecessary* because any human life will involve stress, discomfort and things going wrong . . . *and* lots of pain and suffering can be softened, or even prevented entirely, if we work to cultivate healthy ways of living.

Let's consider how this self-compassionate approach can help in managing anger. We'll spend time exploring how to understand and work with anger triggers. But our anger triggers don't happen in isolation. They occur within the contexts of our lives – contexts that can dramatically shape how much power these triggers will have to impact our emotions. For a brief analogy, let's imagine a driver irresponsibly flicks a lit cigarette butt out of their window. That's the trigger, and if that trigger lands in a field full of grass dried by drought conditions, it's likely to start a fire that could spread quickly, with devastating results. On the other hand, if the butt lands in a pond – or even a green field, fed by abundant rain – it's likely to burn out, with no harm done. Managing anger isn't just about working with anger triggers – it's also about our lives as we live them every day, because that's where the triggers are 'landing'. We can't always control whether triggers will happen, but we can build lives designed to minimise their impact.

To that point, I'll share a bit of my story. As I've mentioned, anger and irritability have been a personal struggle of mine. When this has caused problems for me, it's often been through the vehicle of *impulsivity* – something triggers me, and I've quickly said or done something I ended up regretting almost immediately (like sending an email – I produce words at a rapid rate . . . great when you're an author, not-so-great when you struggle with anger!). I've found several things helpful in working with my anger, but probably the single most helpful thing I've found is exercise. A few years ago, I committed to regular exercise because I enjoy activities like skiing that I'd like to continue late into my life. Over time, I noticed that I was becoming physically stronger and my clothes fitted better, which was great. But I also noticed something I hadn't expected – since I'd begun exercising regularly, I was remarkably more emotionally stable.

Over the years, I'd developed strategies for working with triggers and curbing my impulsivity . . . so *most* of the time, I managed things well. But a few months after I started working out, I noticed I *wasn't having to use* those strategies much any more. Challenging things were still happening, but usually I wasn't even experiencing them as triggering – I just calmly handled them. The real test was when COVID hit, everything locked down, and I (like all academics) had to figure out how to put all my classes online (which I'd *never* wanted to do) with two weeks' notice, and was stuck in my house pretty much 24 hours a day with my wife and son, who both had to deal with their own inconveniences. For someone like me, who'd struggled with anger, this was the perfect storm.

And it was fine. I was handling stuff as it happened, almost never getting bent out of shape. On the days in which I *would* find myself getting triggered . . . I noticed that, almost without exception, those were days I *hadn't* exercised. It turns out for me (and scientific research shows it's not *just* me), vigorous exercise helps reduce impulsive emotional responses.[1]

If that weren't proof enough, the pandemic intervened to provide a bit more evidence. After two years of avoiding COVID, I took a risk and attended one of my favourite conferences. It was a great conference . . . *and* I ended up getting COVID. My initial illness wasn't awful – I isolated and had mild flu symptoms for a week or so. But the virus hit my lungs hard, and it was more than two months before I was able to exercise again. Those two months were, emotionally speaking, two of the most difficult months of my life – despite being off for the summer and not having much I had to do. It wasn't *just* the lack of exercise, as my lingering COVID symptoms were certainly stressful, but once I'd recovered and was able to exercise again, the emotional stability I'd become accustomed to returned as well. The point here isn't to say that 'it worked for me, so you should exercise too', but there are a couple of observations that I think are relevant for working with anger.

First, if we want to be at our best, paying attention to factors that contribute to general wellness is key. Second, building these things into our lives takes *intentional effort*. While there are lots of things that can help us be healthy and more resilient in the face of stress and anger triggers, the list below provides a start:

- Getting sufficient sleep (for most people, seven to eight hours per night).

- Eating relatively healthily (lots of fruits and vegetables, limiting highly processed foods).

- Moving our bodies regularly (optimally, twenty to thirty minutes per day of physical activity).

- Avoiding doing things that are harmful, like overindulging in alcohol, using hard drugs, smoking cigarettes . . .

- Creating time for fun, rewarding and relaxing activities.

- Creating opportunities for meaningful, fun connections with others.

- Refraining from exposing ourselves to unnecessary sources of threat and stress.

This form of self-compassion requires intentionality and discipline, and often some creativity. For years, my 'fun' time occurred in the later evenings . . . and I'd often resist going to bed, leaving me not getting enough sleep. I'm also almost completely unable to resist the lure of snacks – crisps, biscuits . . . if they're there, I'll eat them! Finding balance required some planning. While I don't rigidly schedule my life, I've learned it helps to go to bed between 10 and 10.30 p.m. during the working week, so I can get the sleep I need and still get up in time to exercise before starting my day. As I've mentioned earlier, regarding healthy eating I rely on something behavioural psychologists call 'stimulus control' – I try to fill my home with healthy foods, not bring home foods I struggle resisting, and to avoid grocery shopping when hungry. If I've got crisps in the kitchen, I'll often grab a handful when I'm walking through . . . but, no crisps, no handful!

Planning how to get enough sleep and exercise and to eat healthily are beyond the scope of this book, but there are *lots* of resources out there – books, apps, podcasts, videos, different types of professionals – specifically focused on helping us get these parts of our lives on track. The key is to make the compassionate commitment to focus on these things, find the resources that will help, and *keep going*. It's not easy, but it gets much easier as these habits become woven into our lives, and it can be a game changer in helping us to manage emotions like anger. Self-care is part of working with anger – just as laying a foundation and using insulation is part of building a solid and comfortable home.

Refraining from addictive behaviours (or working to free ourselves from them) can be particularly important for people who struggle with anger. Addiction is driven by what psychologists call 'aversive control', which means the behaviour (using the substance) is performed to reduce unpleasant experiences (withdrawal symptoms). When we're addicted to a substance like tobacco, alcohol or other drugs, withdrawal symptoms create irritability (among other unpleasant experiences), making us more sensitive and potentially reactive to anger triggers. So if you're someone who smokes, for example, right now might not be the time to swear off smoking, but you may find that connecting with resources or treatment programmes to help you break the cycle of addiction might be an important part of your long-term anger management strategy.

I've also included fun activities and meaningful connections on the list of basic wellness factors. These experiences are important if we're to have healthy emotional lives. We need time when we're doing 'want to' vs. 'have to' activities and it's worth putting the effort in to make them happen. We want to create lives that aren't about trying to avoid uncomfortable or threatening experiences, but about *moving towards* experiences we want to have. Remember those three systems of emotion? We can use leisure activities to activate both our drive (doing stuff that's *fun*) and safeness systems (doing stuff that's *soothing*). We can target multiple systems at once, by doing enjoyable activities with other people – people who like, accept and value us. We can get creative and choose activities that hit several wellness domains at once: playing casual sports (exercise, fun) with people we enjoy (meaningful connection), or going hiking or swimming in natural areas (exercise, soothing) with people we like (meaningful connection). We can plan an afternoon or evening with friends (connection) in which we share a healthy meal (eating healthily), and play games, music or watch an enjoyable film together (fun). The key here is to prioritise *helpful* activities and build the habit of intentionally bringing them into our lives. When we've done that, we may find ourselves getting angry a lot less often.

The final piece is about not exposing ourselves to unnecessary threat and stress. We'll all face challenging situations in our lives – deadlines, illnesses, vehicle breakdowns, etc. We don't want to avoid those; compassion is about facing them head-on, acknowledging the challenges and finding helpful ways to work with them. But sometimes we unnecessarily expose ourselves to experiences that leave us feeling less safe and more stressed. During the last US election season, I noticed myself spending lots of time watching cable news and scrolling the internet for updates – although almost nothing changed from day to day. All the while, my stress level was creeping up, until I noticed my jaw aching (a consistent sign I'm stressed). So I put a limit on it, deciding I'd 'check in' with the news for no more than fifteen minutes per day and limit 'doomscrolling' on social media. It's worth considering how we may invite unnecessary stress and threat into our lives, and how we might change that. This can sometimes mean making difficult choices, like spending less time (or having an assertive conversation) with people we like but who are linked with unhelpful activities like malicious gossip or substance abuse.

The idea is to pay attention to how we engage with the world around us – how we spend our time, how we use our bodies, what we consume (both physically and mentally) – and approach the process of living *intentionally* and *compassionately*. It's about taking responsibility for how we spend our lives, time and efforts, gradually and intentionally filling our lives with things that are *helpful* and pruning away things that are unhelpful.

What are your thoughts on what we've covered in this module? What stood out for you? Are there any positive changes you'd like to make in your life?

James: *I need to focus on sleep and exercise. Sarah does a good job of grocery shopping, so I eat healthily, but I stay up late and almost never exercise. I want to change that. I enjoy time with friends and want to do more of that. I'd also like to do more fun things with my family, which is linked with managing my anger. The bit about avoiding unnecessary stressors stood out because, although I have some friends I enjoy spending time with, with others our time is spent getting pissed and complaining about things. I don't really enjoy it, and Sarah doesn't appreciate me coming home late stinking of beer. It's not the example I want to set for the kids.*

Antwan: *I get the focus on having fun – my best days are when I'm playing footie or doing fun stuff with my friends. The pieces on addiction landed as well. My dad drank and smoked, and he was irritable all the time. I bet some of that was withdrawal. I have friends who vape, but Mum let me know early on what she thought of that, so I've avoided it. I've drank and smoked weed in the past. Also, I don't get seven to eight hours of sleep every night. I usually stay up late just doing stuff on my phone, playing video games or watching YouTube. I enjoy that stuff, but I can be tired and grumpy in the mornings.*

Jordan: *I've done a pretty good job with sleep and diet, as I've worked with my therapist on those. Exercise is hard because I'm not entirely comfortable with my body. It can be uncomfortable thinking about going to the gym or even wearing activewear, which can feel really unflattering. I get why it's important, though, and I'm working on it. The inclusion of fun activities and connection surprised me – I often hear about 'diet, sleep and exercise', but those seemed different. I want to put more effort into that. Often my whole day is spent going through the 'to do' list. Over time, life can feel pretty blah, with nothing to look forward to. I think doing more fun things with friends would make my life better. I can do that – I just need to be intentional about making it happen.*

What are your thoughts on what we've covered in this module? What stood out for you? Are there any positive changes you'd like to make in your life?

_____

_____

_____

_____

_____

_____

_____

Establishing healthy habits is challenging and can present us with lots of little obstacles. James wants more fun activities with his family, but his history of anger has made that tricky. Antwan enjoys evening activities that get in the way of his sleep. Jordan wants to exercise more but has discomfort with her body that makes this difficult. These are _real obstacles_, and they're _valid_. In the next module, we'll explore how to work with such obstacles.

Final reflection

What was it like reading through this module? Did you find yourself interested in making positive changes in your life, or feel burdened by having 'more things I need to do'? Or maybe a bit of both?

_____

_____

_____

_____

_____

_____

_____

_____

Imagine you were trying to help someone you cared about who was trying to make positive life changes. How might you validate, support and encourage them? How might you offer some of that to yourself as you consider what changes you'd like to make?

_____

_____

_____

_____

_____

_____

_____

_____

_____

Module 16: Working with Obstacles When Making Positive Changes

The previous module explored life changes aimed at helping us manage anger and have better lives. Much of that information probably wasn't *new* to you. Most of us know it's a good thing to get enough sleep, eat well and exercise. So why don't we all just do these things? It's not because we're lazy, stupid or don't have the self-discipline. It's because doing these things is *difficult*. Many of us have packed lives, filled with tasks competing for our attention, personal histories that make things tricky for us, and emotions that can take us off track. This module is about working compassionately with all of that.

We may have attempted to make positive changes in our lives, but then run into one or more of these obstacles, resulting in us getting thrown off track, and then even beating ourselves up for 'failing' – perhaps concluding we 'didn't care enough' or 'don't have the willpower'. A compassionate approach can help break this cycle. Compassion acknowledges that *obstacles will arise* as we try to make changes. Using what we know about ourselves, we can try to anticipate obstacles and plan for how to handle them. When obstacles we *didn't anticipate* show up, we can refrain from beating ourselves up, validate our experience of the obstacles ('it makes sense I would struggle with this . . .'), and adjust our plan. What if we saw every 'failed attempt' as a trial that *teaches us something* about how to make our next effort more likely to succeed?

This is how compassion works – when faced with difficulty, suffering or struggle, we don't give up, avoid or blame – we slow down and look carefully at what's happening, curiously seeking to understand obstacles and how we can act skilfully to address them. What will we need to do? What resources might help us? How can we help keep ourselves motivated to continue? Compassion is about figuring out what will be *helpful*, and doing it. Instead of condemning ourselves when we don't follow through with our plan, we're *validating* ourselves – recognising that building new habits is difficult, and that we'll almost certainly struggle (for good reasons!) when starting out. We can remind ourselves why this change is important to us, consider what might be helpful in addressing the obstacle, and try again . . . repeating, until we've found a way to make it work.

Earlier, I told you about my exercise journey, and how valuable it's been for me to exercise regularly. What I didn't tell you is that this was a *long* journey. I've never really *liked* exercising, I pretty much never *feel like* doing it, and it took a lot of little steps for me to exercise regularly. But I did it and, boy, does it help. The accompanying table presents a summary of how my exercise journey went, organised in steps.

Plan	Obstacle	Outcome
'Exercise more.'	No plan for when or how it would happen.	No exercise.
'Exercise after work.'	I'm tired after work and unmotivated to exercise.	Almost no exercise.
'Exercise in the morning.'	Not much time in the morning to exercise.	Rare exercise.
'Get up early to exercise, plan activities I can do from home.'	I'm tired and don't want to get up early to exercise.	Infrequent exercise.
'Go to bed earlier and get up early to exercise.'	I don't really enjoy exercising in the morning.	Intermittent exercise, feeling a bit better about improvement.
'Remind myself why it's important, lay out exercise clothes the night before, give myself lots of exercise options, go to bed early, get up early to exercise.'	Still often don't really feel like it (but usually wake up and go).	Regular exercise, increased motivation upon seeing gradual improvement. Engaging becomes easier as habit is established and the natural rewards of exercise manifest.

You'll see it took a while before I exercised at all! First, I didn't really have a plan – just a general idea of what I wanted to do. As any good behavioural psychologist will tell you, *vague plans don't happen.*

Then I had a plan, but a series of obstacles got in the way – feeling tired after work, lack of time, and just not feeling like it. By the way, 'not feeling like doing something' isn't a cop-out – it's a genuine obstacle. We can't just *choose* to feel differently, so we shouldn't beat ourselves up for the emotions we feel. How we feel is important . . . *and* we don't want to let those feelings control what we do and don't do.

But at each step, I – *my compassionate self* – worked to notice the most recent obstacle and modify my plan just a little to address it. More obstacles appeared, but something else happened as well – as I slowly began to see some success and establish exercising as a new habit (intentionally reminding myself of why exercising is important to me), my motivation to exercise grew as well. Once I hit the second-to-last stage and was exercising intermittently, I started feeling good about my progress, which helped me *get serious* about it. Inspired by my success, I got creative in modifying the plan in several helpful ways at once – reminding myself of my motivation, laying out my workout clothes in advance so I could immediately put them on while still waking up, and giving myself lots of exercise options to choose from that I can do from home. I've even got an 'in case of emergency' option – Zumba! When I just can't bear to run, lift weights or do an interval training workout, I can often manage to push play on my fun Latin-dance inspired Zumba DVD, and gracelessly boogie my way to a good sweat.

As I mentioned above, this process of working with obstacles captures the essence of compassion. Compassion is about understanding suffering, struggle and challenges, and curiously considering what would be helpful in addressing them. When we're trying to change, instead of beating ourselves up for struggling (or labelling it *failing*), we can compassionately acknowledge that *of course* there will be obstacles when we start something new, and consider how to *help ourselves* succeed in spite of these obstacles. As with me, you may find it takes several run-throughs before you discover the right combination of factors that supports the change(s) you're making. But every time we apply this process to a challenge in life, we not only work to make *this* change, but we refine a strategy for dealing with whatever life throws at us. Over time, this can translate to changes in how we approach life challenges (with curiosity and confidence we'll *find a way* to work with them versus overwhelm) and perhaps even how we relate to ourselves (as someone who sometimes struggles but finds ways of succeeding anyway). As our confidence and repertoire of helpful strategies grow, some of those anger triggers may begin to feel a lot less threatening.

When building new habits, certain factors make it more likely we'll keep going – things like making our goals specific, making our plans as specific and detailed as possible (when, where, how the behaviour will happen), building flexibility into the plan (see my multiple exercise options), finding ways to make it fun, and working with our social support systems so they can support our efforts (or at least not undermine them). Once established, these new behaviours can begin to run on autopilot – as they become a part of our new routine. All these suggestions are based in behavioural science, and are elaborated upon in Dr Katy Milkman's book *How to Change*, which I like because it's specifically organised to help us work with the unique obstacles that come up in *our* lives.[1]

I'd like to suggest a general strategy for working with obstacles as we make life changes (i.e. 'what we do'), and a few elements that might help as we do this (i.e. 'how we do it').

Making positive life changes

1. Decide on the life change you'd like to make, focusing not just on eliminating unwanted behaviours, but on building positive ones. If it's a behaviour you want to reduce (that probably meets a need), consider what you'll replace it with ('I want to drink *less* alcohol and *more* water or tea', 'I want to make critical comments *less* and consider others' perspectives *more*').

2. Knowing what you know about you, consider obstacles that might arise.

3. Make a plan. The more specific the plan (when, where, how it will happen), the better – try to address the obstacles you've anticipated. Try to make it flexible (giving yourself options to choose from), as fun as possible, and see if you can build support from others into the plan (e.g. plan to do the activity with a partner).

4. Try it out!

5. Consider how it went. Get curious! What factors worked or helped, and how might they be built upon? What obstacles got in the way? Celebrate any success you had – no matter how small.

6. Revise your plan, making adjustments to maximise helpful factors and address obstacles. Repeat steps 4–6.

Pretty straightforward, huh? The key is to not let obstacles kick us out of the process, but use them as opportunities to understand ourselves, the challenges that arise when we're trying something new, and how to work with these challenges. It's about persistence, curiosity and not beating ourselves up when we observe we haven't *yet* succeeded. Now for the *how*. In terms of compassionately supporting ourselves in this process, here are few elements you may find helpful in planning to work with obstacles:

- **Validation:** Rather than beating ourselves up for struggling, we acknowledge that making change is hard, obstacles will arise and it makes sense we'd sometimes struggle.

- **Curiosity:** We want to get curious about noticing both obstacles and what is helpful. When we failed, what specifically happened (outside us or within us) that got in the way or made things difficult? To the extent we succeeded, what helped or made it easier?

- **Support:** We consider how we might support ourselves (or anyone we care about) in doing something difficult. What might help us feel safe and more comfortable (or hopeful, seen, understood, valued, appreciated) as we make this change?

- **Encouragement:** We consider how we might encourage ourselves (or someone we care about) to keep our motivation high. What might you remind yourself of? What might inspire or energise you? What might help you take pride in this effort you're making?

- **Reward:** We consider how we might acknowledge or reward ourselves (or some-one else we care about) for this effort. Make the reward contingent on the *effort* you're making, not whether the outcome turns out just the way you'd envisioned.

Have you tried to make life changes only to have obstacles get in the way? Has anything you've read in this module affected how you might approach these in the future?

James: *Definitely, on both counts. Several times I've decided I would 'get healthy', and start exercising and eating better. I've spent lots of money on gym memberships I've almost never used. Reading this, I think I had two problems. First, my plans were vague, just a general 'I want to do more of _____.' Then, something would happen – unscheduled meetings or a holiday would come up – and I'd get derailed. Then I'd either forget about the plan or notice I'd got derailed, beat myself up about it and give up. I also have some friends who weren't always helpful – encouraging me to drink and eat unhealthily when we're out, etc. Today I'm going to make a more specific plan around diet and exercise and see if I can build some consistency. Sarah is always saying she wants us to eat more healthily, so I think she'll be on board – maybe exercise is something we could do together.*

Antwan: *I haven't tried too many life changes except to get my grades up. I sometimes blow off homework because I just don't feel like it. I guess it might help if I set up a time to do it, like right after school, and just do it whether I feel like it or not. I haven't been that motivated around school, but graduation is coming up next year, and I've been thinking about what comes next. The bit about making things fun and social support made sense – last year a group of friends and I would go to the gym together like three times a week, and it was awesome. I've never worked out so much in my life. It would be cool to get back into that.*

Jordan: *I'd like to do more exercise and social activities. Not surprisingly, the biggest obstacle that gets in my way is anxiety. I'm good at making specific plans, but the validation, curiosity, support, encourage and reward pieces at the end were new to me. Thinking about it, when I've made plans to address things that make me anxious (like going to a new, woman-friendly gym), I'd get anxious, and my focus would shift from the plan to beating myself up for being anxious about it . . . and then I back away from the whole thing. I think those last pieces will help me work with that. I also need to remind myself of what I have to gain – a bigger life that isn't controlled by my anxiety!*

The companions' responses demonstrate a few important points: James highlighted several common obstacles (vague plans, getting derailed) and Antwan added another common challenge – simply *not feeling like it*. He also came up with ways to overcome this obstacle – setting a consistent time he'll do the behaviour whether he feels like it or not (homework), and finding ways to make it fun and social (working out). Jordan then noted another common obstacle that James also shared: *self-criticism*. Both highlighted sneaky ways self-attacking can undermine our efforts to change, with Jordan getting sidetracked by criticising herself for having anxiety about the new behaviour, and James beating himself up when he didn't perform it at the level he'd planned. Both demonstrate perhaps a common effect of shame and self-criticism – *it shuts us down*. This is the problem with using self-criticism to motivate ourselves – much of the time, it doesn't work! On the other hand, a compassionate approach to self-change recognises that change is difficult, focuses on what is helpful, and supports, encourages and recognises our efforts to change – and the *good reasons* we're doing it.

Have you tried to make life changes only to have obstacles get in the way? Has anything you've read in this module affected how you might approach these in the future?

_____

_____

_____

_____

_____

Final reflection

For the final reflection, consider one helpful behaviour you'd like to add to your life. It could be one of those mentioned above, or something else you think would be helpful in enhancing your life, like 'spend more time outside', 'speak compassionately rather than critically to myself and/or others'. What's one helpful behaviour you'd like to add to your life?

_____

_____

_____

What obstacles might be likely to get in your way as you create this change?

_____

_____

_____

Make a specific plan to begin this behaviour, considering the obstacles:

What specifically will you do? (Try to give yourself different options.)

_____

_____

_____

When will you do it?

_____

_____

_____

Where will you do it?

_____

_____

_____

How might you make it fun? How could you reward yourself when you do it?

_____

_____

_____

How might you build in social support, connection or companionship in doing it?

_____

_____

_____

When you struggle, how will you validate, support or encourage yourself? What could your compassionate self say or do to help the version of you that is struggling? What would help you refrain from criticising yourself and keep going?

_____

_____

_____

_____

_____

End of section check-in

How are you feeling about your progress so far?

_____

_____

_____

What has been helpful for you?

_____

_____

_____

What obstacles have arisen that should be considered as you move forwards?

_____

_____

_____

What would be helpful for you to keep in mind going forwards?

_____

_____

_____

Compassion practice plan

Now we've completed the third section, let's update the practice plan. Here are a few suggested practices based upon the modules in Section III, along with a few from previous modules:

1. **Check in with your compassionate self** (Module 14): Take five to ten minutes to pause, slow down your breath and step into that deeply compassionate version of yourself: courageous in the face of struggle; committed to doing what's helpful; wise and confident. Using the acting approach described in Module 14, imagine what it would be like to be filled with these qualities. Imagine how your body would feel as this compassionate being – balanced, calm, centred. Imagine what you would pay attention to, think about and care about – noticing difficulty and considering what would be helpful to address it. Imagine how you would go about your day as this compassionate self, and how you would interact with the people around you.

2. **Deepen a compassionate quality** (Module 14): Select one of the qualities described in Module 14 (courage, kindness, wisdom, kind curiosity, acknowledging acceptance, sympathy, empathy, non-condemnation, distress tolerance, confidence). Take five minutes to reflect on how you might bring this quality into your life. How might you apply it to a situation you're facing today?

3. **Check in with your personal change plan** (Modules 15 and 16): Take a few minutes to consider your change plan and how it's going. If you've been following through with the plan, take this time to reward yourself by doing something pleasant. If obstacles have got in the way, consider how you might modify your plan a bit to address them . . . and then reward yourself for doing that!

4. **Connect with a flow of compassion** (Modules 6–12): Take five minutes to connect with the self-to-self, self-to-other or other-to-self flows of compassion. Using what you've learned, recall a time you've struggled and try to offer yourself some compassionate understanding. Consider what this struggling version of you might find helpful. For other flows, select a flow from Module 7 and reflect on the questions. Consider how you might express compassion to another person or how you might engage with others in ways that help them relate compassionately to you.

Every day, do one mindful check-in or three systems check-in, and one other practice. Choose practices from those listed above, as well as those included in the first two practice plans, on pages 64–6 and 107–8. Make sure to do each of the new practices at least once, and don't repeat any practice more than twice per week. Try to fit in soothing activities regularly as well – daily if possible.

Daily practice log

Practice	Sun	Mon	Tues	Weds	Thurs	Fri	Sat
Mindful check-in/ three systems check-in							

Practice notes

Day	What was helpful?	What obstacles came up?
Sunday		
Monday		
Tuesday		
Wednesday		
Thursday		
Friday		
Saturday		

SECTION IV:

Getting to Know Our Anger

This section takes a deep dive into how anger works. As we begin, I want to mention that emotions like anger are *implicit processes*. This is a fancy way of saying we can't just *choose* how to feel. Sometimes people say *happiness is a choice*. If that were true, there'd be no need for mental health professionals, because we'd all just wake up and decide to be happy all the time. What happens is that the parts of our brains that create our emotions receive messages from lots of different places – from the outside world; from our own thoughts, memories and mental images; even from our bodies – and then produce feelings in response to all that.

People who say things like *happiness is a choice* aren't all deluded, by the way. Many use this phrase as shorthand for the much more unwieldy, 'If you want to have a good life, good relationships, and feel good more of the time, create the causes and conditions in your life that will make that more likely.' If we do that – take care of our bodies and brains, intentionally cultivate good relationships, and learn to develop ways of thinking and behaving that are helpful – things are a lot more likely to go our way. If we want strawberries, we can't just stand in the middle of a field, cup our hands and say, 'I choose strawberries!' We plant the strawberry plants in a sunny place and give them what they need to thrive – water and fertilise them, maybe even pull out a few weeds now and then . . . or, at the least, we walk to a market that sometimes stocks strawberries. None of this *guarantees* we'll get strawberries, but it makes it a lot more likely. To do this, it helps to understand a bit about strawberry plants and what they need to thrive. Emotional health works the same way.

Working with emotions compassionately begins with understanding them and how they work, so we can cultivate the skills and experiences we need to manage them effectively. We also want to create experiences that will allow us to have emotional lives that are rich, fulfilling and fit with the sort of person we want to be. In the service of that, let's start by taking a deep dive into understanding anger, how it works and how we can engage with it in helpful ways.

Module 17: Anger Organising the Mind

If you're someone who struggles with anger, you may notice that the version of you that shows up when you're angry is very different to how you are (or want to be) the rest of the time. Basic motives and the emotions that serve them shape our experience in powerful ways. As we touched on earlier, it's like we have different 'versions' of ourselves that correspond to different motives, the emotions that flow from them, and how these organise our minds and bodies. Emotions like anger aren't just about how we 'feel', although that's certainly part of the picture. As we see in Figure 17.1, anger shapes many different aspects of our experience.

Figure 17.1: Anger organising the mind and body

When we consider how anger organises the mind, we can see how easy it is to get stuck in it, and to have a hard time shifting away. This module focuses on the upper-left side of the spider diagram in Figure 17.1, considering how anger impacts our attention, thinking and reasoning, and mental imagery and fantasies.

Attention

Anger evolved to help our ancestors defend themselves from threats. When we're angry, there's a dramatic narrowing of our attention onto whatever triggered the anger (the threat our brains have perceived). Ever try to work or study after something's triggered your anger, and been unable to concentrate, with your attention going back again and again to the hurtful thing the other person said, the thing that didn't go as you wanted or the obstacle that got in your way? Whatever triggered the anger, our brains registered it as a threat that needs attending to *right now*, and anger is designed to help with this by keeping our attention focused right onto the 'threat'.

When you're angry, where is your attention focused? Is it narrow and blinkered, or broad and open?

James: *Narrow and blinkered – like it's all I can focus on. I find myself going over and over what happened – thinking about it, playing it over and over in my mind, ruminating . . .*

Antwan: *Focused on whatever has pissed me off, duh . . . like I can't stop thinking about it.*

Jordan: *My attention is narrowly focused, for sure. It's also difficult to shift to other things. When I do manage to shift my attention, it tends to quickly bounce back to the trigger again.*

When you're angry, where is your attention focused? Is it narrow and blinkered, or broad and open?

_____

_____

_____

As we see from the companions' brief responses, anger *narrows* our attention onto the situation that triggered it. This plays out in our thoughts and mental imagery as well. Ever found yourself angry, thinking about what happened over and again, playing through the situation like it was a movie, repeatedly fantasising about what you *could have* done, what you *should have* said or what you'll say the next time? These are examples of how our threat systems keep us focused on perceived threats in their efforts to help us deal with them.

Unfortunately, the threat system isn't always a good match for the threats we face in modern life, and can even have us responding to 'threats' that exist only in our imagination!

Thinking and reasoning

As mentioned above, anger fixes our attention, thoughts and mental imagery on perceived threats, so we can find ourselves ruminating in unhelpful ways. But anger shapes our thinking in lots of *other tricky ways* as well:[1]

Impaired critical thinking

When we're angry and locked into a threat response, we don't do a good job of thinking critically. We don't tend to question our reasoning ('I wonder if I'm interpreting this situation correctly'). We don't tend to consider other explanations ('Maybe he misunderstood what I said?'). We don't tend to look at things from other people's perspectives ('I wonder what this situation feels like from her side?'). We're also more likely to accept the perspective of perceived authority figures, particularly when their perspective lines up with biases we already hold.

This is one reason inflammatory cable news hosts can be dangerous – they feed us threat-filled narratives of varying accuracy, designed to fire up our threat systems. Once we're fired up, we tend not to question whether what they are saying is even true . . . accepting the narrative, which then serves as fuel to keep us in a state of threat. People are much more easily controlled when we're feeling threatened. This is not our fault; it's how our brains work. When we notice a 'news' host or politician is working hard to make us angry or scared (versus, say, communicating a reasoned argument or doing straight reporting of factual information), it's best to change the channel – because they're trying to use our threat systems to influence our attitudes and behaviour.

We're more likely to accept stereotypes

When caught up in anger, we're more likely to unquestioningly accept negative stereotypes about other people and groups – *whether they're true or not*. We're also more likely to create what Chimamanda Adichie referred to in her brilliant TED talk, 'The Danger of a Single Story'.[2] When we're angry, it's easy to create 'single stories' about other people and groups – experiencing them as being *defined* by the one thing we find threatening – *even if that thing exists only in our minds.* Our angry selves are very good at attaching the 'bad' label to others (and sometimes to ourselves), setting us up to hate or attack them. Those of us who struggle with anger can have an intimate understanding of this, as we may have experienced other people relating to us as 'that angry person', failing to see all the other aspects of our personalities and the good things we do.

Certainty

Anger is linked with feelings of being *certain* our perspective is the correct one. Have you ever had the experience, 'I'm not sure what I think about this, but I'm really mad about it'? That almost never happens. When we're angry, there's a felt sense of certainty – a feeling of *knowing* that we're right.

If we consider that anger evolved to help us fight off physical threats, this all makes sense. If an animal is attacking us and we need to fight it off, we *want* to be single-mindedly focused and able to act with certainty and conviction, not distractedly thinking through all the ramifications ('Is this bear a member of an endangered species?', 'What if the bear-spray blinds it?', 'I love animals . . . this is so unfortunate . . . look at those pretty flowers!'). In organising our minds in these ways – focused on threats, certain in our convictions, ready to act – our anger is doing exactly what evolution designed it to do.

. . . and that can set us up for lots of problems in the modern world. When you combine these factors, it creates a perfect storm, organising us in ways that aren't at all helpful in addressing the complicated problems we face in our lives. Think about it – when we're angry, we feel very certain, but our capacity to weigh evidence and consider different perspectives is impaired. *When we're angry, we're more certain that we're right, even as we're much more likely to be wrong.*

It's not hard to see the consequences of this playing out in our lives and cultures. Suppose someone tells us a threatening lie about a neighbour or another group of people: 'They want to steal your job', 'They want to ruin your way of life.' These are just the sorts of messages likely to get our threat systems fired up quickly. Once the anger kicks in, we're less able to think critically about their message ('Hmm . . . does this sound right?'), more likely to accept it ('That seems to make sense to me!'), more likely to use the information to create or strengthen stereotypes ('I never did trust them. _____ are just problem people'), and more certain that these views are correct. We're also more likely to *notice* little bits of evidence that seem to fit with this threat-focused view ('see them on the street, just milling about . . .'), while ignoring evidence that contradicts it. This is dangerous stuff and right now our society is filled with it.

It's not just dangerous to other people. Because these angry views are shared and repeated so frequently in the media and on social media platforms, they can be in the background almost all the time. We can find our momentary anger transforming into chronic hostility we carry throughout our daily lives. Not only does this make it hard to enjoy life, but it also shortens lives – anger has been linked to increased mortality due to cardiovascular disease and cancer![3]

Let's take a moment to explore your experience of your thinking and reasoning when you're angry:

When you are angry, what do you notice about your thinking and reasoning? Does it fit with the descriptions in the text?

James: When I'm angry, my thinking is completely focused on whatever triggered the anger; it's almost impossible for me to focus on anything else. It's like everything in the world disappears. I also get blamey – like, whatever is wrong, I blame the people around me and can get really critical. Then the shame hits, and the blame reverses onto myself, but with that same feeling of certainty – feeling sure that I'm a terrible father and husband. I also do a little of the stereotyping – thinking my co-workers are idiots who can't do anything on their own, which I know isn't true. A lot to think about.

Antwan: It's weird to think about 'thinking' when I'm angry. At first, I thought that it doesn't seem like I'm thinking anything at all. It's like I'm just reacting, like the part of my brain that thinks just shuts off. I guess that's the critical thinking turning off – when I'm locked in on whoever's pissed me off, the only thing I'm thinking critically about is them. I'm thinking about the other person, what they did, how I want to put them in their place and why they deserve it. The bits on stereotypes and single stories landed, too. I think maybe I stereotype one of my teachers, as a 'bitch who doesn't like me', and she stereotypes me back, as a 'bad kid' or 'troublemaker'. Then we see all the stuff in each other that fits with those stories, and don't see any of the good stuff that doesn't. Damn, you got me on that one.

Jordan: My experience seems a bit different, in that when I get angry, so often the focus shifts from whatever I'm angry about to the fact I'm feeling this way – it's like the anger becomes the trigger, and I react to it by criticising myself and feeling overwhelmed. With that in mind, the text rings true – I'm stereotyping myself as bad, weak or ineffective, I'm not able to think broadly or flexibly, and I'm certain there's something wrong with me. No wonder I feel so overwhelmed! Also, I could relate to the cable news example in ways that aren't so flattering for me. So many times, I've got upset about the political realities we're seeing right now, and it's easy to label everyone who votes for the other side as idiots or terrible people . . . even when deep down I know that isn't true. I've been trying to work on that.

When you are angry, what do you notice about your thinking and reasoning? Does it fit with the descriptions in the text?

_____

_____

_____

_____

_____

_____

_____

_____

It can be a new experience to reflect on how our thinking works when we're angry. I suspect lots of us have experiences that mirror Antwan's initial comment, reacting in anger without an awareness of what we're thinking or how it relates to our emotion. Going forwards, I'd like to invite you to get curious about the thoughts that accompany your anger. Are they definitive statements about reality, or stereotypes about other people ('This is totally wrong!', 'What an idiot!')? Are they blamey, as James identified ('I wouldn't be upset if you didn't _____!')? Are they ruminative thoughts about others, what they did and how to get back at them, as Antwan described? Do they turn into shaming attacks on yourself, in relation to your angry behaviour ('Look, I just screwed it up again!') or criticising your experience ('This isn't okay. I'm so pathetic')? These are examples of how angry thinking _can_ manifest – the key is to get familiar with how it works _for us_, so we can learn to recognise when our 'angry selves' start taking over the airwaves, and consider whether we want to leave them in charge or give our compassionate selves a chance to weigh in.

Final reflection

What was it like to reflect on your thinking when you're angry? Noticing how your thoughts work when you're angry, does it make sense that it would be easy to get trapped in angry ways of feeling?

_____

_____

_____

_____

_____

_____

_____

Did you notice anything you think might be helpful to keep in mind as you work to manage your anger going forwards?

_____

_____

_____

_____

_____

_____

_____

Module 18: Anger Organising Our Body, Motivation and Behaviour

In Module 17, we explored how anger impacts how we pay attention, think and imagine. This module explores the bottom-right part of the spider diagram in Figure 18.1 (which is a repeat of Figure 17.1), considering how anger shapes our felt experience, motivation and behaviour.

Figure 18.1: Anger organising the mind and body

If we begin by considering how anger feels in the body, we can see it is activating us for action.

> When you are angry, what feelings or sensations show up for you? What do you notice going on in your body? See if you can describe the *feeling* of anger.
>
> James: *When I'm angry, there's this huge building up of tension. I've read that your heart rate increases, blood pressure goes up, and lots of other things, but what I notice most is this feeling of being really wound up and ready to go – like a spring that's coiled tight. It's hard to hold back. There's this sense of 'I have to do something right now!' Too often, I give in to that feeling, and say the thing, or send the email or whatever it is that ends up causing problems. It's like my whole system gets hijacked.*
>
> Antwan: *I kinda like how I feel when I'm angry – especially when I give in to it. It feels powerful – like I'm strong and nobody can mess with me. I've got into a few fights, and although I don't really want to hurt people, it feels good to put assholes in their place ... to punch that guy who's mouthing off or to tell the teacher who keeps riding me what I think of her. There's hell to pay later, but while it's happening, it's fun in a messed-up sort of way, sort of powerful.*
>
> Jordan: *For me, feelings of anger and anxiety get swirled together, and it can be hard to distinguish between them. If someone says something that makes me angry, I get this feeling of tension in my whole body, particularly my stomach and my shoulders. My heart starts beating fast and I feel out of control. Then it blurs into anxiety, and that's usually when I start to cry. I'll often get a headache, and my guts get wrapped up in knots. It's like there's all this energy building up with no place to go. I hate it.*

When you are angry, what feelings or sensations show up for you? What do you notice going on in your body? See if you can describe the *feeling* of anger.

_____

_____

_____

_____

_____

The companions' responses above capture how anger can show up in the body – as activation, with physical symptoms such as increased heart rate, blood pressure and muscle tension. We also see how angry arousal – this 'energy building up', as Jordan puts it – can be experienced very differently, with Antwan experiencing it as powerful and sometimes pleasurable, and Jordan experiencing it as feeling unpleasantly out of control. James's description of anger involving a feeling of urgency is a nice transition to our next exploration: how anger organises our *motivation*. Let's explore that now:

When anger arises in you, what is your motivation like? What do you find yourself wanting to do?

James: *As I mentioned, when I'm angry, I get critical and blamey, as well as defensive. I find myself wanting to explain myself, to justify my position – to let others know why I'm right and they're wrong. It goes with that sense of certainty from the last module. I write these long, drawn-out emails or lecture my wife and kids about what they did wrong, explaining my position or whatever. But it's not a conversation – it's just me ranting. I can see them tuning out, which makes me even more angry. Later, I feel terribly ashamed . . . oh, the emails I wish I could get back. But as it's happening, I have a hard time holding back.*

Antwan: *When I'm angry, I want to fight. Usually there's another person involved, and at that moment, I want to go at them. Physically, verbally, whatever – depending on the situation. That's my motivation.*

Jordan: *When I'm angry, I feel trapped between wanting to engage the world and whatever triggered me, and to shrink and hide. It's like both motivations are going at the same time. So I shut down and wallow, usually in self-criticism. I'm curious what would happen if I could just be angry without all the anxiety and shame piling on.*

When anger arises in you, what is your motivation like? What do you find yourself wanting to do?

_____

_____

_____

_____

_____

In exploring the motivation of anger, we can recall that anger is an evolved threat response designed to help us defend ourselves – literally preparing the 'fight' part of 'fight or flight'. Considering this, we can see it's not our fault if we experience it as an aggressive motivation. It's *designed* to be aggressive. Working with anger is about how we allow this motivation to play out in terms of our behaviour. Let's take a moment to explore that aspect of anger:

Considering the motivation you described, how does your anger play out in terms of your behaviour? Are there specific behaviours you engage in when angry that you'd like to change? How would you like them to change?

James: *I went through a lot of the behaviours before – sending long, convoluted emails, lecturing and over-explaining my position to prove I'm right, snapping at my family, blaming others for things I'm upset about. Although rare, I've even yelled at my family when I've really lost it. I'm ashamed of that – I feel like a terrible father. In terms of change, I guess I'd like to find ways to discharge the anger, so I don't cause problems. If I had my choice, I'd never raise my voice in anger again. Also, I don't know if it's a behaviour, but I do a lot of thinking that doesn't help – the stuff we talked about last module. I'd like to change that, too. Even if I'm not acting it out, it still makes me miserable.*

Antwan: *This bit gets me in trouble. Like I said, sometimes I've got into fights. Other than a split lip, it hasn't been a big deal – usually when things cool down, my friends and I work things out. But I'll be an adult soon, where there are serious consequences for that stuff. I've also had problems mouthing off to teachers and, like my mum says, if you do that at your job . . . no more job.*

Jordan: *I feel trapped between the energy of the anger/anxiety and the critical voice that tells me I'm stupid and should stop being so childish, irrational or whatever. So I shut down and cry. In terms of new behaviours, I'd like to speak out more – stand up for myself, be assertive, whatever the situation calls for. Without running myself down. That would be nice.*

Considering the motivation you described above; how does your anger play out in terms of your behaviour? Are there specific behaviours you engage in when angry that you'd like to change? How would you like them to change?

_____

_____

_____

Lot of tricky behaviours can show up when we're angry. Both James and Antwan describe unhelpful behaviours that manifest the aggressive side of anger – snapping at others, blaming, lecturing, yelling and even physical aggression. Jordan demonstrates another type of challenge with anger – when it's so suppressed that the energy of anger isn't available to fuel appropriate assertive behaviour or is turned inwards to attack the self. Both James and Jordan mention what psychologists sometimes call 'covert' behaviour – things we do (like thinking) that others can't observe directly. James describes ruminating in ways that keep the anger burning hot, and both describe shame and self-attacking – for James, related to his angry behaviours, and, for Jordan, self-criticism around both *feeling* the anger and her inability to address the situation that triggered it. This is a nice set-up for future modules, in which we'll explore tricky thought–emotion loops that can keep us stuck in anger and shame.

Final reflection

What was it like to explore how anger shapes your feelings, your motivation and your behaviour? How is the motivation of your angry self different from the motivation you tend to have when you're not angry?

_____

_____

_____

_____

_____

_____

Module 19: Threat Systems Bouncing – Anger and Relationships

Whenever two people are interacting, there are at least two layers of communication happening. The first is the level of *content* – the actual words or verbal information that are being communicated. A second layer involves the *emotional exchange* occurring between the two people. When we interact with another person, we're exchanging words, but the *way* we interact with them creates an emotional exchange as well. Things like our tone of voice, body posture, facial expression and the words we choose communicate things about how we're feeling, and can trigger emotional responses in the other person.

These two layers of information often interact. Several years ago, I was walking up the stairs to my office at Eastern Washington University, a few steps behind a couple of female students. They were clearly friends enjoying a lively conversation. At one point, one of the women smiled, looked at her friend, and in a light-hearted and friendly tone of voice said, 'You bitch!' The other woman laughed, and they continued their conversation on the way to class. Imagine how differently this conversation would have gone had the woman said, 'You bitch!' using an angry tone of voice and a hostile facial expression. The meaning of the words spoken was clearly modified by the woman's tone of voice and facial expression, and how these fitted with the two students' relationship history.

In this way, communication between people can be complex. To communicate effectively, we must choose words that express the meaning we want to convey, but also be aware of the emotional messages we're sending out (which are affected by how we're feeling), as well as noticing and responding to what the *other person* is feeling. One way to approach this emotional exchange involves considering the three systems of emotion (threat, drive and safeness/soothing). During the interaction, which system is running the show for us? Are we in threat, feeling defensive (angry, fearful or anxious)? Are we acting out of our drive system – excited, engaged and interested? Or are we feeling safe, soothed and connected? As we engage with the other person, *the way* we engage them is then likely to trigger experiences of threat, drive or safeness in them. Awareness of how such emotional exchanges impact communication increases our chances of having successful interactions . . . and, when we're ignorant of this, things can go sideways in a hurry!

This is particularly true with anger. As we've explored, anger is a threat emotion, and angry tones of voice and facial expressions communicate that we're dangerous and not to be trifled with. Our threat systems – and everyone else's – are pattern-recognition machines finely tuned to detect threats – like angry faces and tones of voice! When we engage other people angrily, *we will almost certainly activate their threat systems*, prompting them to feel emotions like anger, fear, anxiety or disgust, which then shape their experience of us and how they'll engage with us.

When we're angry, our angry selves may not care so much about this – I mean, we're upset, so why shouldn't they be upset too? But let's consider what we know about anger. When our threat systems are running the show, humans don't operate at our best – our attention, thinking and imaginations are narrowly focused on threats; we're not good at thinking flexibly or creatively; and our motivation is to protect ourselves. When we engage people in ways that are likely to trigger *their* threat systems, they'll tend to respond in defensive ways that can then further fuel *our* threat systems – lashing back at us, showing signs of disapproval, withdrawing and avoiding us, shutting down. We can end up with *threat systems bouncing* back and forth, each person engaging the other in ways that almost guarantee the situation will escalate, or at least will not be resolved well (for example, if the other person shuts down or withdraws).

It doesn't take many such interactions before a relationship begins to deteriorate, as one or both people come to associate the other person with feelings of threat. When we've fallen into a pattern of threat-based communication with another person, every interaction can become strained – because even if the purpose of the interaction might be a pleasant one, there can be the constant anticipation of threat based on the history of difficult interactions. Have you experienced anything like this?

What do you take away from this discussion? Have you experienced 'threat systems bouncing' in your own relationships?

James: *I sure have. Although I've had angry interactions with my family, most of the time it's not like that. But it's happened enough that I think they're always wary around me. They just don't know what they're going to get. I also sometimes get upset because it sometimes feels like my wife doesn't care about me or isn't on my side. Reading this, I realise that the way I express this to her – with an irritable tone of voice and often in a critical way – is almost certain to get her threat system going! It's like I'm expressing a need for affection in a way that makes it impossible for her to give it to me. Why would she want to be close or affectionate to me when I'm coming at her like that? It is 'threat systems bouncing' – I get irritable, she withdraws, I escalate, she withdraws further... I've got to work on this.*

Antwan: *I get this. It's like that at school sometimes. I've got this teacher, Mrs Saunders, who is always on my case. I can be just sitting there, thinking about what to do next, and she's on me like 'Antwan, you need to get back to work.' That pisses me off – ah, triggers my threat system – so I'll snap back, 'I'm not doing nothing!' Well, she doesn't like that, so things go downhill from there.*

Jordan: *In my own life, I don't see as much 'bouncing' of threat systems because I tend to pull back and shut down – I don't really bounce things back. But looking out into the world at things like politics, it happens all the time. One side engaging the other in a hostile way, the other side returning fire. The politicians and even the people – I've heard about families not speaking to each other for years after arguments about Brexit and so forth. Even in international relations, nations posture back-and-forth in ways that seem designed to threaten the other. It's no wonder we've got so many problems with things. Everyone's too busy defending themselves and threatening the others to figure out solutions.*

The companions' comments reveal several examples of 'threat systems bouncing'. James describes family members avoiding or 'walking on eggshells' when they've learned to anticipate anger or irritability. Antwan's anger triggers are interpersonally cued (signs of disrespect from others), so when his teacher engages him in ways that feel disrespectful, he 'snaps back', prompting a harsher response from her, and things escalate. Jordan's situation is a little different, but she notes that this pattern of 'threat systems bouncing' can be seen in many places in our cultures – living in the United States, as I do, it sometimes feels like *most* of our politics has become defined by threat-based communication (attacking, threatening, blaming, criticising . . .). We may avoid taking responsibility for working with our own anger when we're constantly seeing it modelled by powerful people in our culture – it can seem *normal* to interact in these hostile ways. But, *normal or not, it's not helpful*, particularly if we want to have good relationships. Finally, I wanted to highlight something else James said: often, people who struggle with anger may be expressing *legitimate needs*, but in angry or hostile ways that make it almost impossible that others will be able to care about or meet those needs – because when another person is triggering our threat system, our focus is on protecting ourselves, not meeting *their* needs.

What do you take away from this discussion? Have you ever experienced 'threat systems bouncing' in your own relationships?

_____

_____

_____

_____

_____

_____

This discussion is about bringing awareness to emotional exchanges between people – considering how _the ways we express our feelings_ can shape others' emotional experiences, which shapes how they will react to us. Sometimes I hear people say things like, 'I can't _make_ anyone else feel anything', or 'You're not responsible for how anyone else feels.' At face value, those statements are true. But we _are_ responsible for our own behaviour, and when we behave and communicate in ways that we can reasonably expect to trigger threat in other people . . . well, those 'technically true' statements end up sounding like a cop-out. Interacting with others in ways that trigger threat in them makes good communication almost impossible. If we want to have helpful, productive and positive interactions with others, we need to drop the blame game and take responsibility for engaging in ways that are likely to help them feel safe and interested in engaging with us. We'll explore ways of doing this in future modules, but for now I'd encourage you to consider how you interact with others, how you want them to feel when you're around, and how this fits with the relationships you'd like to have with them.

Finally, it's important to bring compassionate understanding to all this. When I first realised I sometimes interact with my family in ways that trigger their threat systems, I felt sad and ashamed – that's not how I want them to experience me at all. I want them to feel safe, respected and cared about when interacting with me, even when I'm expressing disagreement or frustration. This is tough stuff, in ways that aren't our fault. Anger is designed by evolution to produce just the sort of facial expressions and tones of voice that will put other people into threat. But we don't have to let these evolved threat responses control our relationships with others. Once we understand how this works and how tricky it can be, we can stop 'bouncing' and start working to create the relationships we want to have.

Final reflection

What was it like to consider your own relationships in relation to this module's discussion? If you recognised any of the patterns discussed, how did it feel to notice that?

_____

_____

_____

_____

_____

_____

In thinking about your own relationships, is there anything you'd like to keep in mind or change in how you approach communication – say, around making requests, expressing your needs or otherwise communicating with others – that might help you keep from getting into 'threat systems bouncing' situations with those you care about?

_____

_____

_____

_____

_____

_____

Module 20: Understanding Our Triggers

Module 2 explored how our experiences are reflected in patterns of activation in our brains – creating and strengthening patterns of cells linked to different aspects of the experience. As we discussed, with repeated activation over time (doing or experiencing the same thing over and over – like a student studying for an exam), cells in these patterns and the connections between them are strengthened, so that the pattern becomes 'worn in' and more easily activated in the future. Normally this process takes place over time, but in the case of high-threat situations involving emotions like anger, fear and disgust, this learning can take place much more quickly – sometimes in a single learning experience.

A common example of how this can work involves fear. Let's imagine Susan has a car accident – say, another car jumps a red light and hits her vehicle as she's crossing the junction, causing her only minor injuries but scaring her deeply. Our brains are particularly efficient at 'burning in' such patterns in times of threat. It's our brains' way of saying, 'This was very dangerous, so I want to learn as much as possible about this experience so I can spot it quickly next time and avoid the danger.' Learning to quickly recognise and avoid dangerous situations helped keep our ancestors alive in a world filled with lots of physical threats – dangerous animals, poisonous plants, sinkholes, bad sushi . . . you get what I'm saying.

In this case, all the sensory information coming in during the accident can be woven into the pattern – the fear Susan felt, the act of driving, the junction where it happened, the other car; even things like the song on the radio or the colour of the other car, which had nothing to do with the accident (but our brains' threat centres don't know that). This isn't Susan's fault, by the way – it's just her brain trying to learn everything it can about this dangerous situation, to protect her in the future. But, once the patterns are laid down, she can find herself feeling scared whenever she needs to drive, when she's near the junction where it happened, even when she hears the song again. To Susan, this may seem crazy . . . why should she feel afraid when a song comes on the radio? But it's all a part of how her brain is working to protect her. This is how 'triggers' are born.

Just as fear and anxiety can have learned 'triggers' that bring fear up almost immediately, we can learn anger triggers as well. You may notice certain experiences that bring anger up in you very quickly and very powerfully, with little or no warning. Like Susan, *it's not your fault*. As with fear, anger is one of our brains' threat responses, and once patterns are laid down connecting angry feelings with certain experiences (such as things not going the way we'd hoped, feeling attacked or disrespected, or having our progress blocked), we can find ourselves feeling a powerful rush of anger whenever a version of these experiences happens in our lives. Our anger can even be triggered by the experience of *other emotions*. Several men in anger groups have told me anger arises very quickly in them when they notice themselves feeling anxiety, sadness or shame – finding themselves *angry at themselves* for feeling such vulnerable emotions, or 'using anger so I don't have to feel all that stuff'.

Whatever the trigger, when our experience triggers a part of this pattern that's been laid down in our brains, the pattern lights up and – boom – we're angry! When this happens, we're not *choosing* to get all bent out of shape. But, chosen or not, if we just go with the anger, we can find ourselves behaving in ways that cause real problems in our lives. The good news is that while we can't control that our brains work this way, we can recognise these patterns and *take responsibility* for learning how to work with them so our *behaviour* reflects the sort of people we want to be, rather than a threat-based pattern rooted in experiences we may have had years ago.

Can you identify any of your anger triggers – situations that activate anger in you? What experiences in your life may have helped lay down those patterns in your brain?

James: *I've got lots of triggers. A big one is when things don't go as planned – I'll have an idea of how things are going to go, and then when something goes wrong or just changes things, I get angry. Even small things, like when I'm cooking dinner and I burn something, or if I'm trying to fix something and a screw gets stripped, and I can't get it off. I'll raise my voice and rattle off some choice curses. It doesn't last long, but when it happens, my family looks at me like I'm from another planet. Then I get ashamed – like I can't even bear to be around them or to have them see me – and that can ruin the whole day. I know just where I learned it . . . I saw my own father do this all the time.*

Antwan: *I've got some triggers. For me, a lot of it is about being disrespected. When I get angry at school, or even with friends, it's usually when I feel someone has talked to me like I'm stupid, talked down to me or told me what to do. I'm not having that. I know where that comes from. My dad left when I was young, but I remember one time he said to me, 'No matter what you do, Antwan, don't let nobody disrespect you.' I took that shit to heart. Thinking about him is also a trigger. I can't believe he left us. And when something happens that reminds me of him, it's like I'm filled with emotions – like I want to scream and cry and punch something all at once. That sometimes ends with me blowing up.*

Jordan: *This whole discussion of patterns and triggers, and how things can get linked up in our brains and activated later, has been helpful, and I can see that I've got some deeply entrenched patterns. As I've* mentioned, I work in a setting in which my co-workers will sometimes cross my boundaries. Sometimes it's by making work-related demands that aren't realistic, and sometimes it's inappropriate comments that I don't appreciate. When that happens, I feel a surge of anger or irritation – but it's really quick, like you might not even notice it. As soon as that happens, I immediately go into shame, and start thinking that somehow it's all my fault, that I shouldn't be feeling this way. The book talked about people turning fear and shame into anger, but I think I do the opposite – the moment anger comes up in me, I turn it into shame and anxiety.

The companions' comments above highlight different triggers and different life experiences that can pave the way for these experiences to trigger us. I want to particularly highlight the second half of Antwan's reflection. His comments about his abandonment by his father and reflection that his anger can be triggered by reminders of this abandonment highlights that unresolved *grief* can set us up to struggle with anger. As Antwan describes, grief (in this case, from the loss of a primary caregiver who chose to leave rather than take care of him) can leave us overwhelmed by a complex combination of emotions – grief, sadness, fear, anxiety – which can play out in terms of angry explosiveness. In such situations, it's important to explore the profound loss and different emotions underlying the anger. This is difficult work, and if you recognise that grief seems to underlie your own anger, you may choose to enlist someone like a therapist who's trained to help us untangle this complicated web of feelings. It takes a lot of courage to do this work, but it's worth it.

Can you identify any of your anger triggers – situations that activate anger in you? What experiences in your life may have helped lay down those patterns in your brain?

The second question above is designed to help us bring compassion on board in relation to our triggers. We don't *choose* to be triggered by these things – we *learn* to be triggered through our life experiences. It's not our fault. But once we recognise we've been shaped in this way, it's our job to figure out how to work with these emotions so that we don't behave in ways that create problems in our lives or harm people we care about. You're probably noticing a theme to compassionate coping: we can *refrain from blaming* ourselves for our struggles while *taking responsibility* for how we respond to triggering situations.

Final reflection

What was it like bringing curiosity to your angry patterns and awareness to things that trigger them? Given your history, does it *make sense* that these things would trigger your threat system?

_____

_____

_____

_____

_____

_____

_____

Module 21: Tricky Brain Loops

In Modules 17 and 18, we explored different aspects of our 'angry selves' – how anger shapes our attention, thinking and reasoning, mental imagery, felt emotion, motivation and behaviour. These different aspects of our experience can interact with one another to keep us stuck in anger. In this way, anger can be quite 'sticky' – once we're in it, it can be a challenge to work our way back out. In this module, we'll explore these interactions.

Our emotional brains are powerful, but not very wise

It turns out that our 'emotional brains'[1] – a term I'll use as shorthand for the relatively ancient parts of our brains that produce emotions – are very *powerful*, but they aren't very *wise*. Brain structures like the amygdala – an almond-shaped structure right in the middle of our brains – are very good at rallying our brains and bodies to fight off threats, focusing our attention and thoughts, creating feelings of urgency, and so on. These structures are good at getting us going.

But these emotional brains aren't good at telling the difference between real physical threats that must be addressed *right now* and complex situations that are better served by calming down and carefully considering the most helpful way to respond. Even trickier, these emotional brains *aren't very good at telling the difference between real threats in the outside world and threatening ideas and fantasies we create in our own minds.*

If someone were to come up to me and say, 'Russell, I don't like you', I wouldn't feel good about it. I'd probably have some hurt feelings ('What's wrong with me? What did I do?') and maybe some anger ('Who do they think they are, to say that to me?!?'). Luckily, that doesn't happen so often. But imagine that I'm walking across campus at my university and wave at a new colleague I've recently met at a university function. Imagine this colleague walks by without even acknowledging my greeting, and I have the thought, 'Wow, they completely blew me off – they must not like me.' How do I feel? If I take that thought at face value, I'd probably have similar feelings as if they'd actually *told* me they didn't like me – feelings of rejection, wondering if I'd done something to put them off, that sort of thing. Our emotional brains are like pattern-recognition machines that respond to the inputs they're given. In this case, the input is a thought that may have no basis in reality (they're probably just distracted, thinking about the lecture they'll give in their next class) – but my amygdala doesn't know that. All it knows is that it's received the message 'they don't like me', and it starts firing off emotions in response to that threat.

Tricky 'loops'

Regardless of whether our emotional brains are responding to real or imagined threats, once they've fired off a threat emotion like anger (or anxiety), other aspects of the anger experience can kick in. An anger trigger occurs, we feel an emotional reaction and then start generating thoughts and images (as well as bodily arousal) related to the anger. *Those thoughts and bodily arousal then become information that is fed back to our emotional brains, fuelling the very anger that triggered them.* Figure 21.1 demonstrates how these loops can work.

Figure 21.1: Tricky loops in the brain

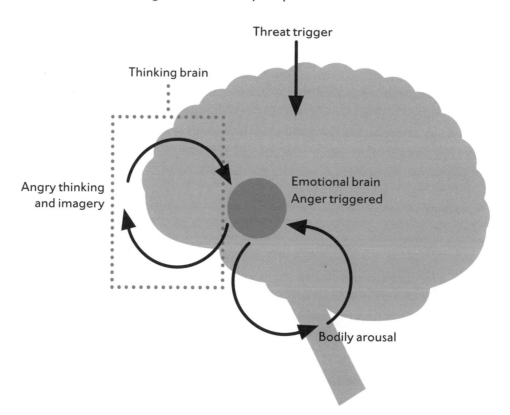

Let's explore how this can work, using a trigger I share with James – having a plan for how things will go, and then something happens to disrupt the plan. Often, behind the plan, my mind's formed a fantasy of an idealised version of what I want to happen – I think that's what's 'threatened' when things go a bit sideways. As I write this, it's autumn in Spokane, a beautiful time of year when Spokanites commonly visit an area north-east of town called Greenbluff, where large fruit farms hold an autumn festival. Our family likes to visit the festival and stock up on organic apples and pumpkin donuts, listen to some music, and maybe grab a pint at the brewery. Let's imagine that this autumn, we've planned to go on Sunday afternoon, leaving at noon when my son returns home from a morning shift at his job. On the day, let's imagine he's forgotten the plan to go to Greenbluff and has agreed to stay an extra hour to help a co-worker – and, since he's turned the sound off on his phone while working, he doesn't respond to my texts and calls.

Keeping Figure 21.1 in mind, we can imagine how this situation might play out. First, the trigger: I'm waiting at home at noon, excited to get going, and about 12.30 I receive a text from my son saying he'll be working late. I text him back repeatedly and try to call, but he doesn't respond. This input is received by my brain as a threat (to my idealised day with my family ... which you may not understand if you haven't tried those pumpkin donuts!) and anger fires off. This emotion then begins to shape my awareness, focusing my attention on the perceived threat and triggering a barrage of thoughts – that the day will be ruined, that my son is being irresponsible (he's not, most of the time) and blowing off this family event. These thoughts then feed back to my emotional brain, where they are perceived as additional threatening information. In this way, the thoughts I'm having in response to this situation end up *fuelling* the anger that triggered them in the first place.

The anger also triggers arousal in my body: stress hormones released, heart racing, blood pressure increasing, muscles start to tense ... This information then loops back up to my emotional brain, becoming more input that fuels my growing experience of threat. It's like my emotional brain is saying, 'Wow – my body is going wild ... I must be *really* angry!' If the process carries on uninterrupted, looping back and forth from emotional brain to body to thinking brain and so forth, the escalation could take me into wild territory: I could find myself lost in anger, fantasising a world in which my family *never* gets to do anything fun together, in which my son *completely disrespects* me and just *doesn't care* about our family, and in which the day, the week ... hell, the entire autumn, is now *ruined*.

We could draw another loop at the top of the diagram in Figure 21.1, going out into the world, as I vent my frustration to my wife, who would probably be taken aback that I'm getting so bent out of shape because my son is a bit late getting home from work, perhaps expressing irritation at my overreaction. Her irritation could then become *another* input to my emotional brain, adding a new nuance to my angry thoughts – 'Oh, now *you're* against me, too. Why am *I* always the problem? I'm the only one who actually seems to care about our family having quality time together, and now I'm getting blamed for it getting screwed up?!?'

As all these loops feed back on one another, we see that my really-powerful-but-not-terribly-clever threat system isn't just responding to the relatively minor stressor of my son being a bit late and not immediately answering my calls. It's now faced with the mentally created experience of *having a son who doesn't respect me, my day/season being ruined* and, oh yeah, *my entire family being against me as I try to create quality time for us* (for some of us, one shame-avoidance strategy can take the form of martyrdom!). If these imagined threats are taken as real – which our emotional brains can easily do – well, it's easy to see how things can escalate even further. This is tricky stuff.

You may find this example a bit exaggerated for effect, which it is . . . *somewhat*. The point is that different parts of our brains interact in ways that can create 'loops', creating an inertia that makes it hard to shift out of emotional experiences. This is deepened by the nature of angry thinking – which is threat-focused (leading to catastrophising, as our threat-focused brains work to anticipate the worst ways things could go wrong), poor at critical thinking and seeing things from different perspectives, and carries a felt sense of certainty – a feeling of *knowing* our interpretation of the situation is correct and that things *really are* this bad (even when our interpretation is likely to be incorrect, and things probably won't be that bad after all). Add in some arousal feeding back from the body, and messages of disapproval or rejection coming in from the outside world, and it can create a perfect storm that keeps us cycling in the anger, sometimes for hours.

This isn't our fault. We didn't design our brains to work this way. But, understanding how this works, we can help keep ourselves from getting hijacked. Doing this involves the two core aspects of compassion: *sensitivity* to suffering and difficulty (to notice what is happening in us), and the *motivation* to figure out and do what is helpful.

What do you make of the information on 'brain loops' – how our emotional brains, thinking brains and bodies can interact to keep us stuck in our anger experiences? Did this discussion relate to your life experience? What feelings came up while reading it?

James: *I've never had a pumpkin donut – something I'm keen to remedy – but reading this module felt like someone had gazed into my life. I can't count how many times something like this has happened, and I've escalated in just this way. What it didn't mention is the shame I feel after. At some point – usually once my wife has really had enough of me – I snap out of it and see what I've done, and how unhinged I must have looked. Then I feel like the worst father and husband in the world. This helps me see both sides of it. I can see how crazy-making my escalation must seem to them, and thinking about these loops helps me understand how I can get caught up and so upset without meaning to. It's hell. In terms of feelings, it's a mash-up of the shame of seeing myself in the example, relief about understanding what's happening, and hope that I'll learn how to do something about it.*

Antwan: *This was interesting. Thinking about my life, I could see different parts show up at different times. At school, I see the thinking loop play out. Like, a teacher will say something to me, and I'll be a little annoyed, but then I think, 'She's talking down to me. She doesn't disrespect other kids like that.' Then I get really pissed off. When I've got into fights, it's all the body loop. Someone will say something or start something, and it's like there's a rush of adrenaline and I'm ready to go, son. I kind of like that feeling, but I can see how it feeds into what we're talking about.*

Jordan: *I could relate to the loops. Something happens – I have lots of triggers – and I'll get a burst of irritation or anger. But as it loops to my 'thinking brain', it gets turned around by my thoughts, 'If I say something, I'll cry and they'll think I'm hysterical or oversensitive', 'Am I making a big deal out of nothing?' And when those thoughts feed back, it's like some of the anger is turned into anxiety and shame – so they're all there at the same time. It's overwhelming!*

What do you make of the information on 'brain loops' – how our emotional brains, thinking brains and bodies can interact to keep us stuck in our anger experiences? Did this discussion relate to any of your life experience? What feelings came up while reading it?

Final reflection

In future modules, we'll explore these loops and how to work with them in your lives. Is there anything you've learned so far (or other ideas that you didn't learn here) that you think might be helpful to keep in mind as we approach working with these loops?

_____

_____

_____

_____

_____

_____

_____

_____

Module 22: Exploring Triggers and Loops

In this module, our focus is on unpacking how the loops we introduced in Module 21 play out in *your* life, so we'll get straight to the reflections. As depicted in Figure 22.1 (which is a repeat of Figure 21.1), let's start by revisiting your typical threat triggers.

Figure 22.1: Tricky loops in the brain

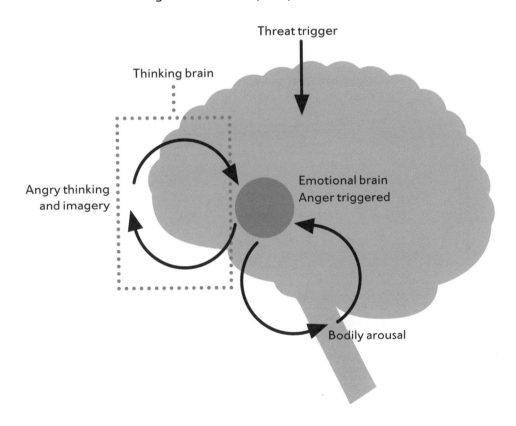

What experiences and situations most frequently trigger your anger?

James: *I've been thinking about this. For me, there are two big domains – the first is to do with things not playing out as I want or hope (when things don't go as I've planned, others don't do as they've said they will), and the second involves how other people relate to me, feeling rejected or unwanted, and feeling unheard or not cared about. Those are the biggies.*

Antwan: *My anger triggers involve either feeling like I'm being disrespected or challenged, or being made to do stuff I don't want to do. Sometimes, like at school, it's both at the same time. Also, anything that reminds me of my father puts me on edge as well.*

Jordan: *In terms of anger triggers, a big one for me is injustice and thoughtlessness – people intentionally doing things that make life harder or uncomfortable for others. Things like sexism, racism, homophobia and body shaming. This sometimes plays out directly in my own life, like when co-workers mansplain to me or make sexist comments, but I also get triggered seeing it in the culture. I think there's also feeling unseen – having my work not acknowledged or even seeing the credit given to someone else when I (and they) know I'm the one who did the work.*

What experiences and situations most frequently trigger your anger?

_____

_____

_____

_____

_____

As we see in Figure 22.1, sensory information about the trigger is transmitted to the emotional parts of our brains, which fire off a threat response involving anger, irritability, frustration or hostility. When these emotions arise in us, they tend to be followed by thoughts and imagery that fit with (and then work to fuel) the anger. Let's explore these now:

Select one of your most common (or upsetting) triggers. What thoughts and imagery (words, images and 'movies') accompany the anger provoked by these experiences?

James: *I feel I've written a lot about what happens when things don't go my way, so I'll choose the relationship trigger instead – when I feel people disapproving, pulling back or avoiding me. This is difficult for me. When that happens, two kinds of thoughts come up. The first tends to be hostile: 'F*** them!', 'Who do they think they are?', 'Why do they always make me into the bad guy?' The second is more focused on being excluded and involves imagining things – picturing others having fun without me, talking about me behind my back, imagining their lives would be better off without me. Wow . . . I'm noticing myself getting upset just writing this stuff down.*

Antwan: *When a teacher gets at me about something, I think about how unfair it is, how they don't talk like that to kids they like, even though those kids do the same stuff. I guess underneath that is the idea that they don't like me or respect me. They talk about caring about us and our futures, but it seems like that caring only applies to kids that fit their idea of how a kid is supposed to be. Others they just seem irritated by. If you're gonna treat me like you don't like me, I've got nothin' for you. Just writing about this is getting me stirred up. I'm tired of adults who say they care about you but then don't show up. Like my father. It was his job to take care of us . . . and then he just left. Who does that? I picture him out there with some other family, or hanging out with his deadbeat friends, while we're just trying to get by. I guess other thoughts I have are about not being able to trust people – that the only person you can really count on is yourself. That makes me angry, and it makes me sad, too.*

Jordan: *Lots of thoughts come up in response to triggers and the feelings that follow. There's often an initial thought that 'This is wrong! This is not okay!' And I think these thoughts are probably spot-on a lot of the time. But then things get all topsy-turvy. I start doubting myself, thinking I'm overly sensitive or wondering if I'm making a big deal out of nothing. These are things my mother said to me when I was growing up, and several men have said to me in my adult life. I imagine them laughing at me and talking about me, seeing me as this hysterical woman they don't need to take seriously. After I get paralysed by all these thoughts and start crying, I get self-critical – 'I'm so weak. I can't even stand up for myself.' So yeah, I have a lot of thoughts going on.*

Select one of your most common (or upsetting) triggers. What thoughts and imagery (words, images and 'movies') tend to accompany the anger provoked by these experiences?

_____

_____

_____

_____

_____

_____

_____

_____

Considering our companions' exploration of their thoughts and imagery (and, probably, your own), we can imagine how – if accepted as true – they could fuel the anger that triggered them. However, all the companions mentioned thoughts that could potentially trigger other threat emotions as well. Sometimes anger can mask other experiences, like grief, anxiety, shame or sadness.

Let's unpack this thought–emotion loop a bit further:

Keeping in mind the thoughts and imagery you just described, let's fill in the thought–emotion loop. As these thoughts and images feed back to your emotional brain, what feelings (perhaps not just anger) do they fuel in you? What feelings do they trigger?

James: _Well, thinking of myself being rejected and avoided fuels anger, but it definitely brings up other feelings. When I picture my family excluding me or having fun together without me, sadness and anxiety show up. And shame . . . lots of shame. Like 'Maybe there is something wrong with me. Maybe I am a terrible father and husband.' That feels terrible. I can feel tears coming up as I write, which makes me feel weak._

Antwan: _When I think about my teachers treating me unfairly or looking down on me, it just pisses me off. But I guess it's also a little sad, you know? Like, why do they like those other kids and not like me? With my other triggers – being reminded of my dad and how he left – things are more complicated. I don't like to talk about it. I'm sad he left – didn't he love me? I mean, he didn't just divorce my mum . . . he just disappeared. And I wonder if part of it was my fault; if I did something wrong that drove him off? I'm scared I'll be like him and hurt the people I care about. If he cared about us at all. It's like all this stuff is swirling around in my head and I don't know what to do with it. I just get so angry. I want to yell and scream and fight, but none of it does any good._

Jordan: _Here's where it gets messy for me. I start out with anger, which then triggers all the thoughts . . . which then trigger lots of other feelings. The anger's still there, but then there's anxiety and worry that I'm overly sensitive or will be seen that way, frustration and sadness about the fact this happens to me and so many women, and feeling hopeless and overwhelmed – like I can't do anything about any of it. Then it's like I'm still angry, but now I'm angry at me, because I didn't do anything. I feel pathetic._

Keeping in mind the thoughts and imagery you just described, let's fill in the thought–emotion loop. As these thoughts and images feed back to your emotional brain, what feelings (perhaps not just anger) do they fuel in you? What feelings do they trigger?

_____

_____

_____

_____

_____

_____

Considering loops from our companions, we see the complexity that can show up when working with anger. Often, it isn't *just* working with anger. For each companion, as thoughts and images associated with their anger play out, they not only fuel ongoing anger but also give rise to other challenging feelings like grief, anxiety, sadness and shame. Shame – a sense of being bad, flawed or having 'something wrong with me' (or having others see us like this) – is a deeply painful experience, and is quite often wrapped up with anger.[1] This is one reason compassion – particularly compassion for the self – can be helpful in working with anger, as shame can get in the way of taking responsibility and engaging helpfully with our anger.

For now, let's consider that lower loop in Figure 22.1. In Module 18, we explored how anger plays out in our bodies, with common experiences involving heightened arousal (heart rate, blood pressure), feelings of urgency, muscle tension and sometimes other symptoms (for example, we can't know if Jordan's irritable bowel syndrome is related to her anger, but it *could be*).[2] In terms of the loops, this information from the body is transmitted back up to the brain – where it can impact our emotional brains and the feelings that flow from them. We can imagine how this heightened arousal, muscle tension and other experiences described might combine with angry thoughts and fantasies to fuel ongoing experiences of anger and other threat emotions, creating another threat-focused loop.[3]

We could even draw *another loop* – from ourselves out to the outside world (through our behaviour), and back from the world into our emotional brains – through our senses, giving

172 The Anger Workbook

feedback on how other people and the world are impacted by and reacting to our angry behaviour. As we explored in Module 19, when caught in anger we may find ourselves engaging with others in ways that are likely to *trigger their threat systems*, setting them up to engage with us in ways that will further trigger ours in turn.

To wrap up, when we're angry, it's not just about feelings – it's about how our feelings, thoughts, bodily experiences and interactions with the external world can impact one another to fuel our anger and keep it going. This is tricky stuff – but it's also *good news* that our emotions, thoughts and bodily experiences interact with one another, giving us lots of avenues through which to intervene. *Each of these loops represents an input to our emotional brains that we can use to create the emotional experiences we want to have.*

Final reflection

What were your takeaways from the discussion of the 'brain loops'? Did you learn anything that you'd like to keep in mind going forwards?

_____

_____

_____

_____

_____

_____

_____

End of section check-in

How are you feeling about your progress so far?

_____

_____

_____

What has been helpful for you?

_____

_____

_____

What obstacles have arisen that should be considered as we move forwards?

_____

_____

_____

What would be helpful for you to keep in mind going forwards?

_____

_____

_____

Compassion practice plan

Now we've completed the fourth section, let's update the practice plan. Here are a few suggested practices based upon the modules in Section IV (and a couple of reminders from Section III):

1. **Un-bounce a relationship** (Module 19): Take five minutes to reflect on a relationship in which you've had 'threat systems bouncing' – in which you and another person interacted in ways that fuelled each other's threat systems. Consider how you might approach interactions with this person in a way that might change this dynamic. How might you interact with them in a manner that will help them feel safe (or at least not put them into threat)? How might you help yourself feel safe and calm during the interaction, however they engage with you?

2. **Reflect on a trigger** (Modules 20–22): Take five minutes to recall a situation (or type of situation) that commonly triggers you. Consider your history, and how it makes sense that this experience would be triggering for you. Think about how your compassionate self might respond to this trigger: how would this kind, wise, confident version of you respond? What advice might your compassionate self offer the vulnerable version of you who struggles with the trigger?

3. **Mind the loops** (Module 21 and 22): Take five to ten minutes to reflect on the 'loops' from Modules 21 and 22. Consider a recent triggering situation (or simply notice what's happening *right now*), and try to curiously notice all the aspects of that experience. Notice the information coming in through your senses about what is happening outside. Notice the emotions that arise in you in response to that information. Notice the thoughts that come up with these emotions. Notice the feelings prompted by these thoughts. Notice what's happening in your body as well, and the urges or behaviour that may or may not arise. Consider if there's anything helpful to be done.

4. **Check in with your compassionate self** (Module 14): Take five to ten minutes to pause, slow down your breath and step into your compassionate self: courageous in the face of struggle, committed to doing what's helpful, wise and confident. Using the acting approach described in Module 14, imagine being filled with these qualities. Imagine how your body would feel as this compassionate being – balanced, calm, centred. Imagine what you would pay attention to, think about and care about – noticing difficulty and considering what would be helpful to address it. Imagine how you would go about your day as this compassionate self, how you would interact with the people around you.

5. **Deepen a compassionate quality** (Module 14): Select one of the qualities described in Module 14 (courage, kindness, wisdom, kind curiosity, acknowledging acceptance, sympathy, empathy, non-condemnation, distress tolerance, confidence). Take five minutes to reflect on how you might bring this quality into your life. How would you apply it to a situation you're facing today?

Every day, do one mindful check-in, three systems check-in or brief 'mind the loops' practice for the present moment, and one other practice. Choose practices from those listed above, as well as those included in the first three practice plans on pages 64–6, 107–8 and 135. Make sure to do each of the new practices at least once, and don't repeat any practice more than twice per week. Mix in soothing activities regularly – daily, if possible.

Daily practice log

Practice	Sun	Mon	Tues	Weds	Thurs	Fri	Sat
Check-in practice of choice							

Practice notes

Day	What was helpful?	What obstacles came up?
Sunday		
Monday		
Tuesday		
Wednesday		
Thursday		
Friday		
Saturday		

SECTION V:

Working Compassionately with Anger

Module 23: Bringing Mindfulness to Anger

Recent modules have explored how anger and other emotions can involve mental 'loops', in which thoughts, imagery, bodily sensations and interactions with the outside world can trigger our emotional brains, which then can activate more angry thoughts, bodily sensations and behaviours. These interactions can fuel anger and keep it going long after the original situation is over. I suspect most people who struggle with anger or other threat emotions can relate to 'playing a situation in my head like a movie' over and over, continually reactivating the anger (or anxiety or fear . . .). In this module, we'll introduce a way of working with this, with the goal of shifting from anger-driven loops like those pictured in the previous modules to something that looks more like Figure 23.1.

Figure 23.1: Creating compassionate loops

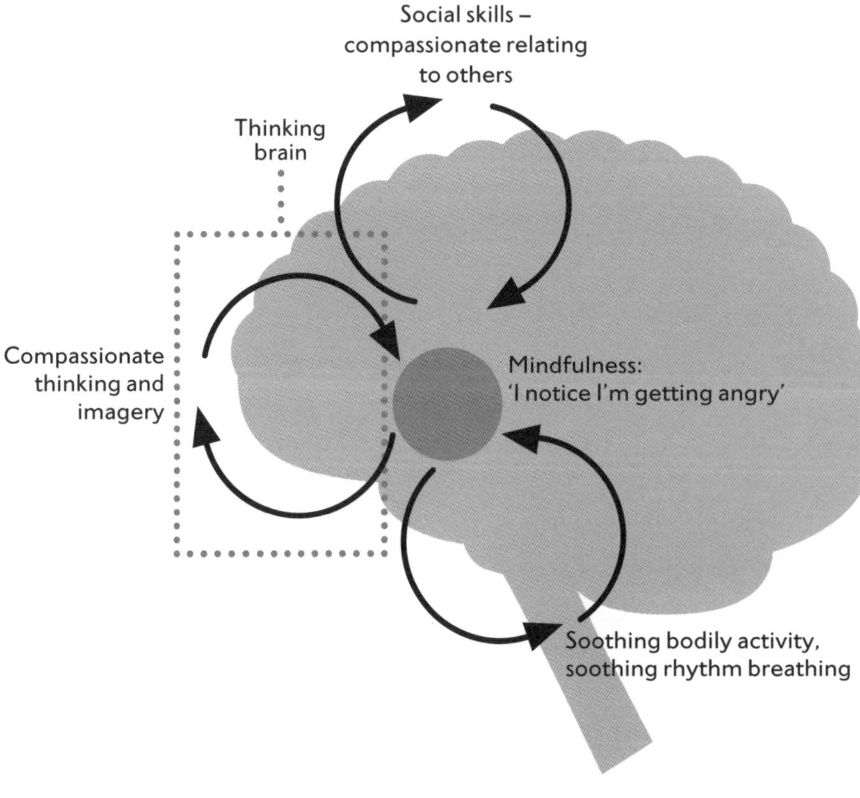

Sometimes we may try to manage anger or other threat emotions by attempting to avoid contact with things that trigger those feelings. There are a few problems with this approach. First, we can't control what other people do (or many other things that happen in the world), so on a practical level it's almost impossible to avoid all potential triggers. Second, such efforts are based on avoidance – *running away* from things that challenge us or make us uncomfortable. When we create patterns of avoidance in our lives, our worlds get a bit smaller, and the power of the things we're avoiding grows. When we avoid, it's like we're teaching our emotional brains that 'This is really threatening, and I can't handle it.' So when we *do* inevitably come across the trigger, it's even more threatening and activating than before.

Our approach is different. We're going to *assume* we *will* be triggered sometimes, *plan* how we're going to respond and *prepare* by developing the skills to help ourselves cope when the time arrives. Looking at Figure 23.1, we see the threat trigger, provoking an angry emotional response. But there are also lots of *other* things happening that can help us keep things from getting out of control. In this module, we'll focus on the centre of Figure 23.1 – mindful awareness – which we introduced in Module 5.

Mindful awareness

There are lots of benefits to being able to curiously notice our experience without getting caught up in it, rejecting it or beating ourselves up for having it. With anger, a mindful response can begin in a variety of ways:

- Noticing the trigger – 'Ah . . . there it is, one of my typical triggers!'

- Noticing the emotional reaction – 'I'm noticing myself feeling angry. I wonder what that's about. Oh yeah, one of my typical triggers just happened.'

- Noticing bodily sensations – 'Something just happened – my body just got really activated. I'm tense and feeling myself flush. Let's see if I can figure out what's going on.'

- Noticing thoughts and imagery – 'Look – I just had the thought that she disrespected me. That's likely to fuel my anger.'

Mindfulness can help us get one step ahead of our anger, as we learn to notice early signs that it's arising. Every time we notice a sign of anger coming up in us, it's an opportunity to step out of the anger loops and consider what might be helpful to do instead.

Writing this, I recall that last week was Halloween, and I was meeting with a group of high-school students, discussing this exact topic. Together we came up with an analogy that compared working with threat triggers to the experience of watching a horror movie. Being triggered is like finding yourself spontaneously dropped right into the middle of the horror movie. If you're *in the movie,* it's very scary (or, in this case, anger-inducing), and easy to get caught in an out-of-control threat response – in horror movies, there's lots of threat-filled, not very helpful running about! On the other hand, if we're *watching the movie,* we can notice the threats and other things happening, but there's a degree of separation. Sometimes I even find myself trying to coach the characters . . . *What are you doing? Don't you know that having sex during a horror movie is the fastest way to get yourself killed?!?* Mindful noticing helps us *step out of the movie,* so instead of just reacting and getting caught up in the loops, we can see them playing out. This sets our compassionate selves up to *coach* our angry selves, just as I try to coach the characters in those scary movies – and with much more success!

If you've been following the practice plan, you'll probably have got into the habit of 'checking in' with yourself a few times a day – pausing to notice what is going on in your body, and what thoughts, images and emotions are playing through your mind. If you've let that drop off, no worries . . . here's a gentle reminder to give it another go. In the rest of this module, we'll introduce a strategy to train your mindful awareness to notice your triggering situations and help yourself 'step out of the movie'. First, let's pause and reflect on the discussion so far:

What thoughts do you have about how you might bring mindful awareness to your anger and 'step out of the movie'?

James: *It felt hopeful to me that I just need to notice one part of the experience to recognise what's happening and 'step out' of it. I'd like to get to know my triggers and the feeling of anger well enough that I could recognise what's happening before I get swept away. It's reassuring to know that at any point I can notice some part of what's happening – my racing heart, thoughts or images – that can help me wake up and hopefully do something about it. I'm interested to learn more.*

Antwan: *I love horror movies, so that was fun to read. It made sense. When I'm caught up in anger, I'm in it, energy running through my body and everything, like the movie characters are running around terrified. I can see how recognising what's happening could help you step out of it, so some of the energy is still there – which is why I like watching horror – but you can think more clearly about what to do. I think it clicked with me because characters in horror movies are always doing stupid stuff, just like I do when I'm angry.*

Jordan: *I don't like horror movies, so I'm going to change the analogy to being caught in a dream and waking up. That fits for me, because when I'm doing my anger ⟶ anxiety ⟶ self-attacking loops, it's dreamlike in that I've gone* way beyond *what happened to trigger me. Sure, something happened and I may need to do something about it. But so often, that's not what I'm reacting to. Most of the time, I'm reacting to stories I've made up about it in my head, or beating myself up for being angry or sensitive, and it just keeps looping. If I could notice I'm doing that, 'wake up' from it, and just consider how to deal with the actual situation, it would really help. I can remember times I've been in the middle of scary dreams and recognised 'wait a second ... I'm dreaming', and it immediately stopped being so scary. I think my thoughts drive a lot of it, so maybe learning to notice when I'm criticising myself or making movies in my head about what happened would be a good place to start.*

What thoughts do you have about how you might bring mindful awareness to your anger and 'step out of the movie'?

_____

_____

_____

_____

_____

_____

_____

Looking at the reflections above, our companions discussed several important points, but I wanted to highlight something Jordan did around working with obstacles. As I enjoy horror movies (the vampire/werewolf/ghosty ones – not the really gory ones!), I was taken with that and used it as an example. Jordan, like a lot of people, doesn't care for horror movies. But instead of skipping over the material or 'powering through' even though it wasn't a good fit for her, she acknowledged that horror movies aren't her thing, and considered how she could make it helpful for her . . . using the analogy of a dream instead of a movie. In doing this, she explored the material in ways that deepened its usefulness for her, and probably for some of us, too. You may have noticed that James also used the term 'waking up'. This ability to notice obstacles and then consider *what might be helpful in working with them* is a huge part of applying compassion to our struggles. We can begin to *collect* helpful strategies – intentionally noticing things that work well in helping us cope with different situations, and building these strategies into our repertoire of skills we can draw upon in the future.

Monitoring our anger

Speaking of helpful strategies, I'd like to share a practice you might find helpful in learning to notice different aspects of your anger as they arise. Behavioural psychologists often use an intervention called 'self-monitoring', which is a fancy way of saying 'keeping track of something you do or experience'. Self-monitoring has several benefits,[1] one of which is that it helps *train the brain to notice the behaviour that's being monitored*. Self-monitoring can be a helpful tool for addressing sneaky habits we may not notice initially – things like nail-biting, for example – because it teaches the brain 'this behaviour is something worth noticing'.

In training our minds to quickly notice angry patterns of attention, feeling, thinking, imagery, motivation and behaviour, we'll take a page from the self-monitoring playbook. To do this, it's good to have a notebook, journal or even a notes app on your phone; it needs to be something we have access to all the time. Whenever we find ourselves experiencing any aspect of our anger – *whenever we notice it* – we stop and make a note of it. We want to keep it brief, as the key is to do it consistently – preferably *every time* we experience anger – and if it ends up taking half an hour each time, we probably won't do it. Shorthand is fine. The point isn't the written record – it's that the act of writing it down will train the brain to notice these parts of our experience, with the goal that we'll notice anger triggers, thoughts, bodily experiences and feelings *before getting caught up in the loops and taking actions that cause us problems*. As soon as you notice an anger trigger, angry feeling, angry thought or bodily activation that you recognise as related to anger, take a moment to jot down the following:

Trigger: [What happened? Briefly note the situation, experience or interaction that triggered your anger.]

Emotions: [Briefly record your feelings – anger/irritability/hostility and any other feelings that show up, like anxiety or shame.]

Thoughts and imagery: [Briefly write down any thoughts, images or 'movies' playing in your head.]

Bodily experience: [Briefly note any sensations you notice in your body – racing heart, tension, etc.]

Later, we'll explore how to work compassionately with anger triggers – although you can feel free to use this monitoring activity as a jumping-off point to consider 'I wonder what would be helpful to do right now to manage my anger or address the situation?' For now, though, the goal is simply to notice and briefly record the trigger, emotions, thoughts and bodily experiences whenever we experience anger. We're teaching our brains that these experiences are worth noticing . . . because the sooner we *notice* our anger beginning to take shape, the sooner we can work to manage it, using methods we'll cover in the rest of the book.

For our final reflection, let's make an initial plan for how you'll consistently monitor your anger. I say 'initial' because, often, unanticipated obstacles will get in the way. If this happens, don't beat yourself up about it – instead consider ways to address the obstacle so you can do the self-monitoring. New habits can be challenging to establish, but this one is worth it.

Final reflection

How do you plan to record your anger observations (for example, in a notebook, on your phone, in a journal)? To be effective, the monitoring needs to be done *as soon as possible* **– optimally,** *as soon as you notice any part of the experience* **(trigger, bodily experience, thought or feeling) . . .** *and* **later is better than never.**

What do you think might help you stay motivated to do the monitoring, so that it happens? (For example: reminding myself why I'm working with my anger; reminding myself of my values and of the sort of person I want to be; rewarding myself – doing something enjoyable towards the end of the day if I complete the monitoring form.)

_____

_____

_____

_____

_____

_____

_____

Module 24: Working with the Body

Module 23 focused on training ourselves to notice the arising of anger – triggers, thoughts and images, feelings, bodily sensations – with the goal of becoming aware of what's happening before we're carried away by it. In this module, and in the rest of the book, we'll use what we know about the 'loops' to engage behaviours to help break the cycle of anger and create the mental states we want to have. In this module, we'll focus specifically on the role of the body in our anger, and how we can work with it. Let's revisit the figure from the previous module depicting these loops:

Figure 24.1: Creating compassionate loops

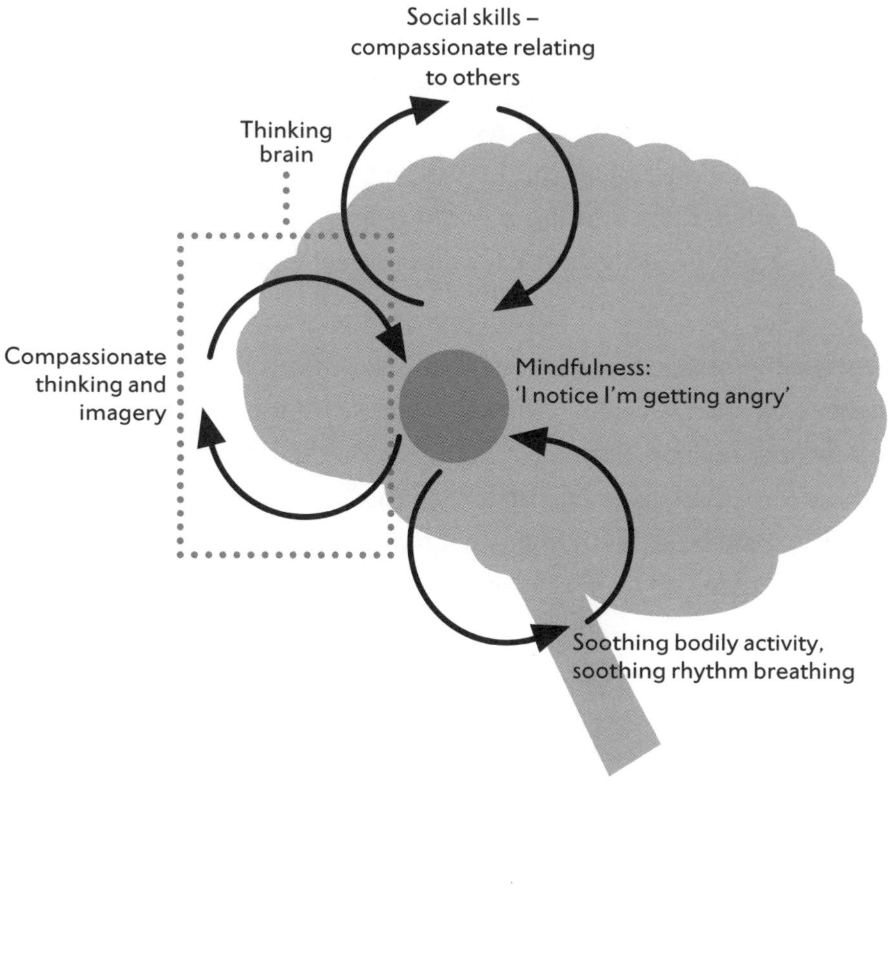

Social skills –
compassionate relating
to others

Thinking
brain

Compassionate
thinking and
imagery

Mindfulness:
'I notice I'm getting angry'

Soothing bodily activity,
soothing rhythm breathing

As we've discussed, anger activates our bodies, and this activation in the body can then fuel the anger that created it. This module focuses on working with the body to create new, soothing inputs for our emotional brains. This will help soften our anger and pave the way for more helpful, compassionate and pleasant mental states.

I've been a clinical psychologist for nearly twenty-five years, and if someone asked me, 'What is the single most powerful "psychological technique" there is?', I'd almost certainly say 'learning to slow down the breath' (the other thing I might mention – also involving the body and the reason for the 'soothing bodily activity' in Figure 24.1 – is 'exercise'). There's a large body of science documenting the benefits of learning to slow down the breath.[1] We won't delve into that here, but I wanted to mention it because, as powerful as breathwork is, lots of people resist doing it. I've had clients respond mockingly to the suggestion: 'Oh, you want me to *slow down my breath*? I'm sure that's going to help . . .'. I even know *therapists* who hardly ever use breathwork with their clients. (By the way, if you're a therapist, use breathwork more with your clients. Seriously.)

If you're not completely stoked about breathwork just yet, I understand. But here's the thing – slowing down the breath isn't *just* about creating change in the body (although it does that in very helpful ways). It's also about *using the body as a tool for working with the mind*. When we do *soothing rhythm breathing* (abbreviated to SRB, the CFT term for slowing down the breath), we send soothing information up from the body to the emotional brain, which helps shift our emotional state. This in turn helps shift our thoughts, etc. via the looping process we've explored. We can think of slowing down the body as a powerful tool for helping us slow down or soften anger (or other threat emotions like anxiety or fear) in the brain.

The act of intentionally shifting our attention to the breath can be challenging but also quite helpful. Remember, the threat system narrowly focuses our attention, thinking and imagery onto perceived threats, fuelling our anger. Soothing rhythm breathing requires us to shift our attention away from those angry triggers, thoughts and imagery and towards the breath and body, cutting off some of the thought-fuel that keeps our anger burning hot. As our threat systems are designed to keep our attention locked onto perceived threats, we may find ourselves having to let those angry thoughts and images go and move to the breath again and again . . . but this practice is helpful, too, helping us get better at noticing our attention and directing it where we want it to go, rather than having it controlled by our threat systems.

Soothing rhythm breathing

In soothing rhythm breathing, the goal is to *slow down* the breath. Below, I'll present some guidelines, but you can also access guided audio versions of the practice online here: www.compassionatemind.co.uk/resource/audio, at the website for the Compassionate Mind Foundation. There are also several breathing apps that can be downloaded onto your phone. I find these particularly helpful for clients whose histories make focusing on their bodies tricky (for example, people with a trauma history involving their bodies), as you can 'breathe along' with an image on the app (for example, a balloon-like figure expanding and contracting) instead of focusing attention on the body.

In any case, the goal of SRB is to slow the breath down – optimally to a rate of four to five seconds on the inbreath, and five to six seconds on the outbreath. Some people find counting as they breathe ('breathing in – 1, 2, 3, 4 – breathing out – 1, 2, 3, 4 . . .') helpful, while others find that focusing on 'getting the count right' creates anxiety or tension that gets in the way of it being soothing for them (another reason apps can be nice – you may find it less distracting to 'breathe along with the balloon' than to count). *The point is to find a rate of breathing that is slow, comfortable and soothing for you.* After lots of practice, I know when I've found the right rate of breathing, because I find it enjoyable . . . there's a pleasant 'settling in' sort of quality. If you listen to different versions of the practice, you may notice some variations in the instructions. I recommend you don't worry about that, except to try to notice which ones work best for you, and using those. As with everything in this book, it's about *learning what is helpful* and building that into your life.

Soothing rhythm breathing (SRB)

- Sit or stand comfortably in an upright position you can maintain for a few minutes. Hold your upper body in an upright, dignified posture, to keep your airways nice and open. Once you're familiar with the practice, you might close your eyes.

- Take a moment to check in with your body. If you notice you're holding any tension, see if it's possible to allow your body to relax and release a bit of that tension.

- Breathing in through your nose and out through either your nose or mouth, gently bring your attention to the sensation of your breath, noticing it entering, filling you and departing again.

- Resting your attention on the breath, allow your breathing to settle into a comfortable rhythm. Try to let go of the desire to control the breath and allow it to take on a rhythm that is comfortable and soothing. If your attention wanders from the breath, gently bring it back, again and again. Don't worry if it wanders – coming back is part of the practice.

- Once you've found a comfortable rhythm, see if it's possible to allow your breath to slow down a bit further. If you're counting, count to four or five seconds during the inbreath, and five or six seconds during the outbreath.

- Spend a few minutes just breathing slowly like this, enjoying the soothing quality of the breath.

To begin, I usually encourage people to do soothing rhythm breathing for two minutes or so, and then as they become comfortable with the practice, to extend it to five minutes. Some people turn it into a meditation and spend twenty to thirty minutes breathing. Here are a few points I think are helpful to know about this practice:

- Some readers may have had experience with mindful breathing, which involves focusing the attention on the breath and bringing it back again whenever it wanders. While mindful breathing can *look* very similar to SRB, the difference is the focus of the practice. With mindful breathing, the focus is on awareness – working with the attention to grow our ability to keep it stable (focused on the breath) and notice the arising of different experiences (thoughts, images, etc.) in the mind. In this way, mindful breathing is actually a very active mental training process. With SRB, the focus is on soothing and relaxation. While we do bring our attention back to the breath whenever we become distracted, the purpose here is to settle in to the experience of *slowing down* the body and mind.

- As the goal is slowing down and soothing, try to let go of the need to tightly control what you're doing or to *do it just right*. While well-meant, these efforts can undermine the purpose of the exercise, which is about soothing and calming.

- If you find yourself nodding off a bit, that's no problem . . . maybe take a nap!

- If you find yourself feeling uncomfortable and restless, that's also not a problem. Frequent use of modern conveniences like smartphones may have trained our brains to expect high levels of stimulation, and it can be unsettling at first when they're deprived of all that activation. If this is the case for you, maybe start small – thirty seconds or so at a time – repeated several times throughout the day. Gradually extend the time until you're at five minutes (or longer if you like). You're helping your brain adapt to a different level of stimulation, which will be worth the time invested.

- As with many things, breathwork becomes much more effective the more we practise it. Given that, I'd encourage you to do SRB a few times each day. In addition to doing it whenever you notice your threat system taking over, you might also create a practice routine – if you're a TV watcher, maybe do a minute of SRB during the first commercial break of each programme you watch. I know people who set two or three reminders per day on their phones to practise. With practice, SRB can become a valuable tool that is there when you need it . . . and, without practice, it will probably slip off your radar when triggers show up.

What did you think of the soothing rhythm breathing (SRB) practice? Did you notice anything that might be helpful to keep in mind going forwards?

James: I liked it, although it'll take some getting used to. There were points of resistance that came up, like 'I already know about breathing, when are we going to get down to business?' And then I realised that although I know about slowing down my breath, I don't use it . . . which is the point. Once I got over myself and focused on slowing down the breath, it helped. I was able to relax and ended up enjoying it and going longer than I'd planned. If I can remember to do this when I'm triggered, I think it will help slow things down.

Antwan: At first, I thought this was dumb. I've had teachers try this stuff in classes, and it always seemed like bollocks to me. But the way it fitted in with the diagram made sense, so I tried. I didn't like it at first – I was restless and uncomfortable, wanting to check my phone or do something. But I kept going and it seemed to get easier after a while.

Jordan: My therapist has encouraged me to do slow-breathing exercises in the past, and I've done them on and off, with it being helpful at different times. I found some of the supplementary instructions helpful. It was good to be reminded that the point isn't to do it perfectly, but to settle in to the experience of soothing – it's easy for me to get so preoccupied with 'getting it right' that the practice becomes something else to be anxious or self-critical about. That still came up, but next to it was a mental voice reminding me that I don't have to be perfect – that the point is to relax into the breath and enjoy it. That helped.

What did you think of the soothing rhythm breathing (SRB) practice? Is there anything you noticed that might be helpful to keep in mind going forwards?

_____

_____

_____

_____

_____

_____

The companions' comments highlight common themes – initial resistance and dismissing the practice, feelings of restlessness, and self-criticism or concerns about 'getting it right'. I'm sure in your life you've done things you weren't initially excited about, but which got easier and paid dividends as you kept going. I'm a born-again exerciser, but if I get derailed, it's a slog during that first few weeks back at the gym or on the trail before I start seeing the positive effects again . . . but once I start seeing them, I'm quite keen to keep going. I'm hoping that even if you experience resistance around SRB or the other practices we explore, you'll try them out and give them a chance to work. Finally, Jordan's comment referenced a helpful 'mental voice' that encouraged her, reminding her of the purpose of the exercise and helping her release the self-criticism. That's what it looks like when you bring your 'compassionate self' on board to help.

Final reflection

Do you have ideas about what might be your preferred way to engage in the SRB practice? For example, using the guidelines in this module, listening to guided audio from the link or downloading a breathing app?

_____

_____

Module 24: Working with the Body   193

_____

_____

_____

_____

When might be good times during the day to practise SRB? What would help you remember to practise for a minute or two at these times?

_____

_____

_____

_____

_____

_____

Can you think of any other things you might do involving your body to help work with the intensity of your anger when you've been triggered (for example, go for a walk in a natural area, stretch, go for a run, work out, take a bath or shower)? No hitting things, by the way – we don't want to teach your brain to link anger with aggressive behaviour!

_____

_____

_____

_____

_____

Module 25: Self-compassion through Validation

As you make your way through this book, I hope you'll be collecting a repertoire of *helpful strategies* to use when you notice your anger arising. The previous module presented an excellent option: slowing down the breath. In this module, we'll explore a straightforward but powerful step in compassionate thinking: *validation*.

I'll use the term 'compassionate thinking' to refer to thinking that happens when we've observed that we or someone else is struggling – for example, when we notice our anger has been triggered, or that another person is hurting. Compassionate thinking is driven by consideration of what is *helpful* – both in how we relate to the person who is struggling or suffering, and how we address the situation itself.

To 'validate' means to acknowledge a person's struggle, suffering or experience as real and valid – that it *makes sense* that they (or we) would have this experience: 'I've been triggered and am feeling my anger surging. This is really tough.' In contrast, to 'invalidate' means to dismiss, to not take seriously, or to relate in a blaming or shaming way to the individual who's struggling: 'This is so stupid . . . here I am overreacting again. I'm a terrible parent' or 'I don't know why you're overreacting – it's not a big deal.'

Working with struggles and suffering in helpful ways begins by acknowledging that the experience is real, is difficult and is worth taking seriously – setting us up to figure out what would be helpful in addressing the situation. Invalidation shuts down that process because it doesn't even acknowledge the situation as genuinely challenging. Invalidation happens a lot, perhaps because it seems easier to dismiss or fail to acknowledge difficulties and uncomfortable emotions than to *deal with them*. But avoiding or failing to acknowledge pain and the situations that cause it doesn't erase them – it sends them to the gym!

I think validation is particularly important for working with anger. In my experience, we may tend to overreact or ruminate on difficult or threatening situations when we *don't feel heard or seen – when we don't feel validated*. This can occur when a difficulty isn't acknowledged and understood by others . . . or by ourselves. Sometimes I'll have a client who is 'on loop', talking about the same thing over and over, seemingly unable to move past it. I've learned this most often happens when they *feel like I haven't got it yet* – I haven't fully understood their experience and how painful it is, or at least I have failed to communicate that understanding to them. Once I slow down to really grasp how difficult this experience is for them and show that I understand, it's amazing how many clients then quickly shift to things like problem-solving how they're going to work with the situation.

Validation activates our soothing systems. Remember, we evolved to feel safe through caring connection. Often, I've had people tell me about something that was really bothering them and found that simply responding with a 'Wow – that really sucks! I'm sorry you have to deal with that' is all they needed from me: 'Yeah, it does, but I guess I'll figure it out.' Having our experience simply be heard and accepted by others (or even by our own compassionate selves – seriously, we can validate ourselves!) can be powerful.

On the other hand, invalidation can fuel our threat systems. Ever share something that's really bothering you and have the other person minimise your experience? 'Yeah, but that's not really a big deal. You should just . . .'. How did that make you feel? Probably worse than you did before! We can think of validation as a crucial first step in working with anger and other difficult experiences.

This also demonstrates why self-compassion can be helpful for working with anger. If we're going to manage anger well, we'll probably need to learn to validate *our own* experience and, at least initially, not have to rely on getting validation from others. It can be easy to get blamey around this, thinking that because our family and friends *don't* tend to validate us, it means we have lousy family and friends. But it's not so simple. Unlike the physical signs that accompany emotions like sadness, which can trigger caregiving responses in others, expressions of anger can motivate others to avoid us, withdraw or resolve the situation quickly to pacify us (for example, by minimising it or offering solutions – both of which tend to be *invalidating* when we're genuinely upset or struggling with something).

It's not other people's fault when they fail to approach and validate us when we're struggling with anger. They're doing exactly what evolution designed their brains to do when confronted with someone expressing anger – recognising the person as a threat and seeking ways to avoid or minimise the threat. Here we see another facet of compassionate understanding – recognising that *both* our difficulty managing anger *and* others' difficulty responding to us when we're angry *are real and valid*. These are the challenges that come with having a tricky human brain. In working with these challenges, it can be helpful to learn to *validate ourselves* when we're struggling with anger, so we don't have to rely on others to do it for us.

What stands out from the discussion on validation? Did any of it relate to your own experience? Is there anything you'd like to keep in mind going forwards?

James: *This helps me understand things that happen in my family when I'm struggling with anger. One thing that's been hard is feeling that they don't care about me, or that I'm always the bad guy. They shut down or go running for the hills every time I get irritated, even when it has nothing to do with them. This helps me recognise that it isn't about me – it's about the feelings of threat that come up in them when they see my anger. That makes sense. I think keeping that in mind will help me keep from blowing up small situations into big ones. Sometimes I'll get irritated about something small, and then get more upset when I notice how my family is reacting to me. I think having a little compassionate understanding for them and me might help me pause and recentre when that happens. If I didn't become so irritable, I think they'd probably have an easier time validating me when I'm struggling, which would mean the world.*

Antwan: *When it started talking about compassion and validation, I thought, 'Here's the wimpy stuff I've been waiting for', but then it started to make sense. I get mad at school sometimes when it feels like teachers don't listen to what I have to say, or don't care about it . . . like they're invalidating me. On the other hand, I've had times when I shared with my friends about something hard that happened to me, and they say something like 'That sucks.' It helps. It helped me realise that some things really are hard, that it isn't just me.*

Jordan: *This reminded me of a seminar I went to on 'toxic workplaces'. They talked about work environments where people were constantly pressured to perform, but none of their human needs were recognised, and how that tends to erode productivity and cause employee-loss over time. I feel like that as a woman sometimes, too – like there's this stuff that happens that you're not supposed to be upset about, and if you complain, you're told you're being 'too sensitive'. I've even internalised some of that stuff and say it to myself sometimes. On the other hand, a couple of years ago we got a new manager who actually listens to us and takes our concerns seriously. Although my job still isn't perfect, he's probably the reason I'm still working there. I can deal with a lot if I have people who believe in me and are on my side. Finally, I can relate to the part where people reflexively back off and avoid you if you show anger – I do that with other people, but I also do it with myself. If I notice myself getting angry, it feels really threatening, and I immediately shut down and try to avoid it. Learning to validate that angry part of me will take some practice.*

What stands out to you from the discussion on validation? Did any of it relate to your own experience? Is there anything you'd like to keep in mind going forwards?

_____

_____

_____

Let's consider what this can look like. I've provided a few examples of self-compassionate validation along with blanks for practice. Many of us may not be used to communicating with others or ourselves in this way. Feel free to come up with variations of the examples given – you may find it easier if you imagine situations in which you've felt anger or other strong emotions.

Validating statements when our anger (or other emotion) has been triggered

1. 'This is one of those situations that's hard for me. Given my history, it makes sense that this would trigger my anger.'

2. 'Of course I would feel threatened right now . . . this situation genuinely sucks!'

3. 'I feel really disrespected and want to lash out right now. I think a lot of people would probably have a hard time with this.'

4. _____

   _____

5. _____

   _____

6. _____

   _____

Instead of avoiding, justifying or condemning our anger – or beating ourselves up for having it – we're recognising that we're feeling it, acknowledging it is real and that, given our histories and the situation, *it makes sense* that we would have these feelings. We can apply this validation to any other emotion we might feel as well.

One hope I have for this book is that by learning to manage your anger better, you'll also improve your relationships with people you care about. Think of that upper loop on the compassionate loops diagram from previous modules – our behaviour impacts those around us, which shapes how they respond to us. If we're hostile, others will probably withdraw, avoid, condemn or even come back at us with hostility. On the other hand, if we engage others in ways that communicate validation and caring for their wellbeing, they'll feel safer with us, and are likely to engage with us in more helpful ways.

This relates to that self-to-other flow of compassion we've explored: we can't control what others feel, but we can recognise that how we interact with them can powerfully influence their emotional experience, and do our best to help them feel safe, seen and valued. With that in mind, let's consider validating statements we can extend to others when they are struggling or in pain. The point is to accept what they're telling us about their experience, acknowledge it as real, and communicate that it makes sense to us that they would feel or struggle in this way.

Validating statements for others

1. 'That's fair.'

2. 'That sucks. It makes sense that you would feel *frustrated* [reflect back the emotion they've shared with you] about that.'

3. 'That sounds really hard. I'm sorry you have to deal with that.'

4. 'Given what you've gone through in your life, does it make sense that this would be hard for you?' (When the other individual is being self-critical.)

5. 'I've been irritable lately, and I know that must be frustrating for you. I'm sorry about that, and I'm going to do better going forwards. I don't want to act in ways that make you want to avoid me.'

6. _____

   _____

7. _____

   _____

8. _____

   _____

There's some variety in the statements above. I learned the first statement from working with teens – I love how efficiently 'That's fair' communicates 'I accept that – that makes sense to me.' The second one is a direct validating statement – acknowledging the person is going through something difficult, and expressing it makes sense to you that this would be hard for them. The third statement adds in an expression of sympathy: 'I'm sorry you have to deal with that.' The fourth statement represents one of my favourite ways to validate my clients – through a question that *invites them to validate themselves* . . . with the fact that I'm asking the question implying that their experience *makes sense to me*. The final example is tailored to the experience of many who struggle with anger – validating the experience of someone we've been irritable with when angry. You'll see how it combines an apology with validation. Assuming the apology is sincere (and we never want to apologise if it isn't), combining an apology with validation can help it feel real – because it's anchored to the *other person's experience* – and not just focused on us and our behaviour. With any apology, if we say we're going to do better, we have to put in the effort to follow through and behave differently in the future. Otherwise, we're just teaching the other person that our apologies are meaningless.

Final reflection

What was it like to come up with validating statements for yourself and for others? Was validating yourself or others more challenging? What do you make of that?

_____

_____

_____

_____

_____

_____

_____

Can you think of situations in which making validating statements to yourself or others might be helpful?

_____

_____

_____

_____

_____

_____

_____

_____

Module 26: Soothing Imagery

Another way to work with emotions uses imagery. Our brains produce emotions based on inputs they receive from the outside world, from our bodies, and from our own thoughts, memories and mental images. For this reason, imagery can be a powerful way of working with emotions.

Sometimes clients baulk at using imagery: 'Oh, you want me to *imagine* things? Like that's gonna help!' They may associate imagery with daydreaming or childishness but tend to get on board once they recognise they are *already* using imagery to stimulate their emotional brains. Remember those new-brain/emotional-brain loops from a few modules back? Often, when we are feeling angry, anxious or excited about something, we are *creating imagery* in our minds that fuels these emotional states.

Think about it – what pictures or movies play through your mind when you are angry? Playing the situation that triggered your anger over and over in your mind? Imagining what you wish you'd said or done, or what you might say or do next time? Imagery is already an important part of how we experience emotions. We can take advantage of this, intentionally using imagery to help produce emotional states we want to have, instead of having the pictures in our minds controlled by our angry mood-state.

A brief orientation to imagery

I suspect that when many people hear the word 'imagery', they think 'vivid pictures in your mind'. That's what I used to think, but we're going to approach imagery in a slightly different way. Can you bring up vivid pictures in your mind, imagining things as if you are looking at them? My wife can. When we were in graduate school, she once told me that in exams she'd mentally 'scan through her notes' for the answers. I've never been able to do that. I can mentally play about any song I'm familiar with in my head like a jukebox, but I struggle to 'picture' anything vividly in my mind – the best I can do is a fleeting sense of what something might look like. I've heard from others who have this experience, too.

Luckily, we don't need to be able to picture vivid images in our minds to benefit from imagery. It's sufficient to get a good 'mental sense' of something, in whatever way makes it feel most real to us. To demonstrate, let's try a brief practice I learned from my friend and CFT founder Professor Paul Gilbert. I'm just going to suggest a few things, and I'd invite you to read each prompt, close your eyes for a few seconds and imagine the experience in whatever way works best for you.

- Wherever you are right now, recall how you got here. Maybe you walked to the couch, or drove to your office, or took the tube to the park to sit on a bench while you read . . . bring to mind how you came to be here today, reading this.

- Bring to mind a favourite food . . . something you enjoy and perhaps would like to have in the near future.

- Bring to mind a place. It can be somewhere you've been and would like to return to, or someplace you've never been but would like to visit.

What was it like to do the imagery exercise above? Were you able to bring the different situations and experiences to mind? What form did they take?

James: *I've never thought about it, but I think I struggle forming vivid pictures in my mind. When reading, I stopped and tried a few times, and although I could kind of get an idea of the things I was trying to imagine, it was never very vivid or stable. But doing the exercise, I got a sense of all three things. It's hard to describe what it was like. It was part visual, part other senses (I could imagine some of the sounds in my 'place') – but I had an experience of each thing that felt very real and familiar. It seemed to work, as I found myself wanting to return to the place I'd pictured.*

Antwan: *I can visualise things – was able to do all three. When I'm picturing things, it's not a stable image, but I get a good sense of things. I pictured a bacon sandwich, and even imagined how it tasted. It made me hungry!*

Jordan: *I liked it. I enjoy imagery, and I'm lucky enough to be able to vividly picture things in my mind. All three experiences came easily. I'm reading this on my chair at home at the end of the day, so imagined coming home after work, making my tea and settling in. My food was a piece of cake from a delicious hipster coffee shop down the road, and my place was the beach in Greece – I've never been, but I was recently looking at pictures of potential holiday spots and was able to bring it easily to mind. Beautiful!*

Our companions described very different experiences of the imagery, ranging from highly visual to James's 'mental sense' of things, which was hard for him to describe yet felt very real. That's what we're shooting for. If you can 'see' the images clearly in your mind, that's great . . . but if not, no worries. The point is to just get a mental experience of what we're imagining.

What was it like to do the imagery exercise above? Were you able to bring the different situations and experiences to mind? What form did they take?

_____

_____

_____

_____

_____

_____

Now let's turn our focus to creating *helpful* imagery to help us work with emotions and difficult situations. Our focus here involves using imagery to help reduce angry arousal and get our safeness system working when we've been triggered (or before entering a situation in which we anticipate we might be triggered). There are several audio versions of this practice (titled 'safe place imagery') available for free online: www.compassionatemind.co.uk/ resource/audio.

Soothing space/safe place imagery

In this imagery-based exercise, we're creating a place in our minds – one that helps bring up feelings of safeness and calmness. When we're angry, depressed or distressed, those can be difficult feelings to connect with, but the act of trying and the sense of this place being the sort of place you'd like to be is the important thing. Remember, it's *trying* the practice that is important – the feelings may follow later. After you've gone through it a few times and are familiar with the practice (or are using a guided audio version of the practice), you'll probably want to do the entire practice with your eyes closed.

Soothing space/safe place imagery exercise

- Imagine feeling completely comfortable, safe and at ease. Slow down your breath, and imagine being filled with feelings of calmness, soothing and safeness. If you notice any bodily tension, see if it's possible to relax that part of your body just a bit. Perhaps make a contented smile, allowing your face to soften as you slow and relax your body (pause and do some soothing rhythm breathing for at least thirty seconds).

- Imagine you are in a place that supports these feelings of being calm, soothed and safe.

- Imagine what this place is like, bringing to mind a range of sensory details:

    o   What do you see?

    o   What bodily sensations do you notice?

    o   What do you hear?

    o   What do you smell?

- **Example:** Your place may be a beautiful forest where the leaves dance gently in the breeze. Light shines through the trees to sparkle on the ground. Imagine the feeling of the gentle wind on your face, hearing the rustle of the leaves, and the fresh smell of the air.

- **Example:** Your place may be a beautiful beach with blue sea stretching out to the horizon. Feel the soft white sand under your feet and hear the gentle rhythm of the waves. Imagine the warm sun on your face and the light dancing on the water.

- **Example:** Your safe place may be a warm cottage, with a log fire and a cup of tea or hot cocoa at the ready. Imagine being filled with feelings of warmth, hearing the crackle of the logs as they burn and smelling the pleasing aroma of the fire.

- These are just examples of places – experiment to find mental 'places' that work best for you. The key is that imagining this place helps bring up feelings of being safe, comfortable and valued, just as you are. Once you find your place, try to get a mental sense of what it feels like to be there, connecting with different sensory details.

- Your place may or may not include others – other people, animals or celestial beings. If there are other beings there, imagine they welcome you. They accept you just as you are. They are happy to see you. Imagine that this place itself accepts you warmly, delighting in your presence, almost as if you complete it. It is happy you are here.

- Spend a few minutes (feel free to go for as long as you wish) imagining being in this place, enjoying the feelings of being calm, comfortable, safe and valued.

As you allow the imagery to dissolve, return to the slow, comfortable rhythm of your breath. Spend thirty seconds or so enjoying this slowness before allowing your attention to return to the world around you.

What was your experience of the soothing space/safe place imagery exercise? What was helpful? Did any obstacles come up? If so, how did you work with them?

James: *It took a little while to get into it . . . I kept trying to pick a place in nature but couldn't quite make it work. Then I landed in my favourite pub, and it did the trick – I could imagine soft light coming in through the window, the dark old wood, laughter and pleasant voices, and the smell of a hot meal wafting up to me. I can feel myself relaxing as I describe it.*

Antwan: *At first I didn't take it seriously, like, 'Oh, you want me to "imagine my safe place" . . . won't that be nice . . .'. But once I tried, I was able to do it and it felt pretty good. I pictured myself playing footie in the summer with my friend Ethan, who's a great guy. It was a sunny and warm day. I pictured us shooting and laughing, then heading to get a burger. I imagined being totally relaxed and happy, not a care in the world. Not sure if I did it right, but it relaxed me.*

Jordan: *I wasn't new to this practice, as my therapist introduced something similar a few years back, but I really enjoy it. My 'place' was a trail along the coast, seeing the sea in the distance to my right, the hedgerows to my left, hearing the wind through the trees. It's beautiful and relaxing. It was new to imagine the place welcoming me. I had fun with this – imagining the trees smiling down at me, the wise hedgerows and dry stone walls containing the wisdom of hundreds of years, understanding everything I was feeling. It was lovely. No real obstacles this time – I remember that when starting out with this practice I'd worry about 'getting it right', but now I just let myself imagine it. I should do this one more often!*

The companions' responses highlight several helpful points. James noted trying out several 'places' before settling on one that worked for him. Antwan struggled a bit in the beginning as well – with taking the practice seriously enough to give it a shot – but then found it enjoyable. He also did something quite skilful – using his *memories* and experience of feeling safe and comfortable to help him generate imagery that worked for him. Jordan was familiar with the practice but noted having had a common obstacle in the beginning – worrying about 'getting it right' – before giving herself permission just to try the practice out and see how it went.

What was your experience of the soothing space/safe place imagery exercise? What was helpful? Did any obstacles come up? If so, how did you work with them?

_____

_____

_____

_____

_____

_____

Imagery can be a powerful tool for working with our emotions and planning new ways of engaging with situations in our lives. Just as our 'angry selves' fuel our anger by imagining the trigger situation and ruminating about what happened, our compassionate selves can use imagery to soothe our angry arousal and practise different ways of responding to tricky situations. Here are few examples of ways we can use imagery:

- Imagining how we'd respond if someone we cared about and wanted to help was triggered and struggling with the sort of things we struggle with. How might we validate, support and encourage them?

- Imagining someone who cares about relating to us when we're struggling – imagining them understanding us, accepting us, and offering us compassion, validation, support and encouragement.

- Imagining ourselves responding to trigger situations in new, more helpful ways.

- Trying out new communication skills – imagining practising things like assertive communication, apologising and asking for more information rather than reacting.

It can feel a bit awkward at first, but the more we use our imagination in this way, the better we'll get at it. Try to practise the soothing space/safe place imagery exercise a few times over the course of the next week to help it begin to feel more natural.

Final reflection

What did you notice about the imagery practice? What changes might you make to help the practice work even better for you next time?

_____

_____

_____

_____

_____

_____

_____

Module 27: Compassionate Thinking

Thinking can play a major role for those of us who struggle with anger, with anger being fuelled by thinking that is narrow, threat-focused, rigid, often hostile and blaming, and that involves feelings of certainty (being sure we're right) and urgency (the experience that we must act *right now*). This makes sense when we recall that anger is our *fight* response, designed to rapidly motivate our ancestors to match the intensity of real physical threats. The world we live in now is much more complex, so we need more sophisticated ways of dealing with the threats and obstacles. That's where compassionate thinking comes in.

With compassionate thinking, we're not recruiting our compassionate selves to *argue* with our angry selves. Our angry selves are very good at arguing and are unlikely to change their minds even when faced with overwhelming evidence they've got things wrong. Our anger isn't *bad*, it's just a threat response that is often ill-suited to the job at hand. Rather than arguing with our angry selves, we want to help them – to understand where the anger comes from, consider what would help our angry selves find balance, and figure out how to engage with the triggering situation in ways that fit with our values and don't cause problems in our lives and relationships. Instead of arguing with our angry selves, we can mindfully notice their chatter, slow down our breath and bodies, create some space for ourselves and, when we're feeling a bit more centred, consider what our compassionate selves have to say about things.

Mentalising

A primary goal of compassionate thinking is *understanding*. Many anger triggers involve other people, and our angry selves can experience others as threats, setting us up to relate to them in hostile, critical or aggressive ways. As Jordan and James have explored in their reflections, sometimes this hostility and attacking can be directed towards the self as well. Neither tendency is helpful. *Mentalising*[1] involves looking at our actions, or those of others, and trying to understand how they reflect underlying needs, desires, feelings and beliefs. Rather than attributing someone's behaviour (or our own angry reaction) to them being some version of a 'bad person', mentalising helps us pause and consider *what the behaviour means* and how it makes sense in relation to what's happening in the mind of the person doing it.

Mentalising involves pausing to ask questions. Let's consider how it might be applied to *our own* anger. Imagine something has triggered our anger. Instead of losing ourselves in the experience of certainty that anger carries with it, what if we paused to ask some questions?

Mentalising for the self

- How am I interpreting this situation?

- What meaning am I attaching to this situation? How am I interpreting what it means about how others might be thinking of me?

- How does it make sense that this situation would be triggering for me?

- What feelings are coming up in me besides anger? Anxiety? Shame? Sadness?

- What do I fear might happen if I don't act on my anger? If I do?

- What motivations, needs and desires in me are being served by my anger?

- What would help me feel safe? What do I need to feel less threatened?

Mentalising can help us understand our own anger responses, so that when we're triggered – say, because someone has said something rude to us – instead of lashing back or beating ourselves up for how we reacted (or failed to respond), we can direct understanding, sympathy and empathy to the version of ourselves that's feeling hurt or attacked. It can help change the focus from *How do I get back at them?* to *What's going on in my mind, and how can I help myself deal with these feelings of being hurt, attacked or blocked?*

Mentalising can also help us understand one another's behaviour. Let's imagine that I recently approached my son to ask (for the third time this week) if he's done his homework yet (because I know he's smart and capable of good grades and want him to be able to get into a good university). Imagine he snaps at me: *'Would you stop hassling me about my homework!?'* Now, my angry self might be triggered by the tone he's directing at me when, from my side, I'm just trying to be a good father. This is the moment of truth: I can snap back at him, chastising him for all the time he spends playing online video games with friends – a response I know from experience will only lead to further escalation. *Or* I can do some mentalising:

Mentalising applied to others

- What might they be feeling?
- How might their reaction make sense?
- What needs or desires might be motivating their behaviour?
- How might they be perceiving me and what my behaviour might be implying about them?
- What might help them feel safe so that we can have a helpful conversation?

Asking these questions can help us shift from a position of condemning and reacting to others' behaviour to *understanding* it. This understanding can help bring our compassionate selves online, reminding me that I really love my son, that he's generally not disrespectful to me, and helping me understand that his reaction probably indicates he's feeling attacked. While I'd like to say I asked, '*Whoa . . . it sounds like you're feeling attacked. Can you tell me about that?*', what really happened is that I paused just long enough for my son to continue in a way that aided my mentalising: '*Dad – you know I've got good grades and I get my homework done. I'm working hard at that this year. You don't see me doing it because I work to get as much as I can done at school so I have some free time when I get home.*'

Hearing about his experience helped me understand where he was coming from, setting me up to respond as the sort of father I want to be: '*You're right . . . I'm sorry. I really am proud of how hard you're working, and I can see how hassling you about homework must not feel good. What might be a better way for me to handle it when I want to check in?*' You'll note my compassionate response – informed by understanding his experience – included an apology. Although we could argue that there's nothing to apologise for when a parent asks their child if they've done their homework, I apologised because *he was right* – he'd been taking care of his end of things – and my repeated asking communicated to him that I didn't trust him to do that. I also let him know that as a parent, I *will* sometimes check in on how his schoolwork is going and invited him to let me know helpful ways of doing that. This is an example of how compassionate thinking and mentalising can transform potential conflicts into opportunities to collaboratively figure out more helpful ways of doing things.

'What would my compassionate self think?' Contrasting threat-based thinking and compassionate thinking

Our compassionate selves operate from a very different perspective than our angry selves, driven by very different motives. Where angry thinking is driven by threat-based, defensive motives, compassionate thinking is rooted in the desire to work with suffering and challenging situations in helpful ways. The table below, adapted from *The Compassionate Mind Approach to Managing Your Anger*, contrasts compassionate thinking with threat-based thinking:

Threat–based thinking	Compassionate thinking
Narrowly focused on threat or anger trigger	Broad and flexible, considers many aspects of the situation
Rigid, inflexible and ruminative	Flexible, creative, focused on finding what is helpful
Activates threat system; fuels anger	Activates safeness system; helps us feel safe, comfortable and confident
Hostile towards others and/or ourselves	Directs kindness and understanding towards others and ourselves
Judgemental and critical	Understanding, empathic and non-condemning
Focused on dominating and punishing	Focused on helping; finding solutions that benefit everyone and harm no one
Focused on past and present transgressions and problems	Focused on what would be helpful, both now and looking to the future

Source: Adapted from Kolts, 2012, *The Compassionate Mind Approach to Managing Your Anger*, with permission from Robinson.

As we've explored, threat-based thinking tends to fuel the experience of ongoing anger. It tends to be rigid, hostile and, when combined with the felt urgency that comes with anger, can set us up to escalate things and take actions we'll regret once we've cooled down. Compassionate thinking, in contrast, is flexible, creative and empathic – focused on understanding the situation we're in, the perspectives of everyone in it, and figuring out how to address the challenge in a helpful manner.

Let's select a common trigger situation, note the angry thoughts that tend to show up, and see if we can generate compassionate thoughts to help us understand the situation, the experience of everyone in it (including us!), and how to respond to it in a helpful way. In doing this exercise, consider the questions described in the section on mentalising and the contrast between angry and compassionate thinking described above. Let's start with an example from Antwan:

Situation/trigger: *About a year ago, I was hanging out with friends and this guy looked at me funny – like looking for too long. I was like, 'What's your problem?' Things escalated back and forth from there, and we ended up fighting. That could have gone a different way.*

Threat-based thoughts	Compassionate thoughts
'That punk is staring me down.'	*'That kid is looking at me for a long time. I wonder why?'*
*'What the f*** is he looking at?'*	*'There are lots of reasons he might be looking at me. Sometimes I do that when it feels like I know someone and am trying to figure out who they are.'*
'I'm not going to put up with this.'	*'It makes sense that this would feel threatening, because sometimes people stare at each other as a threat. But he hasn't said anything to me. There's no reason to come at him. Maybe I should just keep talking with my friends and see what happens.'*
'Oh, now he's gonna talk some shit, too?'	*'He probably felt disrespected by how I spoke to him.'*

'That's it, I'm gonna beat his ass.'	'Violence isn't the answer. I don't want to hurt other people, and I sure don't want the consequences that can come from it.'
'If I don't fight him now, people will think I'm a wimp.'	'I don't need to use violence to prove myself. I'm in control of what I do. This is no big deal.'
'My friends will give me shit if I back down.'	'My friends might give me a hard time for like five minutes, but I can take it and change the vibe by saying something funny. They might even respect me for being in control and confident enough that I don't have to prove myself by fighting.'

What was it like to consider the situation from the perspectives of both your angry and compassionate selves? Is there anything you'd like to take away from this to use when similar situations arise in the future?

Antwan: *This took a long time. I tried to make it as real as possible, so for the angry thoughts I tried to think about what was going through my head when that happened. The compassionate thoughts took a while, and I kept going back to the book. But I feel good about how I did. When I started, it felt like I was trying to find justification for wimping out. But when I thought about the man I want to be and went through it, the compassionate side felt like I was in more control, rather than just reacting to stuff that happened.*

Looking at Antwan's example, we see several characteristics of compassionate thinking. He was mentalising – thinking about what might be going on in the other person's mind that might explain how their behaviour made sense. He validated his own experience of threat ('It makes sense that . . .') and then redirected his behaviour towards a non-aggressive alternative (talking with his friends). He continued mentalising and empathising when considering how the situation played out ('He probably felt . . .'), and grounded his responses in his compassionate intention to not be violent – even problem-solving how he could handle it if obstacles arose (using humour to deflect if his friends gave him a hard time).

Use the accompanying form to give it a try. Allow yourself time – you might even begin it and then step away, giving yourself some time (and, as Antwan did, referring back to previous material when needed) to come up with the angry and compassionate thoughts.

The form is also provided in Appendix B for copying and future use, or you can download or print it from https://overcoming.co.uk/715/resources-to-download.

Situation/trigger:	
Threat–based thoughts	**Compassionate thoughts**

What was it like to consider the situation from the perspective of both your angry and compassionate selves? Is there anything you'd like to take away from this to use when similar situations arise in the future?

_____

_____

_____

_____

_____

_____

Coming up with compassionate thoughts can be tricky at first, as it can be very different from how we've approached things in the past. But the more we get used to slowing things down and giving ourselves some space, working to understand rather than react, and then approaching the situation as our compassionate selves, the easier it gets. Every time we do this, we help build and strengthen the brain patterns that make it easier for us to respond compassionately in the future.

Final reflection

Are there any other situations that you think it might be helpful to focus on for the compassionate thinking exercise? Which ones, and how do you think they might be helpful?

_____

_____

_____

_____

_____

Module 28: Our Multiple Selves

Previous modules have explored how different motivations and emotions organise our bodies and minds – how we pay attention, think, feel and imagine – as well as shape our behaviour. As we've explored, it can be like we have different 'versions of the self' – like the angry self and the compassionate self – corresponding to how we're organised by the emotions and motives we're experiencing at any given time. Considering things in this way can be helpful on several counts. It can help us recognise that we *aren't defined* by our anger – there are many other dimensions of us as well. It creates the opportunity to cultivate the 'versions of the self' we want to strengthen, like the compassionate self. And it can help us recognise versions of the self that struggle, suffer and may underlie our anger – versions organised by emotions like fear, anxiety, shame or sadness – and consider what these vulnerable versions of us may need.

Working with these emotions can be tricky. We may prefer the energy of anger over more vulnerable-feeling experiences like anxiety or sadness. But when we look closely at our anger, we may find these other feelings just beneath the surface. In this module, we'll explore how to connect with these different emotional experiences.

Exploring our multiple selves

Let's begin by choosing a recent situation that triggered anger, and use imagery to connect with this experience, imagining it happening and the different emotions that came up. We can choose a recent experience or an example of a situation that has commonly triggered our anger in the past. Then, we'll explore the emotions this experience prompted, starting with anger. We'll connect with these different 'emotional selves' one by one, fully experiencing them in our imagination – imagining how this emotion feels in the body, what this emotional self thinks, feels and is imagining. We'll consider – if this emotional self were in complete control, what would they do? After we've done this with anger, we'll take a few moments to centre ourselves, and then move on to other 'emotional selves', exploring anxiety and sadness and finishing by connecting with the kind, wise, confident perspective of the compassionate self.

Exploring different aspects of the emotional self

- **Thoughts and imagery:** What thoughts are you having as you feel this emotion? What are you imagining?

- **Bodily experiences:** How does this emotion feel in your body? For example, is there an experience of pain, tightness, tension, sinking or temperature?

- **Motivation:** What does this 'emotional self' want to do? If it were in control, what behaviour would it have you do?

- **Desired outcome:** What does this emotional self want? How does it want the situation to turn out?

Using the space in the template provided on page 222–3, you'll explore your different emotional selves in turn. Let's start by considering a challenging situation that has triggered your anger:

- How does your anger – your 'angry self' – experience this situation? Think about typical thoughts you have when angry – perhaps thoughts of unfairness, being dismissed, rejected or threatened. Write down the thoughts you have when angry.

- Consider how your anger *feels*. Where is it located in your body? What is it like? How would it feel if that anger built up in you?

- Consider the action urges that come with your anger. If your angry self were *totally* in control, what would it do? Notice how the threat system tries to shape your behaviour.

- Consider: What does your anger *really want*? Deep down, what would your angry self like to happen?

The idea is to get to know the thoughts, feelings and desires for action that go with the 'angry self'. Rather than disappearing into, avoiding or condemning this angry self, we want to invite it in and learn about its experience.

Once your angry self has had its say, take a few moments to shift gears – perhaps mentally thanking the angry self for sharing its perspective and allowing it to recede. Maybe take a break for a cup of coffee or tea and a snack. Then, in the 'anxious self' part of the form, repeat the exercise, this time considering any anxiety, worry or fears you may feel about this situation. What thoughts does your anxious self have? How does it feel? If it were in control, what would it do? What does it want to happen?

When you're done learning from your anxious self, mentally thank it for sharing its perspective, take a break and, when you're ready, invite your 'sad self' to share. Imagine any sadness you may feel in response to this situation, stepping into the experience of this sad self. In the 'sad self' part of the form, explore any sadness you may have about the situation. What does your sad self think? Feel? What would it do? What does it want?

Lastly, you'll move to the final part of the form and consider your compassionate self. Begin by slowing down your breath; feel your body slowing down, relaxing any tension you may be holding. Imagine yourself as a deeply compassionate being: kind, wise and confident. Create a friendly facial expression and imagine having a kind, confident tone of voice. When you are ready, take a moment to think about the situation that angered you, but focus on thoughts you have when you are being helpful and compassionate. Note how the sense of slowing associated with the compassionate self feels in your body. If that feeling (associated with confidence, wisdom and warmth) were to grow inside you, how would it feel? If your compassionate self were totally in control, what would you do? Consider for a moment, deep down, what does your compassionate self really want?

The captain of the ship metaphor

I've had clients find this metaphor helpful in doing the multiple selves exercise. Imagine you are on a ship at sea, and that on this day a storm arises, as emotional storms can arise in life (like the triggering situation you are imagining for this exercise).

Imagine that the emotional selves you're connecting with are passengers on the deck of this ship, reacting to this scary storm in the only way they know how:

- The angry self is raging: 'Who's in charge here? What the hell is going on? This is unacceptable!'

- The anxious self is worrying: 'We could all die. I can't take this. We could drown.'

- The sad self is lamenting: 'I never told them how much I loved them, and now I'm out of time. It's all over for me.'

Imagine the compassionate self is there too, but this self has an important job – they are the captain of the ship. This compassionate self is *kind*, committed to taking care of the emotional 'passengers' as well as steering the ship to safety. This compassionate self is *wise*, understanding that storms are just a part of sailing (just as difficult and triggering situations are just a part of life), knowing it makes sense that the threat-focused passengers are activated and doing the only things they know how to do, and able to draw upon experience and the assistance of the crew (life resources, therapists, etc.) in figuring out how to navigate the storm. And the compassionate self is *confident* in their ability to comfort the passengers and steer the ship to safety, having seen many storms in their time – just as you have seen many difficult situations in your life.

Imagine how this compassionate captain would help the other emotional passengers feel safe – validating and reassuring them, letting them know the ship was in good hands.

Returning to your situation, imagine your compassionate self as the captain of your 'ship' in the storm of this difficult situation. How would this compassionate version of you engage with your angry self, anxious self and sad self? How would they validate and reassure them? And turning to the situation, how would your compassionate self help you navigate this stormy situation?

Let's begin by considering James's example:

Triggering situation: *I asked Aiden to wash up the dishes after we'd eaten on Tuesday evening, and he replied sarcastically, saying he'd get to them later. I reacted more strongly than I should have, becoming a bit heated and insisting he do them right now. At this point, Sarah stepped in, saying it would be fine for him to do them later. I felt ganged up on and was angry, so I went up to my study and stewed – although I did eventually calm down.*

Angry self	Anxious self
Feelings in my body: *My angry self is filled with energy, like a coiled spring. Lots of tension in my stomach and jaw.*	**Feelings in my body:** *My anxious self is jittery and unsettled. Butterflies in my stomach, and shaky.*
What I'm thinking and imagining: *I'm going over what happened, thinking about how Sarah undermined me in front of my son, thinking about how he treated me disrespectfully and needs to be put in his place. He's the one being disrespectful and they're treating me as the problem.*	**What I'm thinking and imagining:** *I'm worried Aiden doesn't respect me, and that Sarah thinks I'm a bad father. Underneath that, I think there's fear that she'll get tired of me and leave. I guess I'm worried that maybe I am a bad father and husband, and that I haven't made any progress.*
What my angry self would do: *If my angry self was in complete control, it would have yelled at both of them, telling him that he was damn well going to do the dishes when I told him to, and telling her not to interfere when I'm speaking to my son.*	**What my anxious self would do:** *Kind of what I did, I think – my anxious self would retreat . . . only instead of fuming in my study, my anxious self would be worrying, rocking back and forth, going over everything in my mind.*
What my angry self wants to happen: *To be treated with respect and to punish Aiden's belligerence.*	**What my anxious self wants to happen:** *Just for things to be calm, and for my angry self to stop screwing everything up!*

Sad self	Compassionate self
Feelings in my body: *The sadness feels heavy, like a sinking feeling. It's like all the energy has been sucked out of my body.*	**Feelings in my body:** *Calm and settled (it took a lot of breathing to get here!).*
What I'm thinking and imagining: *My sad self is convinced of all the stuff my anxious self is worried about – that my son doesn't respect me and my wife doesn't trust me as a father, and that it's my fault. I've ruined it all with my anger. My sad self wants to give up – like all these efforts to work with my anger haven't done any good at all.*	**What I'm thinking and imagining:** *I know it's not 'thinking', but my compassionate self is feeling bad for my angry, anxious and sad selves. Their reactions all make sense to me, and it's hard to feel that way.*
What my sad self would do: *Honestly, probably just sit there and cry, feeling pathetic.*	*My compassionate self also recognises I actually have made a lot of progress. Just a couple of months ago, instead of retreating to my study, I'd probably have escalated things – raising my voice, insisting Aiden do the dishes right now (when it really didn't matter when he did them), and snapping at Sarah for undermining me or accusing her of thinking I can't parent – which is something she's never said. In fact, she came up to check on me later and kissed me, as if to let me know it was okay. I didn't handle the situation perfectly, but there was a point I could have made things worse, and I didn't. That's big progress.*
What my sad self wants to happen: *Like my anxious self, my sad self wants my angry self to stop screwing things up. And it would like a do-over, a chance to get things right . . . or maybe just for people to see how hard things are for me, and to recognise I'm trying.*	**What my compassionate self would do:** *It seems weird to say, but my compassionate self would reassure my angry, anxious and sad selves – tell them everything is going to be okay, and to let me handle this one. Then I'd go back and apologise to Aiden. I just did this, actually – I apologised for getting heated, and let him know it's because I felt disrespected, but that it still wasn't okay for me to talk to him that way. He actually apologised to me, too – telling me he'd been annoyed by my request because he'd arranged to play video games with his friends right after dinner and didn't want to be late. Things ended well between us.*
	What my compassionate self wants to happen: *Just to stabilise things, so that everyone – within me and outside of me – is on the same team. I think it worked, because I feel a lot better about things, and things seem good with Aiden and Sarah.*

James's experience with the exercise demonstrates some important points. At a pragmatic level, it shows you may want to use your own paper to do the exercise, so that you have all the space you need. In unpacking his various emotional 'selves', James encountered some of his core fears and concerns – fears his family don't respect him, fears his wife might get tired of him and leave, and concerns his efforts to manage his anger haven't amounted to anything. With each, we see the tendency of his threat-based selves to catastrophise – exaggerating the negative interpretations of the experience while failing to notice the positives (that he *didn't* escalate the situation and turn it into a conflict with Sarah; going to his study and giving himself an opportunity to calm down). The interplay between his 'selves' also gives a glimpse into his self-directed fears and self-criticism – both his anxious and sad selves want his angry self to 'stop screwing things up'. In contrast, his compassionate self was able to empathise with and reassure his angry, anxious and sad selves. His compassionate self also noted his progress along with positive signs such as his wife affectionately reconnecting with him after the experience. Finally, his compassionate self – in the exercise and in real life – returned to the situation, reconnected with Aiden, repaired their relationship rupture, and modelled a valuable lesson for his son . . . to apologise when you've handled something poorly in ways that impact another person.

Now, why don't you give the exercise a try? You can use either the blank form below, your own paper or the copy provided in Appendix B (or you can download or print out the form from https://overcoming.co.uk/715/resources-to-download).

Trigger situation:	
Angry self	**Anxious self**
My body feels:	My body feels:
What I'm thinking and imagining:	What I'm thinking and imagining:
What my angry self would do:	What my anxious self would do:
What my angry self wants to happen:	What my anxious self wants to happen:

Sad self	Compassionate self
My body feels:	My body feels:
What I'm thinking and imagining:	What I'm thinking and imagining:
What my sad self would do:	What my compassionate self would do:
What my sad self wants to happen:	What my compassionate self wants to happen:

Final reflection

What was it like to explore other feelings that can accompany or underlie your anger? Were there some feelings/selves that were particularly challenging to connect with? Knowing your history, does it make sense that these emotions might be difficult for you to access or tolerate?

_____

_____

_____

_____

_____

_____

Are there emotions other than anxiety and sadness that sometimes accompany, underlie or follow your anger (e.g. shame, fear, contempt)? What are they, and does it makes sense that you might have these feelings?

_____

_____

_____

_____

_____

_____

_____

End of section check-in

How are you feeling about your progress so far?

_____

_____

_____

What has been helpful for you?

_____

_____

_____

What obstacles have arisen that should be considered as we move forwards?

_____

_____

_____

What would be helpful for you to keep in mind going forwards?

_____

_____

_____

Compassion practice plan

Now we've completed the fifth section, let's update the practice plan. Here are a few suggested practices based upon the modules in Section V:

1. **Practise soothing rhythm breathing** (Module 24): Take five minutes to slow down your breath using the guidance in Module 24 or using a breathing app.

2. **Practise validation** (Module 25): Take five minutes to recall an emotional experience you or someone you're close to has recently had. Drawing on Module 25, take a moment to acknowledge this emotion as real – as a valid experience produced by your (or their) brain in response to what was happening. Even if it's an emotion we don't want to act on (or which others are expressing in ways we don't like), we can acknowledge the validity of the experience . . . and then consider what would be helpful to do. For practice, write the validating statement down.

3. **Do the soothing space/safe place imagery exercise** (Module 26): Take five to ten minutes to do the soothing space/safe place imagery practice from Module 26, using either the guidelines provided or a guided meditation online: www.compassionatemind.co.uk/resource/audio.

4. **Connect with compassionate thinking** (Module 27): Bring to mind a situation you've struggled with and do the compassionate thinking exercise from Module 27. Consider how your compassionate self would understand and respond to this tricky situation.

5. **Notice your multiple selves** (Module 28): Recall a situation that's triggered you recently and consider what 'selves' were activated. What do your angry, anxious, sad or ashamed selves have to say? How about your hopeful, empathic and confident compassionate self? You could mix this exercise with the validation practice above, extending validation to the reactions each of these 'selves' is having.

Every day, do one mindfulness practice (mindful check-in, three systems check-in or brief mind the loops practice) **OR soothing rhythm breathing, and one other practice.** Choose practices from those listed above, as well as those included in the first four practice plans, on pages 64–6, 107–8, 135 and 174–5. Try to do each of the new practices at least once, and don't repeat any practice more than twice per week. Mix in soothing activities regularly – daily, if possible.

Daily practice log

Practice	Sun	Mon	Tues	Weds	Thurs	Fri	Sat
Mindfulness practice							
Soothing rhythm breathing							

Practice notes

Day	What was helpful?	What obstacles came up?
Sunday		
Monday		
Tuesday		
Wednesday		
Thursday		
Friday		
Saturday		

SECTION VI:

Compassionate Communication

Module 29: Setting the Stage for Compassionate Interactions

As we've explored, compassion isn't just something we feel – in fact, the feeling often comes later – it's something we *do*. Compassionate behaviour can take many forms because it's about *figuring out what would be helpful in the given situation and doing it*. Since anger so often manifests itself in interpersonal situations, we're going to explore a few skills that can help us interact with other people in compassionate ways, even around difficult topics.

Laying the groundwork: considering what really matters right now

Psychologist Marsha Linehan[1] introduced a strategy I find helpful in approaching tricky interactions with others, particularly around things like making requests or expressing frustration. The idea is that when we're interacting with another person, there are at least three priorities that can be served by the interaction:

1. achieving the objective or goal of the interaction

2. expressing how we feel

3. our relationship with the other person

Depending upon the nature of the interaction, these priorities will have more or less importance to us. If the interaction is with someone at a bank in trying to secure a loan, we'll probably be served well by highly emphasising the *objective* of the interaction (getting the loan), placing lower emphasis on expressing the *feelings* we have about the process (frustration with the lengthy application process), and placing moderate emphasis on our *relationship* with the loan officer (with whom we have intermittent contact, but who is important to helping us secure the loan). In contrast, if we're at a football game cheering on our favourite team along with hundreds of other fans, we may prioritise expressing our feelings (excitement about the team) over the objective (because we know our cheering probably won't make a big difference in the game) and our relationship with the other people in the stadium (whom we may never see again) . . . although, again, we may want to consider the relationship a bit as well, so as not to have conflict with fellow fans.

Considering these priorities can be particularly helpful when we're interacting with people with whom we're in *important relationships* – friends, family, co-workers. When anger or frustration arises, it can be easy for us to inadvertently behave in ways that *prioritise objectives that aren't really that important* to us or *express frustration or anger in unhelpful ways*, when by far the most important element of this situation is *our relationship with the other person*. Let's consider James's example of asking his son to do the dishes in Module 28. He'd asked his son to do the dishes, resulting in a sarcastic reply, which James didn't appreciate. At this point, his angry self took over, prioritising his emotional expression over either his relationship with his son or the objective (getting the dishes done). As James noted in the exercise, in the past he might have continued to escalate the situation, but at this point (after his partner stepped in) he stepped back, recognising that any further emotional expression while he was still caught up in anger would probably cause problems in his valued relationships. Later, after he'd cooled down, he was able to mend things with both his partner and son, expressing his emotions (in this case, his regret over raising his voice) in a way that made it possible for his son to accept responsibility for his own behaviour (apologising to James for his disrespectful tone). Many of us may have behaved most badly when angry in the relationships we value the most, because those tend to be the relationships in which we can sort of get away with it in the short term (as opposed to, say, getting fired at our jobs), even as such interactions will harm these important relationships when played out over time.

In the rest of this module and in the next, we'll touch on tools for effective communication – assertiveness, apologising, expressing disagreement and forgiving. All of these can help us navigate potentially tricky interactions, but before we approach these interactions, it can be helpful to ask ourselves a few questions related to the current discussion. We can even pause to rank these priorities from 1 to 3, considering how we might then approach the interaction in a way that's anchored to what's most important to us.

Considering interaction priorities

- What is the objective or goal of this interaction? What am I trying to accomplish?
- What impact do I want this interaction to have on my relationship with this person? What sort of relationship do I want to have with them now and in the future?
- How am I feeling about this situation, and how do I want to express those feelings?
- What do I really care about in this interaction? What is most important to me – accomplishing the objective, my relationship with this person or expressing my feelings?

Can you relate this discussion to your own experience? Are there times these priorities have been out of balance in your interactions with others?

James: *Definitely, on both counts. I think I've often inadvertently prioritised things in reverse order from how important they are to me. I have an objective – something I want to happen – I get locked into, and if something isn't going according to plan, I express my frustration in ways that harm my relationships. That's completely backwards from how I feel. My relationships, particularly with my family, are so much more important than 99% of my plans. I do want to be able to express my feelings, but not in a 'lashing out' sort of way that drives people away. I'm learning that if I express my feelings calmly, it's a lot easier for them to hear it and have compassion for how I'm feeling.*

Antwan: *Yeah, this makes sense. As I've talked about, I've got hot quickly when I've felt disrespected, which has got in the way of my goals and relationships. Like, actively worked against me. When my teacher has talked to me in ways I didn't like, my goal was to get her off my back – but when I've snapped back, she just came back harder . . . and it sure didn't help my relationship with her either. The times I've let it go, things went a lot better.*

Jordan: *This one landed for me. I can imagine a lot of people who struggle with anger would say they've prioritised their emotions over their relationships, blowing up in ways that harm their relationships, but for me it's sort of the opposite. I've been a people-pleaser. So often in my life, I've sacrificed my own goals and swallowed my feelings – going along with what others wanted, to avoid rocking the boat. That's driven a lot of anger and resentment for me, which I've then turned on myself. I'm doing better at standing up for myself, but my growth edge is definitely creating more space for me in my relationships – to make room to express my feelings and pursue my own goals. It's hard, but when I've managed to do that, people have seemed to like and respect me more, which has been a really pleasant surprise.*

The companions' responses above show how easy it is to fall out of balance in our relationships, and how we might want to adjust how we approach our interactions with others.

Can you relate this discussion to your own experience? Are there times when these priorities have been out of balance in your interactions with others?

_____

_____

_____

_____

This way of approaching interactions isn't always easy – frequently we'll find ourselves in situations in which we'll have to respond immediately without being able to pause and reflect on our priorities. But if we apply this to interactions we have regularly that we already know are tricky for us, and game-plan ways to shift the balance in helpful ways, we can *build new habits* that will be there when we need them. This can take several different forms. For example, James might imagine something going wrong and practise slowing down and reminding himself that his relationships with his family are more important to him than the plan that's been disrupted. Antwan might imagine his teacher speaking to him in a triggering way, and practise how he wants to respond in a way that doesn't escalate things. Jordan might consider interactions that leave her feeling upset and resentful, and practise how she might be assertive in those situations in expressing her feelings or advocating for her goals. I've used the words 'imagine' and 'practise' repeatedly, because what we're talking about isn't just responding to a specific interaction – it's about *developing skills* that will allow us to communicate in more helpful ways across the range of relationships in our lives. We'll visit a few of these skills in the next module.

Final reflection

Can you think of any specific relationships or interactions that you'd like to 'rebalance' in terms of the priorities we've discussed? Are there skills you think it would be helpful to strengthen or develop as you approach those situations?

Module 30: Skills for Compassionate Communication

In approaching compassionate communication, I want to revisit a common misconception about compassion – that it's about *being nice*; that it always looks and feels, well, *pleasant*. This misunderstanding can be a problem, because compassion is about working with suffering and struggle . . . topics that are not always pleasant to talk about. If our motivation is to keep things nice and pleasant, we can end up not communicating about important things, which can lead to more problems – just as Jordan highlighted in her reflection in the previous module.

Compassionate communication is about having the courage and skills to be able to communicate effectively about difficult feelings and experiences. It involves *kindness* in the sense it is about figuring out and doing what is *helpful*, but this isn't always going to feel pleasant for us or others . . . and will quite often involve taking steps we find uncomfortable. Luckily, there are several skills to make this process much easier.

Expressing emotions and desires

It can be tricky to understand what we're feeling, much less know how to communicate these emotions to others. It can be particularly tricky when we didn't see this modelled for us when we were growing up. In his book *Overcoming Depression*,[1] CFT founder Paul Gilbert describes four steps for expressing angry emotions, which I think work well for feelings other than anger as well:

1. Acknowledge your anger (or whatever emotion you are feeling).

2. Recognise in what way you feel hurt or frustrated and consider if your angry self might be exaggerating the harm done.

3. Focus on where this hurt comes from and your wish the other person could understand and respect your feelings and point of view.

4. Don't insist that the other person agree with you.

The process begins by *acknowledging what we're feeling*, and looking into the source of these feelings, then considering how we'll express this to the other person. For those of us who grew up in settings in which emotions were *acted out* but never talked about, it can feel a bit strange, but if we want to make sure people understand how we're feeling, the easiest way is to *tell them*. Here are a couple of other pragmatic tips:

- Rather than *acting out* the emotion and expecting others to figure it out, we can share how we're feeling directly . . . by *telling* them what we're feeling.

- 'I statements' help to communicate emotions in a non-attacking way – for example, 'I notice I'm feeling angry' versus 'You made me angry.'

This way of expressing emotions is clear, direct and models taking responsibility for our emotions, even as we acknowledge how they may be impacted by others' behaviour. Let's look at a few examples, with some blanks for you to come up with your own:

Expressing emotions

- I'm disappointed our plans fell through.

- I'm noticing myself getting angry right now.

- I'm anxious about _____ .

- I'm frustrated that _____ .

- I'm noticing I'm feeling _____ .

- _____ .

- _____ .

- _____ .

Often, we may be expressing emotions in situations in which we are making a request or want to express disagreement or disapproval. Doing this requires *assertiveness* skills. Approaching these situations in blaming, critical or attacking ways can easily create a 'threat systems bouncing' problem, like we explored in Module 19. The more our manner of communication triggers the other person's threat system, the more likely the interaction won't turn out well. On the other hand, if we can express desires and disagreements in ways that are direct but allow the other person to feel safe (or at least not feel attacked), they'll be more able to care about and to understand our point of view. This is a good time to draw upon other skills we've practised, like empathy, validation and mentalising. In each case, we want to express our feelings directly using 'I' statements, not attack or criticise the other person, and perhaps provide a brief bit of information that helps them understand our perspective.

A handy format for expressing desires and requests can be seen on the walls of many child and adolescent treatment centres, and I think it's gold:

'When ＿＿＿＿＿＿＿＿＿＿＿＿＿ , I feel ＿＿＿＿＿＿＿＿＿＿＿＿＿ , and I would like ＿＿＿＿＿＿＿＿＿＿＿ .'

Let's consider some examples of how this can be used, with a few blanks for you to practise. I've mixed up the order and the language of the phrase to show different ways it can be used – the key is to state what we're feeling and what we want *without* phrasing things in ways that attack the other person.

Expressing desires and requests

- When <u>you interrupt me</u>, I feel <u>frustrated</u>, and I'd like <u>it if you'd let me finish speaking before you respond.</u>

- I feel <u>loved</u> when you <u>text me during the day</u>, and I wouldn't complain <u>if that happened more in the future . . .</u>

- I feel <u>overwhelmed</u> by <u>all the details in this project</u>, and <u>I'd appreciate it if you could help me out with it</u>.

- I feel <u>hurt and disrespected</u> when you <u>make jokes about [insert topic here]</u> and I'd like you to <u>stop saying things like that around me.</u>

- When ＿＿＿＿＿＿＿＿＿＿＿ , I feel ＿＿＿＿＿＿＿＿＿＿＿ , and I would like ＿＿＿＿＿＿＿＿＿＿＿ .

- I feel ＿＿＿＿＿＿＿＿＿＿＿ when ＿＿＿＿＿＿＿＿＿＿＿ , and I'd like ＿＿＿＿＿＿＿＿＿＿＿ .

- ＿＿＿＿＿＿＿＿＿＿＿＿＿＿＿＿＿＿＿＿＿＿＿＿＿＿＿＿＿＿＿＿＿
  ＿＿＿＿＿＿＿＿＿＿＿＿＿＿＿＿＿＿＿＿＿＿＿＿＿＿＿＿＿＿＿＿＿ .

Expressing disagreement

Expressing disagreement can be challenging – it can feel pre-loaded with threat, like it places us in opposition with the other person. It can also be easy for both people to become fused with their own perspective, in that 'I'm right and you're wrong' sort of way that can set our threat systems bouncing against one another. This can particularly be the case when one person is angry, as anger carries with it that felt sense of certainty – of *knowing* we're 'right'. But disagreement doesn't have to mean conflict. The key is to begin by owning our own perspective *and* respecting that the other person may see things differently and may have good reasons behind their own perspective. Even when we're disagreeing with someone who clearly is wrong or behaving unreasonably, things will still go better if we engage them in ways that don't put them in a position of threat-fuelled defensiveness.

This can be particularly important if we're disagreeing about issues that are complicated or already emotionally charged. When the other person feels attacked, there will probably be no argument, data or pile of evidence convincing enough to change their minds . . . and pushing is only likely to get them to dig in more deeply to their existing position. If our goal is to be heard and understood, the first thing that needs to happen is for the other person to feel safe with us. Giving the other person a chance to explain their perspective and *listening* to what they have to say can really help with this. Sometimes, we may even find ourselves changing our minds when we've heard them out. Sometimes when we disagree with others – particularly when we're angry – *we'll* end up being the ones who are incorrect. I can't tell you how many times I've had disagreements with my wife in which I was completely sure of my opinion – only to eventually realise there was a crucial bit of information of which I'd been unaware – information that completely changed my perspective.

Here are some examples of how we can lead by first trying to learn more about the other person's position (use the blanks provided to practise coming up with your own examples):

Connecting with others' perspectives

- This seems important to you. Could you tell me more? I want to understand where you're coming from.

- I can tell you've thought a lot about this. Could you explain it to me?

- _____ .

- _____ .

When expressing disagreement, we want to do it in a way that's non-attacking, respects the other person's right to their perspective, assumes it has a valid basis in their experience, and balances assertiveness and humility.

Here are a few tips for how to approach such interactions compassionately:

Expressing disagreement

- State your perspective, clearly and directly. It's completely okay to say, 'I disagree. I think that _____.'

- Refrain from criticising others or implying that they are short-sighted or stupid for not agreeing with you. This sets the interaction up as a conflict and is likely to result in them digging in to their existing opinion more deeply.

- Be curious about their perspective and why they hold it. Expressing interest in their perspective and asking questions to understand why they feel the way they do will help them feel safe. This will help them think more flexibly and may even increase their willingness to hear why you feel the way you do. If the conversation is one I can anticipate having a high potential for conflict (like talking about political issues), I'll often start with this step before sharing my own perspective.

- Practise in advance! Consider how you might approach the situation in a direct, non-attacking way, and try it out in your imagination. You might even try role-playing with another person, having them take the perspective of the person you'll be talking with, and have them give you feedback on how they're feeling as the interaction plays out.

- Be willing to adjust your approach. Disagreement and working with situations involving conflict are skills that improve with practice and experience.

- If you find yourself getting angry, you'll probably feel the urge to address the disagreement *right then* or to *keep going*, even when the conversation isn't going anywhere. That's the urgency of anger. Often, we're much better served by taking time to cool down, so we can approach the situation as our compassionate selves, think about what we want to say and how to say it, and consider the other person's perspective.

- However well you express your perspective, don't require that the other person change their position or agree with you to consider it a 'successful interaction'. The goal is to assertively express your perspective in a clear, non-attacking way.

Some of us may feel the urge to over-explain – I'm certainly guilty of this. When expressing disagreement, I've often found myself trying to articulate *all the good reasons* behind my opinion ... sure that if the other person would only understand, they'd agree with me. That's often not worked as I'd hoped! Sometimes this can be helpful if we're having a conversation with someone in which we're both unpacking our perspectives for one another – but at other times, it's more effective just to express disagreement and state our perspective directly, perhaps with a brief explanation.

Here are some examples, with some space for you to practise using examples from your life:

Practising disagreement

Statement: *Andrea is such a nasty person!*

Disagreement: *It sounds like you've had a negative interaction with her. That's not been my experience. She's been kind to me and helped me out several times.*

Statement: *Babies should be left to 'cry it out'. They'll stop crying eventually.*

Disagreement: *I strongly disagree with that approach. They may stop crying, but it's really harmful to them. I'd love to chat more with you about that if you're interested.*

Statement: *[Group of people] are just selfish and lazy!*

Disagreement: *I disagree. I don't think that all [group] are the same, and I suspect they're just trying to get by and have good lives just like everybody else.*

Statement: _____

Disagreement: _____

Statement: _____

Disagreement: _____

In this module, we've explored skills for expressing emotions, desires and disagreement. Like any skills, they can feel a bit shaky and awkward when we're learning to use them. Don't give up! The more we practise these skills, the more natural they feel, the more we'll find ways of saying things that work for us, and the more they'll become helpful habits that are there when we need them.

One word of warning: when we've a history of interacting with others in angry, hostile ways, they can naturally be sceptical when we start behaving differently. They may think we're trying some trick on them, expect we'll 'go back to our old ways' (which we occasionally *will* – slip-ups happen, particularly in the beginning), not recognise how hard we're trying, or in some other way respond in ways that are disappointing to us. Don't let that derail you. We're not doing these things to get a desired reaction from others . . . this isn't a manipulation strategy. We're doing it because, over time, it *works better*, and fits with the sort of people we want to be.

Final reflection

Did any of the strategies explored in this module stand out to you? Can you think of situations in your life in which you might want to apply them?

_____

_____

_____

_____

_____

_____

_____

Module 31: Healing Relationship Ruptures

All relationships involve ruptures, and this can be particularly true when one or both people struggle with anger. Relationship ruptures even happen in therapeutic relationships – the therapist will mean one thing and say another, hurt feelings result, and the relationship suddenly feels a lot less safe. When I was a novice therapist I used to fear such ruptures, afraid of losing a client or of being seen as a 'bad therapist'. Now, I recognise such ruptures as valuable opportunities to help clients *learn how to repair ruptures when they happen*, because ruptures *will* happen in any ongoing relationship. But if we know how to repair them, we can find our relationships stronger than they were before, bolstered by new skills and the confidence that comes with knowing that even if things occasionally go sideways, we know how to heal the relationship.

Plan ahead

One helpful way to approach working with ruptures in important relationships is to plan how we will work with them *when we* aren't *having a rupture*. 'Given that we'll sometimes have ruptures, what would be the best way to handle it when that happens, so we can come back together?' Here are some tips for rupture-planning:

- *Communicate about how to help one another feel safe when there's been a rupture, and how you will approach repair.* This involves getting curious and listening to one another: 'What's the best way for me to approach you when we've had a rupture and I'm ready to make up?', 'What could I do that would help you feel safe and willing to reconnect? What should I absolutely not do?'

- *Make a plan to interrupt rumination.* When our threat systems kick in, we may go over and over what happened in our minds, demonising the other person, fuelling defensiveness and making it hard to empathise. Consider how you might interrupt this rumination – for example, by writing a letter from your compassionate self to your angry self to read in the event of a rupture, to remind you what's important. An 'in case we're fighting' letter to your partner can potentially be helpful, too (consult with them on this): 'Andrew, if you're reading this, it's probably because we're fighting. I want you to know I love you and I'm committed to our relationship. Once our hurt feelings have softened, I look forward to working together to heal this rift . . .'

- **Commit to avoiding toxic communication strategies.** The first step in healing a relationship rupture is *not doing things that will make it worse:*[1]

  - **Minimise blaming, criticism and 'zingers'.** Avoid going for 'gotcha' moments. If you're talking about something your partner has done, talk about their *behaviour* using 'I' statements (e.g. 'When you _____, I feel _____') rather than talking about them as a person (e.g. 'You're so hostile!') or about their motives ('You're trying to hurt me!').

  - **Don't sulk or stonewall.** It's completely okay to take a break so that partners can slow things down, but don't engage in passive-aggressive behaviour or refuse to interact, to punish the other person. 'I'm not ready to talk yet, but will reach out to you once I've cooled down.'

- **Cultivate positive relationship strategies:**

  - **Plan positive interactions and make them happen.** Notarius and Markman[2] talk about our 'relationship bank accounts' in which every positive interaction is a deposit and every negative interaction is a withdrawal. Make lots of deposits. Planning fun activities is great, but even small interactions can make a big difference – one of my favourites is *warm meetings and partings.* An honest expression of 'I'm happy to see you' takes only a moment but is a meaningful 'deposit'.

  - **Give sincere compliments.** I'm not talking about flattery but letting the other person know what we sincerely appreciate about them. If we notice ourselves feeling grateful for the other person or something they've done, let's tell them.

  - **Let the other person coach you** about how best to help them feel seen, valued and loved: 'What's the best way for me to let you know that

I _____ you?' We don't need to *guess* how to approach others in ways that help them feel valued and loved – we can communicate about it. This goes for things like sex, too – we can learn a lot about other people when we make it safe for them to let us know what they like and what they don't.

- *Do your homework.* We don't have space in this book to go in-depth into how to cultivate good relationships, but the good news is that a lot of people have put serious work into exploring this, and there are several excellent books and resources on just this topic. I've included a couple of my favourites in Appendix A.[3]

- *Accept that your first 'rupture repair plan' will probably not work perfectly, and be willing to revise it.* As we've explored again and again, unanticipated obstacles are the name of the game when trying to do something new. Expect them . . . and just like the coaching staff after a big game (win or lose), we can come back together when things have cooled down after the rupture and unpack how it went. What did either partner do that was helpful? What was unhelpful? What do we want to do more of in the future? Less of? The goal is to gradually build on strengths and address obstacles, getting a little better each time.

Working with ruptures can be tricky, as it requires us to let go of our egos (not making everything about 'me') and prioritise the relationship ('How can we best address this challenge so we can come back together?'). Here again, self-compassion can be helpful – how can we take care of the hurting or insecure versions of ourselves so we can join with another person to focus on our relationship?

Connect with compassion

It's probably not surprising that I'd recommend this! Connecting with the different flows of compassion sets us up nicely to repair relationship ruptures. Just like working with any other tricky situation, we can start by slowing things down, connecting with the kind, wise, confident perspective of our compassionate selves, and thinking about what would be helpful. Here are a few tips for each flow of compassion:

Self-compassion

- If you're in a rupture, chances are your threat system has been triggered. This is a perfect time to use some self-compassion strategies:

  - **Recognise and validate your distress:** 'Right now I'm feeling _____, and given my history, it makes sense that I'd be struggling with this.'

  - **Use compassionate skills to slow things down:** 'I think now would be a good time to do some soothing rhythm breathing or a soothing space practice.'

  - **Connect with your compassionate self:** 'What would my compassionate self understand about this situation?', 'What would my compassionate self want to happen?', 'What would my compassionate self remind me to do?'

  - **Extend compassion to the version of you that is triggered** and wanting to lash out or withdraw: 'Given my history, it makes sense that this rupture would be hard for me. I wonder what would help me feel safe and find some balance?'

Compassion for others

- **Connect with the compassionate questions** from Module 7:

  - What role do I want to play in this person's life?

  - How do I want them to feel when I'm around?

  - How do I want them to feel about themselves when I'm around?

- **Use compassionate skills** to connect with their perspective:

  - **Empathy** – Consider how they are feeling. Try to understand their experience.

  - **Validation** – Consider how it makes sense that they would feel this way.

  - **Mentalising** – Consider how they are making sense of things, and what needs and desires might be driving their behaviour.

- **Connect with your compassionate self:** What would this kind, wise, confident version of you want for this other person, and your relationship with them? What would your compassionate self know would be helpful (including asking the other person)?

Compassion from others

- **Connect with the questions** from Module 7:
  - What would be helpful for me to receive from others when I'm struggling?
  - What might I need to do so that they will be able to treat me in that way?
  - How might I express my needs to them so that they'll be able to understand my experience?

With each of these flows of compassion, we slow things down and shift from a place of defensiveness to a compassionate perspective that recognises *this situation is difficult* and moves from threat-based behaviours, such as attacking the other person or withdrawing from the relationship, to considering what would help everyone in the situation feel safe and what would help us repair the rupture.

Apologising

Despite our best efforts, we'll all sometimes do things that are hurtful to others. When this happens, it can be easy to go into defensive mode, and do things that aren't helpful:

- Rationalise or blame the other person: *I only said that because you* _____ *!*

- Shame ourselves: *I'm such a terrible [partner, parent, person, etc.].*

- Avoid: Pretend it didn't happen, avoid thinking about it, minimise what happened.

Especially once we've been practising compassion, it can be painful to accept that we've behaved hurtfully to those we care about, and we may find ourselves using these avoidant strategies to keep from facing the pain we've caused. Most people who struggle with anger don't want to hurt others – we want to be recognised, respected, valued and cared about. But when we use these strategies, we double down on the harm we've done, implicitly communicating to the other person that the fact we hurt them *doesn't matter to us*. Connecting with self-compassion in such situations can be helpful – recognising our harmful behaviour as a symptom that we were *struggling* with the situation, acknowledging how *it makes sense* we might struggle in such situations, and considering *what would be helpful* in moving forwards.

Nothing makes it okay that we've behaved hurtfully, but a sincere apology can be an important step in acknowledging what happened, alleviating the harm and healing our relationship with the other person. Let's consider some components of a good apology:

- direct acknowledgment of our behaviour and the harm done

- an expression of regret

- a commitment to not repeat the behaviour in the future

- as time passes, *following through* on that commitment.

Let's look at some examples. Use the blanks provided to practise coming up with examples that fit your life:

Apology examples

- 'I'm sorry I raised my voice to you – that must have been really upsetting. You don't deserve to be treated like that. I'm going to do better at keeping my cool in the future.'

- 'I want to apologise for making fun of your interest in _____ in front of your friends. I was trying to be funny, but clearly it wasn't, and I can imagine it must have been hurtful for you. That won't happen again.'

- 'I'm sorry I criticised you for not putting the dishes away. You contribute a lot around here, and I can imagine it must hurt not to have me see that. Could we talk about how I might approach such situations in a more helpful way?'

- _____

  _____

- _____

  _____

When apologising, we're *taking responsibility* for behaving in a hurtful or unhelpful way, and *committing* to do better in the future. We don't want to approach the situation in either a childlike, overly submissive way or in a hostile, aggressive manner. Although I'm biased, I'd recommend approaching the situation from the calm, committed approach of our compassionate selves. Finally, it's worth repeating that we need to *follow through* on our commitment to do better in the future – apologies become meaningless when we don't change the behaviour we're apologising for.

What stood out to you from the information on healing relationship ruptures? Was there anything you'd like to apply in your own relationships?

James: *What really stood out for me was the suggestion to connect with compassion before trying to repair the rupture. Usually when there's a rupture in my relationship, I'm either in an angry spot or filled with shame, and both make it hard to focus on the relationship. I think slowing down and bringing compassion to everyone involved – including me – will really help. I was also hit by the phrase that was something like 'angry people don't want to hurt others, we want to be valued, respected and cared about . . .'. That so fits with my experience.*

Antwan: *Lots of things stood out, but one big thing was that apologies don't mean anything if you aren't trying to change. That nailed it. My dad used to do that all the time – he'd do all this terrible stuff and then apologise for it, swear he'd never do it again, then a few nights later he'd do the same thing all over again. The apology just became a part of the cycle – it felt worse than if he'd never apologised at all, because we all knew it was a lie.*

Jordan: *It stood out to me that you can actually talk about and plan how your relationship is going to go, rather than just frantically trying to figure it out in the moment. It seems crazy, but I don't think I've ever done that, or seen anyone else do it, either: 'Let's think about how we're going to handle it when . . .', 'How would you like me to approach you when . . .?' This seems like a serious life hack to me! I'm already thinking about how to use it with friends and dating: 'Sometimes, at the end of the day, I just want to curl up at home and not go out, and it doesn't have anything to do with you or how I feel about you. What would be a good way for me to communicate that, so you don't think I'm avoiding you?' I'm strangely excited about this!*

What stood out to you from the information on healing relationship ruptures? Was there anything you'd like to apply in your own relationships?

_____

_____

_____

_____

_____

_____

Final reflection

Building on the last reflection, is there a particular type of rupture that has tended to create distance in one of your important relationships? Are there any skills from the past few modules that you think might be helpful in repairing the rupture? Which ones, and how might you use them?

_____

_____

_____

_____

_____

_____

_____

_____

End of section check-in

How are you feeling about your progress?

_____

_____

_____

What has been helpful?

_____

_____

_____

What obstacles have arisen?

_____

_____

_____

What do you want to be sure to keep in mind going forwards?

_____

_____

_____

Compassion practice plan

Now we've completed the sixth section, let's update the practice plan. Here are a few new practices based on the modules in Section VI:

1. **Consider your priorities before an interaction** (Module 29): Before approaching an interaction with another person, take five minutes to consider your priorities for this interaction. What's the goal or objective being served by the interaction, and how important is it? Are there feelings you want to express, and how important is that to you? What is your relationship with this person, how important is it, and how do you want this interaction to contribute to your ongoing relationship with them? Use this to inform how you approach the interaction.

2. **Practise a compassionate communication skill** (Module 30): Take a few minutes to select a compassionate communication skill from Module 30 that you'd like to work into your repertoire. Practise using the skill, in your imagination, with another person ('Hey, I'm working on my communication skills . . . could you help me practise?') or in a real interaction.

3. **Consider healing a rupture** (Module 31): If you've had a rupture in one of your important relationships that hasn't quite healed, take five to ten minutes to revisit Module 31 and consider how you might approach repairing it. You may want to think about this on a few occasions before trying it out with the other person.

Every day, do one mindfulness practice (mindful check-in, three systems check-in or brief mind the loops practice) **OR soothing rhythm breathing, and one other practice.** Choose practices from those listed above, as well as those included in previous practice plans, on pages 64–6, 107–8, 135, 174–5 and 226. Try to do each of the new practices at least once, and don't repeat any practice more than twice per week. Mix in soothing activities regularly – daily, if possible.

Daily practice log

Practice	Sun	Mon	Tues	Weds	Thurs	Fri	Sat
Mindfulness practice							
Soothing rhythm breathing							

Practice notes

Day	What was helpful?	What obstacles came up?
Sunday		
Monday		
Tuesday		
Wednesday		
Thursday		
Friday		
Saturday		

SECTION VII:
Working with Anger Triggers

We've covered a fair amount of ground so far. This section pulls it all together, as we develop a plan to work with anger triggers in ways that will free us from old patterns and help us respond to challenges in helpful, compassionate ways. Some of the content in the next few modules is adapted from the True Strength group therapy programme, which applies CFT to anger in a 12-session group format. If you're interested, you can download an English-language copy of the manual here: https://overcoming.co.uk/715/resources-to-download.[1] This approach has been used in prison and veterans' hospital settings with good results, with a preliminary study documenting its effectiveness[2] in reducing not only symptoms of problematic anger, but of post-traumatic stress disorder as well. In this section, we'll hear less from our companions, in favour of tailoring our work to your unique anger triggers.

Module 32: The Anger Monitoring Form

Anger triggers activate our threat systems and, as we've explored, when our threat systems are activated, the brain's natural tendency is to focus our attention, thinking and mental imagery very narrowly on perceived threats. When this happens, it's hard to think flexibly, problem-solve creatively and figure out the best way to respond. To counter that, we want to plan ahead. It's like how soldiers train before going into a combat zone, or how elite athletes train before a big match. Their coaches and trainers help them anticipate and identify different situations they'll face – particularly the tricky ones – and then they systematically train and practise effective ways to engage with those situations. That way, when it's happening and their threat systems are triggered, they won't have to start from scratch to figure out what to do – they can rely upon automatic responses they've practised beforehand. This training can also help them keep from being totally overwhelmed by the situation, because although stressful, it also feels familiar. In this way, we want to start by identifying common triggering situations and plan for how to work with them.

Over the course of the book, we've touched on anger triggers several times. Let's take a moment to refresh your awareness of experiences and situations that tend to trigger your anger. These triggers can involve external events (e.g. 'when _____ happens', 'when things don't go as I'd planned . . .'), other people's behaviour (e.g. 'when _____ does _____'), or even internal experiences ('when I'm reminded of _____', 'when I feel _____ or I think about _____'). We want to get *familiar* with all the things that tend to trigger feelings of anger in you, so we can recognise them when they happen (and maybe even anticipate and plan for them beforehand). Let's revisit your common triggers, listing them in the space provided below:

Anger triggers:

1. _____

2. _____

3. _____

4. _____

5. _____

6. _____

The anger monitoring form below – a more elaborate version of the monitoring exercise from Module 23 – is designed to help us get increasingly familiar with our triggers, how they play out in us, and to develop compassionate ways of working with them – to help us reflect on things after they've cooled down, and plan for how we'll work with the trigger in the future. Feel free to photocopy this form, which is also included in Appendix B, or you can download or print it from https://overcoming.co.uk/715/resources-to-download.

Let's briefly unpack the form:

- **Trigger:** What happened? What situation or experience triggered anger?

- **What did I feel?** Including anger, what feelings were prompted by the trigger?

- **What did I think?** What thoughts and images followed the trigger? Pay particular attention to thoughts that *fuel* the anger (rumination, replaying the situation in your mind) and those that tend to *calm* it (considering how the other person's behaviour makes sense from their side; helpful thoughts that assist you to shift perspective or self-soothe – 'Is this more a minor inconvenience or a huge problem?').

- **What did I do?** What did you say or do?

- **How did the situation turn out?** What happened? Unpack the outcome of the situation in terms of the experience and actions of everyone involved ('It got heated and we stormed off in different directions', 'I apologised, things seemed to calm down, and we continued with the game').

- **What does my compassionate self have to say to my angry self?** This part could be expanded into a compassionate letter from your compassionate self to your angry self (which we'll explore in Module 39). Connect with the courageous, wise, kind, confident perspective of your compassionate self, and think about what this compassionate self might offer the version of you that was triggered and struggling with anger. The options are almost limitless – the idea is to find what is *helpful*. Here are some examples:

  ○ **Validation** – 'Given my past experience, it make sense this would trigger me.'

  ○ **Helpful suggestions and distress tolerance reminders** – 'Next time, I'll try to slow down my breath or take a walk before continuing the conversation . . .'.

  ○ **Perspective taking** – 'Which of the three emotion systems was [the other person] in? How does their behaviour make sense?'

  ○ **Reminders of your motivation** – 'It's easy to be triggered by my son's complaining, but I want to be a positive role model for him. I want to teach him helpful ways to respond when things don't go his way.'

- **What might my compassionate self have done differently?** Perhaps building on the previous prompt, explore compassionate ways of responding to the trigger that you can use in the future. If you had the chance to go back and respond to the trigger as your compassionate self, what might you do differently?

Anger monitoring form

Trigger: _____

_____

_____

What did I feel? _____

_____

_____

What did I think? _____

_____

_____

What did I do? _____

_____

_____

How did the situation turn out? _____

_____

_____

What does my compassionate self have to say to my angry self? _____

_____

_____

What might my compassionate self have done differently? _____

_____

_____

Final reflection

Do you anticipate any obstacles that might keep you from filling out the anger monitoring form? What might help make sure you do it (e.g. plan a specific time at the end of every day in which you reflect on the day, whether or not you had a trigger situation, and fill out the form)?

_____

_____

_____

_____

_____

_____

_____

Module 33: The RAGE Model for Working with Anger Triggers

This module introduces an outline for working with anger triggers that we'll explore in subsequent modules. In the effort to organise our approach to applying CFT to working with anger, I'll somewhat cheekily use the acronym RAGE. Let's unpack the RAGE model, imagining that an anger trigger has occurred, with each letter in RAGE indicating a step we'll take in working with the trigger and the feelings that follow it.

R:

- **Recognise** the situation that provoked the anger and the signs of anger coming up in us.

- **Reduce** our arousal by using soothing exercises.

- **Refrain** from engaging in the habitual anger behaviour.

A:

- **Access** the kind, wise, confident perspective of the compassionate self.

- **Acknowledge** that our threat system is **activated** right now.

- **Accept** and endure the discomfort associated with this activation, and with refraining from the habitual behaviour.

G:

- **Give** ourselves permission to experience whatever we are experiencing. Feel it without judging it or acting upon it. We can observe our threat responses without acting on them.

- **Generate** compassionate responses to the situation. This can involve lots of different ways of thinking and behaving, depending on the situation.

E:

- **Enact** compassionate responses. From the perspective of the compassionate self, decide the response we will have to the situation and put it into action.

- **Establish** new patterns in the brain. Every time we engage in a compassionate behaviour instead of a habitual anger response, we're establishing and strengthening brain patterns that shape how we'll respond in the future.

- **Experience** ourselves as a compassionate person. As we observe ourselves acting out of the compassionate self rather than the angry self, we can begin relating to ourselves in a new way: as a compassionate person.

This module unpacks the 'R' in RAGE: **recognising** the trigger and the signs of anger coming up in us; **reducing** our arousal by using soothing exercises; **refraining** from engaging in anger-driven (or other emotion-driven) behaviour that will make the situation worse.

Recognising

The first step in managing triggers is becoming *aware* we've been triggered – or, even better, that we've found ourselves in a situation that has the potential to trigger us but hasn't yet. This awareness can result from our noticing either the triggering situation or the signs of anger (bodily activation, angry thoughts and imagery) coming up in us. Once we *notice* these experiences, we can consider what would be helpful to *do*, rather than having our behaviour dictated by our anger.

We've done several exercises designed to train our brains to notice these experiences. Identifying and noting triggers as they happen, and completing the anger monitoring form, will help us get better at noticing the situations and experiences that tend to trigger us. Similarly, the mindfulness practices presented in Modules 5 and 23 will help us get better at noticing signs of anger arising or looping in us, providing opportunities to unhook ourselves from the anger and consider what might be helpful in working with it.

Reducing angry arousal

Anger and other threat emotions can be fuelled by the engine of bodily arousal, so a good first step once we've **recognised** we've been triggered is to intentionally **reduce arousal** in our bodies. We want to get our safeness and soothing systems going, to balance things out when our threat systems have been activated. Slowing down our bodies and focusing our attention on soothing experiences and thoughts also shifts our attention away from thoughts that fuel anger. This shifting can be hard at first – we may have to do it *over and over*, as our threat systems are designed to keep us focused on whatever triggered us (the perceived threat). But, with practice, it gets easier.

For many people, **soothing rhythm breathing (SRB)**, covered in Module 24, is the best first step in softening threat emotions. I'd encourage you to practise SRB for a few minutes each day, getting into the habit of slowing down your breath and finding a familiar, comfortable rate of breathing you can return to when you notice your threat system is activated. **Soothing space/safe place imagery** (Module 26) can also be helpful in soothing ourselves and reducing angry arousal.

Finally, I encourage clients and colleagues to get curious about noticing experiences they find soothing and to 'collect' them. Try to recall and notice moments in your life when you've felt safe, balanced, calm, soothed and happy. What was happening? What were you doing? Some of these experiences won't be appropriate to use when we've just been triggered by anger, but some may provide options we can use. I've found that listening to certain types of music, watching funny and soothing movies, going for walks – particularly in natural areas – meditating, sitting in a hot tub or bath, and petting my dogs (who love me no matter how tricky I've been) all help to soften my arousal when I've been triggered. Below, I've started a list of potential options you might use to get your safeness system going, and left blanks so you can add to the list. My best advice is for all of us to start collecting soothing experiences now and spend the rest of our lives adding to the list.

We want to relate to our lives with *curiosity* – training ourselves to *notice* and *become familiar* with situations and experiences that trigger us *and* those that soothe us and help us connect with the best versions of ourselves. Everything we do in life happens within *contexts* that activate different motivations and behaviours in us. A big part of working with emotions (and having good lives) involves creating life contexts that activate and support our ability to engage with the versions of ourselves we want to inhabit – our compassionate, patient, committed selves. Activities that remind us of our motivation to work with our anger and of the people we want to be in the world are a bonus, too. I can make suggestions, but *you* are the expert on noticing what is most helpful for *you*.

Activities for reducing angry arousal/soothing

1. Soothing rhythm breathing (Module 24) _____

2. Soothing space imagery (Module 26) _____

3. _____

4. _____

5. _____

6. _____

7. _____

8. _____

9. _____

10. _____

Refraining from anger-driven behaviour

Managing anger is about what we do, but it's also about what we *don't do*. Acting out the aggressive energy and motivation of anger can take already tricky situations and *make them worse*, potentially causing problems in our relationships and other aspects of our lives. While I'm sure you don't need me to explain why physical aggression and violence are unacceptable, in the heat of anger we can also use speech to wound others in ways they'll carry with them for years.

If, like me, you've *already* said hurtful things to people you care about and perhaps noticed pain coming up after reading that last sentence – give yourself permission to recognise this as the pain of compassion. This pain exists because you recognise your past behaviour has been hurtful to others, and that's not okay with you. Rather than using this awareness as a reason to feel bad about yourself (which won't help *anyone*), see if it's possible to use this discomfort as fuel for your commitment to **refrain** from letting your anger hijack you in the future.

Regarding **refraining,** it's almost impossible to just 'stop doing' a behaviour. Behavioural psychologists have the 'dead person rule', meaning we never ask clients to do something a dead person can do. Simply asking people to not behave in a certain way doesn't work, because our behaviours occur within contexts *in which they make sense* – they're triggered by situations, experiences, thoughts, emotions and needs. If we're going to stop behaving in a way that creates problems, we must *develop new, helpful behaviours* to replace the old, unhelpful ones.

In this way, we can see these two last Rs – **refraining from anger-driven behaviour** and **reducing angry arousal** – as working in tandem. It's like one of those healthy eating guides that tells us, 'Instead of eating _____, eat _____.' **Recognising** triggers and angry arousal creates a moment in which a choice is possible. We can use that opportunity to replace unhelpful anger-driven habits with compassionate alternatives. Here are some examples of how that can work, some of which involve **reducing** activities, while others involve helpful alternatives generated by the compassionate self. (We'll revisit this when we get to the G skills.)

- **Instead of** immediately sending that email, **I can** take a few minutes to slow down my breath.

- **Instead of** ruminating and fuelling my anger by replaying the trigger over and over in my head, **I can** take a few minutes to slow things down by imagining my soothing space **OR** go for a walk **OR** spend some time petting my dogs.

- **Instead of** snapping at my child or partner, **I can** pause to consider how it makes sense that they're acting this way **OR** remind myself of the role I want to play in their life **OR** let them know I'm a bit irritated right now, and that I'd like to talk with them about this when I've calmed down.

Several items above feature multiple options, to give us the ability to select the best fit for the situation and how we're feeling. Sometimes we may be in a place where something mental (like imagery) will be helpful, and other times we may be so riled up that we're better served by working with the breath, moving our bodies or doing something soothing like petting a dog. *This search is important* because it reflects that we've *shifted* from being anchored in the threat-focused motivation of our anger to the compassionate desire to *figure out what would be helpful in addressing this challenge.* That shift can open a world of possibilities.

Here's an opportunity for you to practise refraining and replacing:

Refraining options

1.   Instead of _____

      I can _____

2.   Instead of _____

      I can _____

3.   Instead of _____

      I can _____

4.   Instead of _____

      I can _____

5.   Instead of _____

      I can _____

6.   Instead of _____

      I can _____

Although several components are contained within the Rs (recognise, reduce and refrain), they are related: **recognising** that we've been triggered (or are in a situation in which that has historically been triggering for us) creates the opportunity to **reduce** the arousal that fuels our anger, making it a lot easier to **refrain** from engaging in anger-driven behaviour and figure out more helpful alternatives.

Final reflection

What stood out to you from this module? Knowing how your anger works, is there an 'R skill' you think will be particularly helpful for you? In what way?

_____

_____

_____

_____

_____

_____

_____

Considering the 'R skills' (recognising, reducing, refraining), are there any you think may be particularly challenging? Do you have any ideas about obstacles that might show up, and what might be helpful to keep in mind as you apply the skills?

_____

_____

_____

_____

_____

_____

_____

Module 34: Accessing, Acknowledging and Accepting

This module focuses on the 'A' skills in the RAGE model. By this time, we've recognised that we've been triggered, have taken steps to reduce the arousal of our anger and refrained from doing anger-driven behaviours that will make things worse. Now it's time to intentionally begin the shift into working *compassionately* with the situation – beginning with ourselves. Here's a reminder of the A skills:

- **Access** the kind, wise and confident perspective of the compassionate self.

- **Acknowledge** that our threat system is **activated** right now.

- **Accept** and endure the discomfort associated with this activation and with refraining from the habitual behaviour.

The first 'A' skill is **accessing the compassionate self** – shifting from the threat-driven focus of the triggered angry self to the care-focused motive of the compassionate self. This version of us is wise and curious, committed to figuring out what is helpful, and is confident we'll be able to figure out a helpful way to work with it. We can see why the 'R' skills come first – without reducing the arousal of our anger, this 'A' skill would be almost impossible. Once we've slowed things down, it's time to put our compassionate selves in the captain's chair. There are a few ways to approach this, and I'd encourage you to experiment and find the approach that works best for you.

Here are a few options, with blanks for you to note other approaches you've found helpful:

Accessing the compassionate self

1. Do the compassionate self practice from Module 14.

2. Do a guided audio compassionate self practice from www.compassionatemind.co.uk.

3. Keep a small stone or coin in your pocket that you can hold and rub as you remind yourself of the person you want to be and the qualities of your compassionate self.

---

4. Pick three qualities that you can easily remember that capture the essence of your compassionate self (mine are 'kind, wise and confident').

5. Choose phrases that connect you with your compassionate intention (mine are 'How do I want them to feel when I'm around?', 'What role do I want to play in their lives?').

6. Write a note in your phone that reminds you of any of the above – or anything else that helps connect you to the qualities of your compassionate self.

7. Keep a picture, or something else you find inspiring, in your wallet (or on your phone) to remind you of the person you want to be and why you're working with your anger. I use a few, including a picture of my son when he was an infant.

8. Read your compassionate letter (we'll cover this later in the module).

9. _____

10. _____

11. _____

12. _____

Give yourself permission to be curious and creative. The key isn't to 'do it right', it's to find ways of reminding and motivating yourself to connect with the caregiving motive of your compassionate self – shifting from 'How do I attack back or defend myself?' to 'Given that I've been triggered, what would help me be the best version of myself as I deal with this tricky situation?'

Acknowledge your threat system has been activated

As we've explored, anger involves and is fuelled by a range of mental experiences: a felt sense of urgency to do something, feelings of certainty and an aggressive motivation. These are all signs that our brains have registered this trigger as a potential threat and are organising us to defend ourselves against it (or attack it). There are many reasons our brains might do this – reasons that may have everything to do with our history and nothing to do with the current situation. We can find ourselves reacting strongly to situations which actually aren't that big of a deal, and which – if we were in a more balanced space – we might not react to at all, or could deal with helpfully and assertively.

This 'A' skill is about self-compassionately **acknowledging** that, regardless of the situation, our threat system has perceived a threat and is rallying to meet it in ways that aren't our fault (and that set us up to struggle). It's like our inner drill sergeant has been awoken by a mistakenly triggered air-raid siren and is rallying troops to attack the 'threat' when the situation could be better dealt with by pausing, figuring out what is really going on and arranging for the new recruit that triggered the siren to get a bit more training. This **acknowledging skill** is about shifting from a threat-based space of 'I have to respond to this situation right now!' to a more mindful, compassionate perspective: 'Ah, my threat system is really activated. If I rush to respond right now, there's a good chance it won't go well. What would help me manage this threat response so I can respond to the situation in a way that would be helpful?' Having already reduced some of the arousal linked with threat system activation, this step is about connecting with a compassionate understanding of what's happening within us, helping ourselves transition to more helpful ways of working with the situation.

Working with anger triggers can involve a rhythm – first recognising our threat system is activated and disengaging from the trigger to work with our own threat response. Once we feel more balanced, we re-engage with the triggering situation, with a focus on considering what would be helpful in addressing it (rather than a place of attacking/defending), and take appropriate action.

Accepting and enduring the discomfort associated with threat-system activation

Our final 'A' skill is about **accepting** discomfort and finding helpful ways to endure and work with it until it fades and passes. There's no way around it – it's *uncomfortable* when our threat system is activated. This isn't an accident. The discomfort that comes with these emotions was designed by evolution to *get us moving* in the service of avoiding or defending ourselves from physical threats. This discomfort can be magnified by thoughts that we 'shouldn't have' to experience it, or that the fact we are uncomfortable is unfair or means there is something wrong with us. But these emotions are a part of life – unpleasant, but not really 'unfair' (although it can feel that way!), and certainly not a sign anything is wrong with us. Actually, they signal that our system is working to protect us. The goal is to accept and remember that this is a part of life, and to work with the experience the best we can.

In addition to the discomfort of the anger itself, discomfort can arise from **refraining** from our habitual anger-driven responses. Remember, these habits are well-worn patterns in our brains. We can feel like we *want* to respond in the old, habitual ways – think of it as the brain's 'path of least resistance'. Refraining from such habits can be uncomfortable, like not scratching an itch or refraining from smoking. This discomfort signals that we're addressing the real habit – a sign that 'this is the moment of truth', an opportunity to make change as we refrain from acting out the old pattern and instead strengthen a new one. What if we curiously observed and accepted this discomfort as a natural part of changing unhelpful patterns, knowing it will gradually ease as the balance shifts away from the old patterns and towards our new, compassionate ways of being?

Finally, we can remind ourselves why we're doing this. We're choosing to experience this discomfort for *good reasons*. Exercising can be uncomfortable, but we tolerate it to be strong and healthy. Refraining from scratching the itch of a bug bite is uncomfortable – but we *tolerate it* because we know *scratching makes it worse*. We can pause to reconnect with the reasons we want to change our angry habits, and with the people we want to be.

Doing this is the focus of a collection of techniques and coping skills called *distress tolerance*. Distress tolerance skills are good for all of us to have, as most human lives will sometimes involve uncomfortable situations we can't escape, and distress tolerance skills[1] can help us get through such uncomfortable situations.

Like the soothing skills presented earlier, I'd encourage you to get curious and 'collect' things you find helpful as you learn to endure discomfort. Here are a few examples, along with blanks for you to fill in as you find other strategies that are helpful for you:

Accepting and enduring skills

1. **Accepting and acknowledging** what's happening. We can accept discomfort as the cost of doing something important in our lives; taking ownership of the discomfort versus magnifying it with thoughts like 'This is unfair!' or 'I shouldn't have to do this!' Making meaningful change in our lives is difficult, but we choose to do it because we know it will lead us to a better life. Connecting with this understanding can make discomfort easier to tolerate and *choosing to accept* this discomfort as the cost of positive growth can help us feel powerful. We're not victims, we're taking responsibility for our lives and accepting that doing so often isn't easy.

2. **Soothing with attention, activity and imagery.** Replaying anger triggers in our minds keeps anger going (and magnifies the discomfort of refraining from acting on it). Shifting the focus of our attention to other things can be challenging but helpful. Here are some examples:

   (a) Any of the **reducing** skills (e.g. soothing rhythm breathing, soothing space imagery).

   (b) Soothing sensory experiences (e.g. music, sights, smells) and activities (hobbies, things we find soothing and enjoyable).

(c) Bringing our attention to things that 'break the emotional momentum' of the anger – things we find inspiring, funny or beautiful.

(d) Pausing to consider what we feel grateful for in our lives, the things that we appreciate and which make our lives better (this is a great daily habit, by the way).

(e) _____

(f) _____

(g) _____

(h) _____

3. **Reframing with compassionate thinking.** Connecting with compassionate understanding and reminders that soften or reframe our experience of discomfort:

(a) Reminding ourselves of why we're working with our anger, and how that will improve our lives.

(b) Considering how our kind, wise, confident compassionate self would understand and approach this situation.

(c) Asking ourselves 'What would help me be more comfortable as I go through this challenging experience?'

(d) Reminding myself _____

(e) Telling myself that _____

(f) Considering _____

4. **Engaging in helpful behaviour.** Doing things that make use of the angry energy, distract from the experience of discomfort and help us connect with a more compassionate perspective:

(a) Physical activity/exercise.

(b) Going for a walk/engaging with nature.

(c) Doing enjoyable activities (humorous shows or memes, engaging with activities we find fun or soothing).

(d) _____

(e) _____

(f) _____

There is an almost infinite number of potential distress tolerance skills – get curious about what is most helpful for *you* to be the best version of yourself (or at least to not take impulsive action that makes things worse) as you experience the discomfort that comes up as you work with your anger. That 'not making things worse' bit is important, and it's why 'having a few pints', 'doing some drugs' and 'finding something to destroy' didn't make the list. Using substances to mask the discomfort can create dependency (as well as the potential for problem behaviour) and keep us from developing *helpful* coping mechanisms, while *displacing the aggression* can potentially keep us in a threat-focused state of mind. Like all aspects of a compassionate approach, distress tolerance isn't about avoiding or *not feeling* the discomfort, it's about *understanding* it and *finding helpful ways* to work with it that will make our lives better.

Final reflection

Given your history, what has tended to be helpful to you when you've had to do something difficult or go through periods of discomfort? What helped you keep going even when it was hard?

_____

_____

_____

_____

_____

_____

_____

Module 35: Giving Yourself Permission

This module and the next explore the 'G' skills: **giving yourself permission** to non-judgementally experience whatever you're experiencing, and **generating compassionate alternative responses** – two skills that are intimately linked. These skills build on those presented in the previous two modules – relating compassionately to our experience of anger, and working to behave in ways that build new, helpful habits versus falling into our old anger- (or other threat–emotion) driven ways of behaving. You may find some of this material to be a bit redundant with bits from previous modules, but that's by design – we're trying to *grow and entrench* compassionate ways of relating to your anger and the situations that trigger it. We're building new habits and strengthening brain patterns that will help them become part of your daily life.

Giving yourself permission to feel what you're feeling

Threat emotions like anger can feel powerful and very uncomfortable, but they're also designed to be short-lived. In the world faced by our ancestors, these emotions evolved to rapidly switch on when we're faced with a threat (or, in the case of anxiety, the anticipation of one), and then switch back off again when the threat has been dealt with or prevented. As we've explored, one challenge modern humans face is that we can inadvertently *fuel* these experiences of threat by trying to avoid the experience, mentally reliving the threat through our thoughts and imagery, acting out the threat emotion in problematic ways, or criticising ourselves for struggling. In this way, a big part of the problem isn't about the threats themselves, but in *how we relate to the threat emotion*.

This 'G' skill, **giving yourself permission to feel what you're feeling**, presents us with a very different way of relating to threat emotions. As we explored in the previous module, threat emotions like anger are *uncomfortable*, for reasons based in our evolution. I think one thing our modern culture has got wrong is the idea that being uncomfortable means something is wrong (or wrong with us) that needs to be fixed, and that we can't (or shouldn't have to) bear being uncomfortable for any length of time.

Giving yourself permission is an extension of the **accept** and **endure** skills we covered in the previous module. In this 'G' skill, we're taking the acceptance of what we're feeling ('I'm really angry right now') and extending it in a compassionate way: 'I'm allowed to be angry. It's not my fault that I'm feeling this way, and I can bear it. I wonder what would be helpful in working with this uncomfortable feeling?' (cue distress tolerance skills from the previous module). We're tossing aside the idea that we *shouldn't* or *shouldn't have to* feel certain ways and honouring how we actually feel. Instead of *reacting* to the emotions, we're accepting them, acknowledging their validity and valuing them for what they're attempting to tell us (emotions like anger, fear and anxiety are our threat system's efforts to alert us to potential dangers or blocks to our progress, and get us moving to address these threats).

Instead of rejecting, denying or inhabiting our angry selves, we're honouring their intention (to keep us safe and keep us making progress to our goals) *and* recognising that, most of the time, the behaviour advocated by our angry selves probably isn't the best way of responding to the situations we're faced with. It's like having a child or dear friend who is very worked up about something (and adamant that we should respond in a particular way, and *now*) but who doesn't fully understand the situation. We don't want to *reject* our angry selves. We want to compassionately understand them and how they came to be this way. We want to consider what they are telling us, and what they need. We want to help them.

As we approach **giving ourselves permission**, our efforts can be helped by connecting with the caring, wise and confident perspective of the compassionate self, and this intersects with our next 'G' skill: **generating compassionate responses**. This angry version of us is uncomfortable and suffering. It is possible for your compassionate self to extend compassionate understanding to this angry self.

This involves shifting into the kind, wise, confident perspective of the compassionate self, and considering how to help the angry self – validating it, supporting it, considering what it needs, and making helpful suggestions. Imagine your angry self as being triggered, and suffering. We want to activate a different, compassionate version of ourselves to help. What would your compassionate self say to help your angry self when you've been triggered? As the examples below demonstrate, this can involve bringing together many of the skills we've covered so far: we want to *validate* the angry self (communicate that we accept the anger as a real experience that makes sense), *accept and value* the angry self (because it isn't the angry self's fault that it has been triggered – that has to do with our history and our tricky brain), and offer to *help* the angry self in managing this challenging situation. I've included some blanks you can use for practice.

Directing compassion to the angry self

- 'This is really difficult. Given what I know about myself and my history, it makes a lot of sense that this would be triggering. It's not my fault that I'm struggling.'

- 'My threat system is really going right now. This is very uncomfortable. Maybe it would help to slow things down with some soothing rhythm breathing.'

- 'I hate feeling like this. It's difficult to struggle with this anger. I didn't choose to feel this way, but I'm doing my best and I'm doing it for really good reasons.'

- 'I'm really angry right now, and I'm fantasising about lashing out. Of course I would feel this way, but I don't want to make things worse. Maybe I could give myself some space until I'm feeling less heated before I do anything about this.'

- 'I'm doing that thing I do again – beating myself up for getting angry. It's not my fault I'm feeling this – it's my threat system trying to protect me. I wonder what might help my threatened self feel safe so I can come back and deal with this situation?'

- _____

- _____

- _____

- _____

The key is to engage with the angry self – with ourselves when we're struggling with anger – in the same way we'd approach someone we care about deeply who is struggling. Rather than putting the angry self in the captain's chair or banishing it from the ship, we're working to help it feel safe, and taking responsibility for charting a compassionate course.

As we haven't heard from our companions for a few modules, let's catch up with them for our final reflection:

What was it like to explore giving yourself permission to feel whatever you're feeling? How might this be an important step in working with anger?

James: *This was a powerful module for me, and a strange one, but it's helped me make some shifts. I've always been ashamed of my anger. Sure, I'd make excuses, blame other people and pretend it didn't happen . . . but underneath that there was always a sense that something was wrong with me. I guess I've always thought that maybe I'm just a shitty person, and if people find that out, they won't want anything to do with me. I've started to figure out that I'm not that special or different – I'm a guy who struggles, just like everyone else, and the thing I struggle with happens to be anger. There's been a gradual softening. Instead of losing it all the time, I can sometimes recognise I'm getting angry and just tell myself, 'Yeah, you're a little worked up and that's going to happen sometimes.' Part of it is giving myself permission to feel it and not have to react to it, and part of it is recognising my 'angry self' isn't an asshole . . . he's struggling and needs my help. It's weird to talk about it like that, but it helps. I guess it makes it feel like it's not such a big deal – something I can work with. Don't get me wrong, I've got a long way to go. But something's shifted. It's emotional to write about it – in a good way. Like, 'Maybe I can be a good person after all.'*

Antwan: *Like a lot of it, this 'giving permission' stuff seemed silly on the front end, but I think it's helped me face some things . . . to admit I've had problems with how I've handled things. Sometimes I think all that 'you've gotta respect me' and other stuff I learned from my dad set me up to have a hard time admitting when I've done something wrong or, like, to be able to look at what I do and question it rather than automatically try to justify it. He could never do that. I kinda feel bad for him now. It's hard to not ever be able to admit you got something wrong. Thinking about him also makes this 'giving permission' stuff feel scary, because it brings up anger but a lot of other stuff as well. I really wish I had a father who loves me, you know? I see other kids and their dads, and it breaks my heart – makes me sad and angry, all kinds of stuff. I don't know what to do with it. I guess the point is that maybe some things just do break your heart, and you can give yourself permission to be broken-hearted rather than just turning it all into rage. But man, it sure hurts.*

Jordan: *I've been so ashamed and critical of my feelings. I know this book is about anger, but this 'giving permission' stuff has helped with my anxiety, too. It's become clear that I have a really active threat system, and that's not my fault. It's weird to say that: 'It's not my fault.' Anxiety comes up in me all the time, including when I notice angry feelings. Now, instead of just shutting down and crying, I'm trying to tell my anxious/angry/emotional self, 'It's okay . . . you're feeling stuff. People feel stuff. That's not a bad thing.' For a long time, I was so scared of these feelings that I just tried to shut it all down, but I think I ended up shutting down a lot of the good feelings too. It's starting to feel like I've got some more spaciousness in my life. It's nice.*

Final reflection

What was it like to explore giving yourself permission to feel whatever you're feeling? How might this be an important step in working with anger?

Module 36: Generating Compassionate Responses

This module focuses on our second 'G' skill: **generating compassionate responses**. The good news is we've already done half of the work – relating compassionately to our angry selves rather than acting out, avoiding or beating ourselves up for experiencing the anger. Now let's focus on the triggering situation itself, and how we might work with it as our compassionate selves.

Embodying our compassionate selves

Once again, we want to slow things down (beginning with some soothing rhythm breathing) and step into the caring, wise, confident presence of the compassionate self. Dig in to the practice, as an actor would with a role. Imagine being filled with a deep, caring commitment to help address this struggle. Imagine being wise, viewing the situation from multiple perspectives, thinking flexibly and creatively, understanding the challenge and where everyone involved is coming from. Imagine feeling the courage to face this experience, and the confidence that *you will figure out helpful ways to work with it*. Imagine how this compassionate version of you feels: calm, centred and strong.

Embodying your compassionate self, bring your awareness and compassionate motivation to the experience or situation that has triggered your anger, and then consider how you'll approach the situation from this place of compassion. First, bring the situation to mind, and then consider some questions:

- **What would my compassionate self *notice and attend to* right now?** (Looking for signs of suffering and cues about what might be helpful.)

- **How would my compassionate self *understand* what is happening here?** (Curiously seeking understanding rather than assigning blame, considering the perspectives of everyone involved and how their behaviour makes sense from their side.)

- **How would my compassionate self *feel* right now?** (Imagine feeling calm, confident and committed to figuring out a helpful way to engage with the situation.)

- **What would my compassionate self *care about*? What would they be *motivated to do*?** (Imagine shifting from a desire to defend or attack to a focus on addressing the situation in ways that help both you and others, and fit with the person you want to be.)

- **What would my compassionate self *do*?** (Come up with a plan of action – what specifically will you do to address the situation?)

- **Now, imagine that you (as your compassionate self) have encountered this situation. Imagine what you would do and how it might play out.** (For example, imagine different ways of engaging with the situation and how they might go, to help you select the most helpful approach.)

With our companions, let's consider some examples of how this might play out:

James

Trigger situation: *I'll use a common example for me – we've made plans and something goes wrong. Let's say we've planned to watch the World Cup together, but the internet goes out and we can't stream the games.*

Typical anger response: *Historically, I'd get angry – reacting like the day was ruined. I'd probably start complaining about the internet service and how much we pay for it. Then I might get blamey – maybe questioning the kids or Sarah if they'd messed with the Wi-Fi router, even though I know they never touch it. At this point, everyone in the family would probably go their separate ways, and I'd go off in a huff to do whatever, feeling frustrated at what happened and ashamed, knowing I'd made it bigger than it needed to be. I'd come back later and apologise, but it would feel hollow, because it's the same thing I've done again and again.*

Imagine facing the trigger as your compassionate self. What would you be attending to? *First, I'd attend to what was happening in me – noticing myself getting heated, the thoughts of the day being ruined starting to show up ... that sort of thing. I'd notice that this is the moment when I can decide to do the same old thing that will ruin the day, or to handle it differently.*

What would your compassionate self understand about what is happening? *My compassionate self would understand two things. First, it's not surprising that I'm feeling triggered by the situation, as this is just the sort of thing that sets me off. The second is that this situation is not that big of a deal.*

How would your compassionate self feel? *My compassionate self would be calm and not blow things up. The internet goes out sometimes. It makes sense that might happen during the World Cup, with so many people streaming it. My compassionate self would also understand that there are lots of options for watching the games, and confident I'd be able to sort it.*

What would your compassionate self care about? What would they be motivated to do? *Well, obviously to figure out how to watch the games with my family. But my compassionate self would also recognise that the games are much less important than my relationship with my family and the example I want to set for the kids. Given my history, I might recognise this as a chance to show them I've made progress, that I'm not going to overreact to little things like this any more.*

What would your compassionate self do? *I've been thinking about this as we've gone along. First, I'd calm myself down – probably do some breathing and remind myself that this is not a big deal unless I make it one, that I can handle this. I'd then suggest we go to the pub! Every pub in town is going to be showing the games, and it would be a fun time out with the family.*

How do you think it might turn out? *Assuming we found a pub with the game on, I think it would be a fun time that would bring our family closer. Watching the game together at the pub would probably even be more fun than watching it at home – the kids love going out. I think it would bring Sarah and I closer as well, because she's noticed and appreciated when I've handled things like that well. Even if things didn't go smoothly – say, we couldn't find a pub showing the game, or couldn't find a spot – I think there are ways we could still make it a fun day if I didn't ruin it by overreacting.*

In considering James's example, we see how he was able to recognise his historical patterns and figure out how to engage with the situation compassionately. He identified the need to work with his anger first (in his case, by doing soothing rhythm breathing and compassionate self-coaching, reminding himself this wasn't a big deal and that he could handle it) and then moved on to addressing the situation itself.

Let's see how Antwan's example plays out:

Antwan

Trigger situation: *Let's say I'm in class with Mrs Saunders, who's never seemed to like me, and I get a text. Although I check it quickly, she sees me, and says my name in that tone of voice I freaking hate. That's the kind of thing that happens all the time.*

Typical anger response: *If I'm having a good day, sometimes I just let it go. But a lot of times, I'll say something under my breath, so she can just hear it. Then she'll say something else, and back and forth until I snap at her and get sent out into the hall or she writes up a disciplinary report. My mum gets a notification of those, and if you get too many you get suspended.*

Imagine facing the trigger as your compassionate self. What would you be attending to? *I guess there's a lot of things that could go differently. Like, first, I'd notice my phone had vibrated, and I'd think about whether I should check it, rather than just pulling it out of my pocket automatically.*

What would your compassionate self understand about what is happening? *I'd understand I've got a choice. I know she hates it when we pull out our phones in class, even though I see other kids get away with it sometimes. Truthfully, I've done it and not got caught, too. So I guess I'd understand that if I choose to check my phone, I'm kinda disrespecting her and daring her to do something – that it's on me.*

How would your compassionate self feel? *More laid-back. I'd know I have control over the situation. I can choose to wait until class is over to look at my phone. If I can't resist, I can at least wait until she's not likely to see me check it. And, if she does catch me, I could still be chill, knowing it was my choice to play the game and I knew what would happen. Play stupid games, win stupid prizes.*

What would your compassionate self care about? What would they be motivated to do? *To keep from getting caught up in that same old cycle that ends with me getting in trouble. It would be better to do almost anything else.*

What would your compassionate self do? *Knowing me, I probably couldn't resist checking my phone. So I'd probably watch for a time she wasn't looking, check then and hope she didn't see. But if she did see and say something, I could say sorry. She probably wouldn't know what to do! Also, although it's starting to feel less unfair than I've thought in the past, if it really seemed like she was picking on me more than other kids, I guess I could talk to her. Just tell her it seems like she was getting on me for stuff she didn't get on other kids for, and that it feels unfair. I'm not sure where that would go, but at least it would be on the table.*

How do you think it might turn out? *I kinda know how it would turn out, because I've had days I was feeling good and didn't let it bother me. Even if she catches me and says something, if I say sorry or just shut up, it's over. I need to keep that in mind.*

Antwan's responses tell us some important things. When he paused to consider how his compassionate self would understand things, he began to question the narrative his angry self had been running with – that his teacher was relating to him unfairly. He was able to acknowledge that, like other kids, he'd sometimes got away with the behaviour. More than this, he was able to acknowledge that he had a *choice* in how things play out, and that he could take control of the situation to keep it from escalating. He even considered an assertive response he could make should he continue to feel that things in the classroom were unfair.

Now let's consider Jordan's experience:

Jordan

Trigger situation: *One thing that really bothers me is little displays of sexism in the workplace. I've got a couple of male colleagues that say things to me that really drive me crazy. They comment on my appearance in ways that make me uncomfortable, or randomly tell me to 'smile'. I've never seen someone say that to a man, but it happens all the time to me and other women in the office. Standard microaggression stuff, but it drives me crazy.*

Typical anger response: *Usually, I get uncomfortable when I notice myself getting angry. My stomach shrinks into a tight ball, and there's all this tension in my jaw and my forehead. When I notice it playing out, I get anxious. I criticise myself for being too sensitive. I also criticise myself for not doing anything – 'If it's such a big deal to you, you should say something . . .'. It's paralysing. I can end up crying and feeling pathetic. It's awful.*

Imagine facing the trigger as your compassionate self. What would you be attending to? *I think as my compassionate self, I'd notice what happened, and what was happening in my body. I'd feel the sensations coming up.*

What would your compassionate self understand about what is happening? *As my compassionate self, I'd understand the trigger as a sexist microaggression they probably aren't even aware of and don't mean anything by, but which is very real. It's clear I'm not making it up – this stuff has been documented in all kinds of research, books, etc. I'd also recognise I'm having a normal emotional response – it makes sense I would be upset when people treat me in ways I'm not comfortable with. I'd also understand that beating myself up for what I'm feeling and how I'm reacting doesn't help.*

How would your compassionate self feel? *As my compassionate self, I'd still be bothered by what happened, I think. It isn't okay! But I'd accept my reaction, and I think there'd be a calmness underneath everything, as I recognised my experience was valid.*

What would your compassionate self care about? What would they be motivated to do? *My compassionate motivation would be to help myself feel safe first, so I could decide what I wanted to do. Then I'd see what might be done to address the situation.*

What would your compassionate self do? *First, I think as my compassionate self, I'd validate what I was feeling in the way the book describes at different points. It makes sense that this would be a trigger for me. And it makes sense that feeling anger would be uncomfortable for me, because growing up I was taught it was unacceptable for me to be angry. I'd remind myself that what I'm feeling is real, that it's okay, and that it's not my fault. In terms of the situation, I'm not sure what I'd do. I think calling people out directly might be tricky and blow things up, so I might just try to say something in a staff meeting – to let people know it isn't appreciated to comment on women's appearance in the workplace, or to tell us to smile – basically anything you wouldn't say to another man. That would be hard, but I've got a co-worker who's complained to me about the same things happening to her. It might be easier if we addressed it together, either in the meeting or with our manager sometime so that he could address it.*

How do you think it might turn out? *Well, if nothing else, I'd feel better if I stopped beating myself up, whatever I did! But as I finished that last response, it occurred to me that talking with Margot about saying something could make it feel safer for both of us and make it harder for us to be marginalised in that 'Jordan's so sensitive . . .' sort of way. I think we could do it. Although they might roll their eyes behind our backs, my male co-workers are decent guys at heart, and if they understood that it actually bothered us, I think they'd change their behaviour. Even if they didn't, at least I'd have done something.*

Jordan's response gives us a different picture from what we've seen before, in that her struggles with anger don't involve acting out in ways that impact others, but in repressing it and attacking herself. In thinking it through, she noted that a compassionate approach would involve dropping the self-criticism, validating her own experience and considering what might be helpful in addressing the triggering situation. Considering the situation as her compassionate self, she identified factors that help her address obstacles she'd faced in the past – connecting with a co-worker who'd struggled with the same issues to figure out how to proceed together. She also noted that a compassionate response was likely to work better for her *regardless of how the situation turned out*, because she wouldn't be magnifying her distress through self-attacking and rejecting her emotions.

When you're ready, take a few moments to slow down your breath and connect with the committed, wise, confident presence of your compassionate self. Embodying your compassionate self, use the form opposite to consider how you might work with a typical triggering situation (a reproducible handout of the form is also included in Appendix B, or you can download or print it from https://overcoming.co.uk/715/resources-to-download).

Working compassionately with triggers

Trigger situation: _____

_____

_____

Typical anger response: _____

_____

_____

Imagine facing the trigger as your compassionate self. What would you be attending to?_____

_____

_____

What would your compassionate self understand about what is happening?_____

_____

_____

How would your compassionate self feel? _____

_____

_____

What would your compassionate self care about? What would they be motivated to do? _____

_____

_____

What would your compassionate self do? _____

_____

_____

How do you think it might turn out? _____

_____

_____

Final reflection

How are you feeling about this idea of the compassionate self? Is it beginning to feel more natural? Can you think of anything that might help you embody this perspective (for example, bringing to mind someone you experience as having those qualities, and considering how *they* might respond to the triggering situation, or what advice they might give you)?

_____

_____

_____

_____

_____

_____

Aside from the one you selected for the exercise above, in what other situations might it be helpful to apply this compassionate approach?

_____

_____

_____

_____

_____

_____

Module 37: Enacting Compassionate Responses

This module and the next will explore the 'E' skills for working with triggers: **enacting** compassionate alternatives, **establishing** compassionate brain patterns, and **experiencing** ourselves as a compassionate person. These skills are the culmination of all the work we've done – both in learning compassionate ways of working with trigger situations and in transforming our experience of ourselves:

- **Enacting compassionate alternatives:** Implementing our compassionate responses – both in relating to our own emotional experience and the situation that triggered it.

- **Establishing compassionate brain patterns:** Whenever we engage in compassionate behaviour rather than habitual anger responses, we strengthen brain patterns that support our ability to live lives of our choosing, rather than lives dictated by our anger.

- **Experiencing yourself as a compassionate person:** As we observe ourselves acting out of compassion rather than anger, we begin to relate to ourselves in a new way: as a compassionate person. The more we *embody* the compassionate self, the more we *become* a kind, wise, strong, confident, compassionate person.

Enacting compassionate alternatives

In the previous module, you considered a trigger and came up with a plan for how you would understand what was happening, relate it to your own experience and respond to the situation as your compassionate self. Now it's time to put the plan into action. It's important to recognise this isn't a one-time-only process.

Planning for obstacles

As I've emphasised time and again, whenever we try something new there will almost always be obstacles that arise. Our success will often depend on how we respond to these obstacles. Rather than letting obstacles stop us in our tracks, we want to anticipate and plan for them, and when *unanticipated* obstacles occur, pause to consider how we can address them.

Rather than just hoping nothing goes wrong with our plan to work with triggers, we want to get curious – *assuming* things almost certainly *won't* go perfectly according to plan the first few times and, when they don't, trying to learn as much as we can to help our next effort be even more successful. We're sort of making it *boring*. It's not a superhero movie. We're not dramatically pouring all our will into one final, heroic effort. We're spending time thinking about how to approach things (Module 36), then doing our best to enact the plan while curiously noticing what is helpful and what obstacles get in the way. Then we revise the plan and give it another go, again and again . . . making each effort a bit better than the one before. *Every time we do this* – every time we step back, acknowledge an obstacle and consider how we (as our compassionate selves) will work with it – *we're building and strengthening brain patterns that will transform us into more compassionate people.* Like learning any other skill, practising on the very edge of what we're capable of is what helps us get better, quickly.[1]

Below, I've included a form you can use to work through this process. First, let's look at an example from James's experience:

Enacting compassionate alternatives

Trigger situation: *The situation I'd planned for was kind of generic – 'when something unexpectedly goes wrong . . .'. It didn't take long for that to happen. I've been preoccupied by work and working on this stuff, so Valentine's Day snuck up on me. I'd planned to cook Sarah a nice, romantic meal. I used to do this when we were dating and she loved it. But on the day, although I thought I'd have time to stop at the market in the afternoon to buy the ingredients for the meal, a lot of unexpected things happened at work, which blew my plan up.*

My response: *Initially, I started to get upset – that chaotic mix of anger and shame ('I've screwed it up again!') started coming up. This time I recognised it and pulled out my plan from the last module. When I stepped into my compassionate self, it all became clear. I was upset because the meal was blown up . . . but, by slowing down, I was able to recognise it wasn't about the meal. It was about letting Sarah know how much I love and appreciate her. The twenty minutes I had free in my day wasn't nearly long enough for a trip to the market, but it was enough time to write a letter telling Sarah how much I love her, how much I appreciate her standing by me even when I've made it difficult, and how much I cherish our life together. Then I ordered takeaway from our favourite restaurant, including a selection of nice desserts the whole family loves.*

How did things turn out? *We ended up cuddling on the couch, watching our favourite movie together. It was a great night and I feel like it brought us closer.*

What was helpful? What did you do well? *I recovered well. Although, initially, I was starting to get worked up, I was able to recognise it. Once I asked, 'What would my compassionate self care about?' it was all over – my compassionate self only cared about having a good night with Sarah, and my anger couldn't stand up to that. It seemed small in comparison.*

Did any obstacles come up? If so, what were they? *Not sure if it's an obstacle, but if I'd done my shopping in advance rather than assuming I'd have time, I'd have avoided the whole thing. But I can't imagine the evening would have turned out any better than it did.*

What would you (as your compassionate self) want to improve on in your next effort? What might help you with that? *Next time I'll plan ahead if I'm going to do something that takes so much time. I'd also like to get better at recognising my anger and shame a little more quickly – I spent several minutes upset about it and beating myself up. But I was able to snap out of it, reminding myself that I usually do have some time in the afternoon, and I'm proud of how I recovered.*

In unpacking his experience, James recognised how shifting into his compassionate self transformed what was happening – connecting him to what really matters to him. He was also able to extend compassion to himself, acknowledging that he'd failed to leave himself enough time because he'd based his plan on his previous experience, and considered how to avoid such stress in the future.

There's a copy of the form for you to use overleaf (it's also included in Appendix B, or you can download or print it from https://overcoming.co.uk/715/resources-to-download).

Enacting compassionate alternatives

Trigger situation: _____

_____

My response: _____

_____

_____

How did things turn out? _____

_____

_____

What was helpful? What did you do well? _____

_____

_____

Did any obstacles come up? If so, what were they? _____

_____

_____

What would you (as your compassionate self) want to improve on in your next effort? What might help

you with that?_____

_____

_____

_____

_____

As we enact our compassionate plans for working with triggers, it's almost like there's a sequence of steps similar to the behaviour change plan from Module 16: Plan for the trigger or difficult situation ⟶ Do our best to enact the compassionate response ⟶ Assess how it went, revise the plan and repeat. Every time we go through this sequence, we're not just figuring out how to work with *this particular* challenging situation; we're also *learning a process* for working with whatever life throws at us. It's a process defined by the *courage* to face difficult situations, the *willingness* to accept that the process is difficult and will take time to get right, and a healthy dollop of *curiosity* – both about the obstacles that come up and about *what would be helpful in working with them*. Repeated over time, we're building and strengthening whole networks in our brains that will help us succeed in the future, which is the focus of the 'E' skills we'll be covering in the next module.

Final reflection

How does this process fit with how you imagined it would be to work with your anger? What do you like about it? What has been challenging?

_____

_____

_____

_____

_____

_____

_____

_____

What might help you face challenges that arise, and keep going – even when it gets hard? How might your compassionate self validate, support and encourage the version of you that struggles?

_____

_____

_____

_____

_____

_____

_____

_____

Module 38: Establishing and Experiencing

These last two 'E' skills are about tying it all together: considering how our efforts to work compassionately with triggers are building and strengthening brain patterns that support the lives we want to have, and experiencing ourselves in a new way – not as an 'angry person' but as a strong, balanced, compassionate person, who sometimes struggles but who can figure out how to work with everything life throws at us.

Establishing new patterns in the brain

This 'skill' involves reminding ourselves that every time we try a new behaviour, we're changing our brains – building and strengthening connections and patterns that shape how we'll respond in the future, bringing us closer and closer to the version of ourselves that we want to be. It's also a reminder of why change is so hard: because the old, habitual patterns were worn in over many, many trials, and won't simply disappear overnight just because we've decided we don't want to be like that any more. The decision is important, but it's the beginning. We need to *keep going* – and remembering how our brains work can help us stay motivated when things get hard.

Sometimes I use an analogy to talk about this. My home in Spokane backs up against a beautiful forest. Imagine I enjoy going for walks in the woods and that, every day, I walk the same way. Over time, my repeated walking will 'wear in' the path – smoothing out the terrain, deepening it, kicking aside the obstacles. My repeated walking creates a 'path of least resistance' in the woods and, when it rains, where does the water run? Down the path!

Let's say that after a while it becomes clear this path I've worn in has some unwanted consequences – every time it rains, water runs down the path, flooding my back yard. If I want to change this situation, I need to do two things: stop deepening the old path and create a new one to walk (because a fellow's got to get his exercise). So I make a plan – considering where I'd like my new path to go, and how I'll help myself remember to walk the new path rather than the old one. Let's imagine the first week, I do pretty well and walk the new path five out of seven days, only having two days in which I understandably forget and follow the old path out of habit. After that first week, does the forest look different?

Not really. The old path is still solidly there, maybe with a few pine needles having dropped onto it. The new path is barely noticeable at this stage – maybe some underbrush is tamped down so we can make it out, but otherwise it looks just like the rest of the forest. But let's imagine I keep it up . . . rarely getting it perfect, but consistently managing to walk the new path at least a few times per week. Every time I notice I've slipped up and started down the old path (as happens a lot in the beginning), I hop off and head over to the new one.

Over time, the forest gradually changes. The new path becomes more worn in. As this happens, it gets *easier* to refrain from walking the old path (as I get more used to walking the new one, which is becoming more noticeable) and, when it does happen, I begin to catch myself more quickly and change paths. As I'm walking it less and less frequently, the old path begins to deteriorate . . . never completely disappearing but gradually growing over and filling with detritus. Eventually, the balance in the forest shifts – we've *established a new path* of least resistance and, when it rains, the water runs down the new path, sparing my yard from being flooded.

I like this analogy for a few reasons. I think it's fairly useful for considering how change in our brain happens as we establish and strengthen new patterns and allow old ones to weaken over time through lack of use. But, for me, there are two important lessons here. First, *lasting change requires persistent practice over time* to build and strengthen the brain patterns that underlie these new ways of responding. It takes time and effort to change, and knowing that going in, we can offer ourselves some patience and encouragement.

Second, if we continue to behave in the new ways we've planned – for example, sincerely practising compassion over time – we can be confident that we *will* change. It's just how the brain works . . . the more we activate the patterns, the stronger they get. We can't keep walking the same path in a forest *without* changing the forest (which is why we want to stay on trail when walking – so we don't create lots of other unwanted paths). Yes, change is difficult. But we can *know* that if we keep going, we *will* change . . . even as we know that trying something new once or twice and then going back to the same old thing probably won't get us anywhere.

The last thing I want to say has to do with when things get hard. It turns out that new learning happens most efficiently when we're operating right at the edge of what we can do – when we're focused very hard on doing something new, and we're *struggling*. When we're doing the same old things we're comfortable with, we're mildly strengthening old patterns, but we're not building new ones (this is why I spent thirty years as a crappy guitar player before learning how to practise effectively). We *change* by stretching ourselves – by continuing to try when it gets hard. Failure experiences signal opportunities for growth, but we have to seize them. When we try, fail, give up and go back to the same old thing, we learn nothing. But if we fail and then go back to the point where things went awry, *slow things down and focus our efforts*, and try again until we get it right (and then practise it some more, to cement the learning), we're helping our brains build the patterns that lead to future success.[1]

This is important. It's not about getting things exactly right the first time. It's about trying, failing, learning, slowing things down and trying again, getting a little better every time. *This is how we change*. Don't beat yourself up when you slip up. Get curious about the obstacles – how and why you got tripped up – and how you can make the next effort better. Imagery can be helpful, as it allows us to revisit situations again and again, imagining different ways to approach things and how they might turn out. This way, when the situation shows up in our lives again, we're ready for it – we've mapped out the path we want to take. Keep going – your brain will thank you for it later (in the form of making things easier).

Describe your 'new path'. As anger triggers and life difficulties arise in your life, how do you want to respond to them? How would this compassionate version of you respond when things get tricky, or when you aren't met with immediate success? How will you help yourself keep going to build these new paths, even when you get discouraged?

James: *My new path is all about the man I want to be. It's about showing the people I love that they can count on me when they need me, and not becoming part of the problem when things don't go my way. I want to meet challenges with centredness and set a good example for my kids, so they'll be prepared to face difficult things in their lives. I think keeping my focus on what's really important will help the most – triggers are nothing compared to that.*

Antwan: *For me it's about not letting other people push my buttons. Whatever other people do, I want to control how I respond and not react in ways that cause problems. I was thinking about my father the other day, and realised that he demanded respect, but he didn't earn it. I want to earn it. I want to be respected for the kind of man I am – who I am and what I do. If I keep that in mind when people come at me, I think I can hold my ground, in a good way.*

Jordan: *The word 'confident' really jumped out at me. It's still hard to imagine myself as confident all the time, but as I've stopped beating myself up so much it's getting easier to recognise my strengths. I've started speaking up at meetings and sharing my ideas more. People have seemed to respond well. I also spoke with Margot regarding how to address the stuff in the office. Although we haven't decided how we're going to proceed yet, it was nice to share our experiences and commiserate with each other, and I think we're going to end up being friends. My new path is going to be about allowing myself to feel what I feel, not beating myself up, and learning to be assertive in the world. It may sound silly, but I've been thinking of getting a little tattoo – I'm not sure of what, yet – to remind me to go easy on myself when I'm struggling.*

Reflection

Describe your 'new path'. As anger triggers and life difficulties arise in your life, how do you want to respond to them? How would this compassionate version of you respond when things get tricky, or when you aren't met with immediate success? How will you help yourself keep going to build these new paths, even when you get discouraged?

_____

_____

_____

_____

_____

Experiencing yourself as a compassionate person

This is less a 'skill' than a willingness to relate to yourself in a new way. Some people who struggle with anger have had lots of experience feeling like 'the problem'. Even when the things we're angry about are valid, if we express anger in ways that trigger threat in other people, the focus of 'the problem' can shift away from whatever happened and towards us and our behaviour. Over time, we can have many experiences – from receiving direct criticism to noticing others avoid us and walk on eggshells around us – that give us a sense that 'there's something wrong with me'. To avoid this shame, we may find ourselves constantly on the defensive, rationalising everything we do, even when we know we're in the wrong, or pulling back from relationships with others. If we come to relate to ourselves in these ways, it can undermine everything we do.

If you've made it this far, you're clearly not messing around. And if you've been applying the material as we've gone along, I hope you've seen positive changes in your life, or at least in how you understand and relate to some of your experiences. You're now deep into a book that's all about responding to suffering and life difficulties with _compassion_ rather than anger-driven reactivity. What does that say about you? Rather than criticising yourself for your flaws, weaknesses and places where you screw up, what would it mean to give yourself credit for the effort you've made and for the motivation behind that effort . . . *what it means about you that you're making this effort*. What if you gave yourself permission to recognise that you're a human being who will struggle, just like all of us do, but who is committed to working with these struggles in ways that will be *helpful* for both you and others? What if you were to experience yourself not as an 'angry person' or 'the problem' but as a *compassionate person* who is taking responsibility for their struggles and working to improve?

Take a moment to reflect on how you experience yourself. Have you noticed any changes? How would you *like* to experience yourself? What might help you grow in that direction?

James: *I'm coming along slowly. I definitely had a sense of myself as 'the one who screws everything up'. I'd bet if they were completely honest, my family probably saw me like that, too . . . although not completely so. Now I still struggle, but I haven't given up. I guess that means something good about me – that I care enough to try and do better, even when it's hard. I feel good about that. What would help? I think to just keep going, to keep connecting with my compassionate self and to act from that perspective. I was sceptical, but it's really helped.*

Antwan: *Before, I liked to think of myself as a badass, as a guy who wouldn't take shit from anyone. I still don't plan to take shit from people, but I've realised that doesn't mean I have to react to everything they do. That just gives them control. I want to be in control of my own life. Also, I used to feel threatened by stuff as a man. I'd get mad when women would say stuff about men . . . like they were attacking me. Now I know it's not about me. They're probably saying that stuff because men have hurt them, and they're tired of it. I think I'm getting better at listening to stuff without having to make it about me. I guess that's compassion, I don't know. I think that will help me going forward – keeping in mind that a lot of what other people do is about what's happened to them, and I can try to understand that stuff rather than having to react to it.*

This brings up something else for me. I think a lot of my problems are related to my father leaving us. I've got so many feelings about that, and I think that's underneath a lot of my anger. There's a lot of hurt in there, and I don't know what to do with it. I try to avoid it – I've even been in and out of it in these reflections – but it's always there, underneath everything. I've never thought of going to see a therapist before, but if I'm going to be the man I want to be, I think I'm going to need some help with this.

Jordan: *I'm a work in progress! That critical voice in my head still shows up a lot, and sometimes she says some really mean stuff. But now I have another voice as well, and it's a compassionate voice. It helps me realise that I learned to beat myself up and that it makes sense I'd do it, but that it isn't helpful. It also reminds me that it's not my fault that I learned to do that. This new voice sees my strengths and helps me ask 'What do I need?' or 'What would be helpful?' when my weaknesses show up. That's new for me, and to be honest it's a little scary. The idea of giving myself credit or seeing myself as confident, strong or worth caring about still feels weird and a bit fake. But it makes sense that after a lifetime of attacking myself it would be hard for that to feel natural. Overall, I like what I'm seeing so far, so my plan is to keep going.*

Reflecting on our self-experience and how it has changed over time can help us feel good about our progress, and it can also highlight sticking points and areas in which we might want to put in more attention and effort. As Antwan's response highlights, it can also help us recognise areas in which we might benefit from getting some help – his example of grief and loss is one of those areas in which a qualified therapist can help us unpack things that are hard to tackle on our own. This again points out the *courage* of compassion – it takes a lot of courage to ask for help when we're used to trying to handle everything by ourselves.

Final reflection

Take a moment to reflect on how you experience yourself. Have you noticed any changes? How would you *like* to experience yourself? What might help you grow in that direction?

_____

_____

_____

_____

_____

_____

_____

Module 39: The Compassionate Letter

In writing this book, my goal was to be a guide and companion as you apply compassion focused therapy in working with your anger and, as I begin this final module, I find myself a little sad to be shifting out of that role. This module is about *you* stepping into the role of guide and companion – for your compassionate self to serve as guide and companion to help your angry, anxious and struggling selves whenever you feel threatened and need a little help. You've been developing your compassionate self for exactly this sort of task.

One of my favourite ways for us to 'be there for ourselves' involves writing a compassionate letter. In a compassionate letter, we write from the compassionate self to any one of our struggling selves – to read when we've been triggered, find ourselves struggling or must face an experience we know will challenge us. In this letter, we put everything we know will be helpful to our struggling selves, filling it with validation, support, encouragement, and practical reminders and suggestions around what might be helpful. Let's revisit some of the different components of compassion presented in Module 14 and consider how they might manifest in a letter:

- **Sympathy** and **acknowledging acceptance:** *If you're reading this, you're probably struggling. I'm sorry things are so difficult right now . . .*

- **Empathy:** *You're probably having lots of different feelings right now – anger, anxiety, maybe some shame and hopelessness. Given all you've been through, it makes sense that this would be hard, doesn't it?*

- **Courage:** *But you've done hard things before and you can face this.*

- **Kindness/caring commitment:** *Although it might not feel like it now, you're a good person and you're going to find a way through this. I'm here to help you.*

- **Wisdom and kind curiosity:** *You've learned a lot of things that can be helpful when things get hard. What do you need right now? What would be useful for you to remind yourself of as you face this? What might be helpful?*

- **Non-condemnation:** *Remember not to beat yourself up. We all struggle sometimes.*

- **Distress tolerance:** *It feels terrible right now. What might help you manage the* *discomfort while you figure it out? Try some soothing rhythm breathing, some imagery, or call Shane to see if he wants to grab dinner – that always helps you feel better.*

- **Confidence:** *This is hard, but you'll figure out how to work with it. You've done a lot of difficult things in your life.*

Some of my clients have written several compassionate letters to themselves, each one addressing a particular struggle they face. I like this exercise because it packs a lot of benefits into one practice. In writing the letter, we're developing our compassionate selves and using them to work with struggles we face, further strengthening those compassionate brain systems we've been building. We're normalising the fact that we'll struggle in our lives, setting ourselves up to relate compassionately to ourselves when that happens. And finally, we're producing a product – the letter itself – designed to support and help us out when we're struggling the most.

Let's look at one of James's compassionate letters as an example:

Dear James,

If you're reading this, it's probably been a difficult week. It makes sense that you're having strong feelings. You've worked hard at managing your anger, and it's easy to feel disappointed and upset with yourself when it feels you're backsliding. But you've done a lot of challenging things in your life, and there are always setbacks when we do something difficult, aren't there?

Remember that anger is a part of a threat system you didn't choose, and it's not your fault that you experience it. You came by it honestly, seeing it modelled when you were growing up. Habits run deep, and they're hard to change. But you've made a lot of progress, so try not to beat yourself up. The fact this matters so much to you is evidence you are a good husband and father, and Sarah and the kids have commented on how much better things have been since you started working on your anger.

You've shown courage in taking responsibility for your anger and learning to work with it, and you should be proud of yourself. Learning new ways to deal with things is difficult, so of course you won't always get it exactly right. It's okay to feel however you are feeling right now.

The reason you are feeling bad right now is that you care. Your hard work is paying off, even though it's hard to see sometimes. Maybe some of the skills you've learned might be helpful? You've always liked the safe place imagery exercise. Perhaps you could chat with Robert about how you're feeling – he always listens to you and seems to understand. Try to give yourself a break and remember you are doing this to set a good example for Aiden and Jaime. They deserve your love and compassion, and so do you.

Love,

James

James's letter demonstrates several aspects of compassion – validation, sympathy, empathy, encouragement – as well as practical suggestions about what he knows from previous experience tends to be helpful for him when he's struggling.

My compassionate letter

When you're ready, write yourself a compassionate letter. Take time to slow down your breath and connect with the qualities of your compassionate self. Imagine a future version of you, facing a common struggle. Imagine the feelings this struggling version of you might be experiencing. Consider how these feelings make sense and how challenging they are. What would this struggling version of you need in that moment? What could you offer them that would be helpful?

My compassionate letter

Going forwards, you may wish to revisit your letter, adding helpful elements as they occur to you. As I've stated again and again, one of the greatest strengths of our compassionate selves is *curiosity* – an intense interest in *discovering what is helpful*, both to help when we're struggling and in building meaningful, fulfilling lives going forwards. We want to collect helpful experiences, resources, strategies and relationships as we go through life, training our minds to notice and focus on what is helpful rather than ruminating on everything that is threatening.

Final reflection

Can you think of any other situation or struggle you may face in your future life that might merit a compassionate letter? What would you want to emphasise in that letter to your future self?

_____

_____

_____

_____

_____

_____

_____

Summary check-in

What progress have you seen in working with your anger, and how are you feeling about it?

_____

_____

_____

In what areas of your life is there still work to be done? How might you apply what you've learned to those areas?

_____

_____

_____

What might help you to continue to work compassionately with your anger and the challenges that come up in your life?

_____

_____

_____

What would be helpful to keep in mind going forwards, particularly when you struggle?

_____

_____

_____

A Word in Parting

In closing, I'd like to thank you for joining me on this journey. As you know, I've struggled with anger myself, and it's a hard road. I'm still on it, and the six months I've devoted to writing this book is part of my journey. In fact, so much of what my life is about – and any good I've put into the world – has resulted from my efforts to figure out how to work with my anger. I do quite well most of the time, and then sometimes things get tough for a while again. The key is to remember what we've learned and *use it*. If we do that, the benefits of compassion will go way beyond managing our anger – they can be the gateway to a life worth living.

I'm not worried about you. I know that if you keep going – keep considering what your compassionate self might do; keep giving yourself room to make mistakes; keep getting back up, dusting yourself off, asking for help when you need it, and thinking about how to do things a little bit better next time – I know that if you do that, you're going to be all right.

It occurs to me that if you're still with me to read this, you might be willing to consider going a little further.

The world is hurting. Suffering is everywhere. And you now know a lot about compassion and have some skills that are tailor-made to address that suffering. What if you didn't stop with anger? What if you took the same compassionate motivation you've devoted to this effort, looked out into the world and asked, *How can I help?* What might you do? The possibilities are endless.

Just as suffering is everywhere, beauty is everywhere, too. Take it in. Savour it. And don't be afraid to recognise all that is beautiful in you. You aren't perfect. No one is. But you are enough.

I believe in you.

Keep going.

Appendix A: Notes

Introduction

1. Much of the material throughout this book regarding compassion focused therapy, the nature of compassion and the compassionate self is rooted in the work of Professor Paul Gilbert. Interested readers can refer to the following books, which do an excellent job of unpacking these ideas:

   Gilbert, P., *The Compassionate Mind* (London: Robinson, 2009).

   Gilbert, P. and Choden, *Mindful Compassion* (London: Robinson, 2013).

   Irons, C. and Beaumont, E., *The Compassionate Mind Workbook* (London: Robinson, 2017).

2. *The Compassionate Mind Approach to Managing Your Anger* can be seen as a companion volume to this workbook. While this book emphasises engaging the reader in a reflective, interactive process of working with their anger, *The Compassionate Mind Approach to Managing Your Anger* has a greater emphasis on thoroughly unpacking and exploring the ideas of the approach, containing more didactic explanation – as such, it can be seen as a source text for readers working through this book:

   Kolts, R.L., *The Compassionate Mind Approach to Managing Your Anger: Using Compassion Focused Therapy* (London: Robinson, 2012).

Module 1

1. Villatte, M., Villatte, J.L. and Hayes, S.C., *Mastering the Clinical Conversation* (New York: Guilford Press, 2019).

Module 3

1. The compassionate self, and the CFT approach to it, is featured in all core texts in CFT (see note 1 for the Introduction, above).

Module 5

1. Kabat-Zinn, J., *Wherever You Go, There You Are: Mindfulness Meditation in Everyday Life* (New York: Hyperion, 1994).

2. Brach, T., *Radical Acceptance: Embracing Your Life with the Heart of a Buddha* (New York: Bantam, 2004).

3. Dr Elisha Goldstein features in the mindful check-in video noted in the text: www.you tube.com/watch?v=w1EZ_hpnhDM. Dr Goldstein has also written a book you may find helpful if you'd like to delve more deeply into using mindfulness to work with your anger: Goldstein, E., *The Now Effect: How a Mindful Moment Can Change the Rest of Your Life* (New York: Atria, 2013).

Module 6

1. Gilbert, P., McEwan, K., Matos, M. and Rivis, A., 'Fears of compassion: development of three self-report measures', *Psychology and Psychotherapy: Theory, Research, and Practice*, 84 (2011), pp. 239–55.

Module 7

1. There are lots of good resources on the science of attachment and how we're shaped by our early experiences. If you're interested in learning more, the following book explores these ideas: Levine, A. and Heller, R., *Attached: The New Science of Adult Attachment and How it Can Help You Find – and Keep – Love* (New York: TarcherPerigee, 2010).

Module 8

1. This model is based on the work of neuroscientists such as Richard Depue, Jaak Panksepp and Joseph LeDoux:

    Depue, R.A. and Morrone-Strupinsky, J.V., 'A neurobehavioral model of affiliative bonding', *Behavioural and Brain Sciences*, 28 (2005), pp. 313–95.

    LeDoux, J., *The Emotional Brain* (London: Weidenfeld & Nicolson, 1998).

    Panksepp, J., *Affective Neuroscience* (New York: Oxford University Press, 1998).

Module 10

1. Regarding attachment security, see:

    Mikulincer, M. and Shaver, P.R., 'Attachment security, compassion, and altruism', *Current Directions in Psychological Science*, 14 (2005), pp. 34–8.

    Mikulincer, M. and Shaver, P.R., *Attachment in Adulthood: Structure, Dynamics, and Change* (New York: Guilford Press, 2007).

    Mikulincer, M., Gillath, O., Halevy, V., Avihou, N., Avidan, S. and Eshkoli, N., 'Attachment theory and reactions to others' needs: evidence that activation of the sense of attachment security promotes empathic responses', *Journal of Personality and Social Psychology*, 81 (2001), pp. 1205–24.

2. It turns out that having too little *or* too much free time isn't great – the optimal amount is two to three hours per day: Sharif, M.A., Mogilner, C. and Hershfield, H.E., 'Having too little or too much time is linked to lower subjective well-being', *Journal of Personality and Social Psychology: Personality Processes and Individual Differences*, 121 (2021), pp. 933–47. https://doi.org/10.1037/pspp0000391

3. There's a large amount of study that's been put into understanding the ways our experiences and relationships impact our brains. Dr Dan Siegel is a pioneer in this area, and a good place to start is with his seminal text, *The Developing Mind*. I've listed a few other references below as well. Dr Siegel's audio CD set, *The Neurobiology of 'We'*, provides a particularly accessible entry point into this area of study.

    Cozolino, L., *The Neuroscience of Human Relationships: Attachment and the Developing Social Brain* (New York: Norton, 2006).

    LeDoux, J., *The Emotional Brain* (London: Weidenfeld & Nicolson, 1998).

    Schore, A., *Affect Regulation and the Origin of the Self* (New York: Taylor & Francis, 1994).

    Siegel, D.J., *The Developing Mind* (New York: Guilford Press, 2001).

    Siegel, D.J. and Hartzell, M., *Parenting from the Inside Out* (New York: Tarcher/Penguin, 2003).

    Siegel, D.J., *The Neurobiology of 'We': How Relationships, the Mind, and the Brain Interact to Shape Who We Are* [audio learning course] (Boulder, Colorado: Sounds True, 2008).

4. Mikulincer, M. and Shaver, P.R., *Attachment in Adulthood: Structure, Dynamics, and Change* (New York: Guilford Press, 2007).

Module 11

1. See notes 1 and 3 for Module 10, above.

2. Regarding oxytocin reducing amygdala activation, see:

Domes, G., Heinrichs, M., Glascher, J., Buchel, C., Braus, D.F. and Herpertz, S.C., 'Oxytocin attenuates amygdala responses to emotional faces regardless of valence', *Biological Psychiatry*, 62 (2007), pp. 1187–90.

Sobota, R., Mihara, T., Forrest, A., Featherstone, R.E. and Siegel, S.J., 'Oxytocin reduces amygdala activity, increases social interactions and reduces anxiety-like behavior irrespective of NMDAR antagonism', *Behavioral Neuroscience*, 129 (2015), pp. 389–98.

Module 15

1. Regarding exercise and decreased impulsivity, see: Ghahramani, M.H, Sohrabi, M., Kakhki, A.S. and Besharat, M.A., 'The effects of physical activity on impulse control, attention, decision-making and motor functions in students with high and low impulsivity', *Biosciences Biotechnology Research Asia*, 13(3) (2016). http://dx.doi.org/10.13005/bbra/2318

Module 16

1. Katy Milkman's book provides excellent guidance for helping us make life changes: Milkman, K., *How to Change: The Science of Getting from Where You Are to Where You Want to Be* (New York: Portfolio, 2021).

Module 17

1. The literature on how anger can impact our judgement and decision-making is nicely summarised in the following chapter and articles:

Bodenhausen, G.V., Sheppard, L.A. and Kramer, G.P., 'Negative affect and social judgment: the differential impact of anger and sadness', *European Journal of Social Psychology*, 24 (1994), pp. 45–62.

Litvak, P.M., Lerner, J.S., Tiedens, L.Z. and Shonk, K., 'Fuel in the fire: how anger impacts judgment and decision-making'. In Potegal, M., Stemmler, G. and Spielberger, C. (eds.), *International Handbook of Anger* (New York: Springer, 2010), pp. 287–310.

Tiedens, L.Z. and Linton, S., 'Judgment under emotional certainty and uncertainty: the effects of specific emotions on information processing', *Journal of Personality and Social Psychology*, 81 (2001), pp. 973–88.

2. Chimamanda Ngozie Adichie's excellent TED talk can be found by searching 'Adichie danger of a single story' or through this link: www.ted.com/talks/ chimamanda_ngozi_adichie_the_danger_of_a_single_story/comments.

3. Regarding anger and mortality risk, see:

Chida, Y. and Steptoe, A., 'The association of anger and hostility with future coronary heart disease: a meta-analytic review of prospective evidence', *Journal of the American College of Cardiology*, 17 (2009), pp. 936–46.

Trudel-Fitzgerald, C., Reduron, L.R., Kawachi, I. and Kubzansky, L.D., 'Specificity in associations of anger frequency and expression with different causes of mortality over 20 years', *Psychosomatic Medicine*, 83 (2021), pp. 402–9.

Module 21

1. A note about terms: You'll notice that I use the term 'emotional brain' in Module 21 and elsewhere in the book. In previous CFT resources, we've used the terms 'old brain' and 'new brain' to talk about the parts of our brains that perform different functions like thinking and feeling – recognising that some brain areas and functions are evolutionarily more ancient, while others (like those involved in complex thinking) appear to be 'newer'. In the psychology field in recent years, this way of talking about things has come under some controversy, as neuroscientists have correctly pointed out that the way the brain works is much more complicated than this. This is true – whatever we choose to call them, we don't actually have multiple different brains inside our heads . . . *and* in CFT, we've found that using terms like 'old brain' and 'new brain' (or 'emotional brain' and 'thinking brain') is a useful heuristic – a helpful *way of talking about* the tricky ways different aspects of our experience can interact and fuel one another in a simplified way that doesn't require us to use lots of distracting neurological terminology. I hope you find it helpful as well.

Module 22

1. Regarding shame and anger, see:

Tangney, J.P., Wagner, P.E., Fletcher, C. and Gramzow, R., 'Shamed into anger? The relation of shame and guilt to anger and self-reported aggression', *Journal of Personality and Social Psychology*, 62 (1992), pp. 669–75.

Tangney, J.P., Wagner, P.E., Hill-Barlow, D., Marschall, D.E. and Gramzow, R., 'Relation of shame and guilt to constructive versus destructive responses to anger across the lifespan', *Journal of Personality and Social Psychology*, 70 (1996), pp. 797–809.

2. Stanculete, M.F., Pojoga, C. and Dumitrascu, D.L., 'Experience of anger in patients with irritable bowel syndrome in Romania', *Clujul Medical*, 87 (2014), pp. 98–101.

3. The ability of physical symptoms to combine with cognitive attributions to shape how we feel is the subject of one of the best-known studies in psychology. The Schachter–Singer study has been the subject of controversy, but certainly has value in demonstrating how our physical experience can play a role in how we experience our emotions: Schachter, S. and Singer, J., 'Cognitive, social, and physiological determinants of emotional state', *Psychological Review, 69*(5) (1962), pp. 379–99. https://doi.org/10.1037/h0046234

Module 23

1. The following article summarises several studies on the strengths and weaknesses of self-monitoring interventions: Orji, R., Lomotey, R., Oyibo, K., Orji, F., Blustein, J. and Shahid, S., 'Tracking feels oppressive and "punishy": exploring the costs and benefits of self-monitoring for health and wellness', *Digital Health* (2018). https://doi.org/10.1177/2055207618797554

Module 24

1. Regarding breathwork, see: Zaccaro, A., Piarulli, A., Laurino, M., Garbella, E., Menicucci, D., Neri, B. and Gemignani, A., 'How breath-control can change your life: a systematic review on psycho-physiological correlates of slow breathing', *Frontiers in Human Neuroscience*, 12 (2018), article 353.

Module 27

1. Regarding mentalising, see:

Fonagy, P. and Luyten, P., 'A developmental, mentalization-based approach to the understanding and treatment of borderline personality disorder', *Development and Psychopathology*, 21 (2009), pp. 1355–81.

Fonagy, P., Gergely, G., Jurist, E. and Target, M., *Affect Regulation, Mentalization and the Development of the Self* (New York: Other Press, 2005).

Module 29

1. Linehan, M., *Cognitive-Behavioral Treatment of Borderline Personality Disorder* (New York: Guilford Press, 1993).

Module 30

1. Gilbert, P., *Overcoming Depression* (London: Robinson, 2009).

Module 31

1. Much of the material in this section was informed by this excellent book: Notarius, C. and Markman, H., *We Can Work It Out: How to Solve Conflicts, Save Your Marriage, and Strengthen Your Love for Each Other* (New York: Perigee, 1993).

2. Ibid.

3. Gottman, J., *The Relationship Cure: A 5-Step Guide to Strengthening Your Marriage, Family, and Friendships* (New York: Three Rivers Press, 2002).

   Gottman, J., *Why Marriages Succeed or Fail: And How You Can Make Yours Last* (New York: Simon & Schuster, 1995).

Section VII

1. https://overcoming.co.uk/715/resources-to-download

2. Grodin, J., Clark, J.L., Kolts, R. and Lovejoy, T.I., 'Compassion focused therapy for anger: a pilot study of a group intervention for veterans with PTSD', *Journal of Contextual Behavioral Science*, 13 (2019), pp. 27–33.

Module 34

1. The work of Marsha Linehan has elaborated many distress tolerance skills. See, for example: Linehan, M.M., *DBT Skills Training Manual* (New York: Guilford Press, 2014).

Descriptions of many of these skills can be found at this website: https://dbt.tools/distress_tolerance/index.php.

Module 37

1. Daniel Coy's *The Talent Code* (New York: Bantam, 2009) explains the science of how we can maximise the efficiency with which we learn new skills.

Module 38

1. Coy, D., *The Talent Code* (New York: Bantam, 2009).

Appendix B: Reproducible Forms

Daily practice log

Practice	Sun	Mon	Tues	Weds	Thurs	Fri	Sat
Mindful check-in/ three systems check-in							

Practice notes

Day	What was helpful?	What obstacles came up?
Sunday		
Monday		
Tuesday		
Wednesday		
Thursday		
Friday		
Saturday		

Situation/trigger:	
Threat–based thoughts	**Compassionate thoughts**

Trigger situation:

Angry self	Anxious self
My body feels:	My body feels:
What I'm thinking and imagining:	What I'm thinking and imagining:
What my angry self would do:	What my anxious self would do:
What my angry self wants to happen:	What my anxious self wants to happen:

Sad self	Compassionate self
My body feels:	My body feels:
What I'm thinking and imagining:	What I'm thinking and imagining:
What my sad self would do:	What my compassionate self would do:
What my sad self wants to happen:	What my compassionate self wants to happen:

Anger monitoring form

Trigger: _____

_____

_____

What did I feel? _____

_____

_____

What did I think? _____

_____

_____

What did I do? _____

_____

_____

How did the situation turn out? _____

_____

_____

What does my compassionate self have to say to my angry self? _____

_____

_____

What might my compassionate self have done differently? _____

_____

_____

Working compassionately with triggers

Trigger situation: _____

_____

_____

Typical anger response: _____

_____

_____

Imagine facing the trigger as your compassionate self. What would you be attending to?_____

_____

_____

What would your compassionate self understand about what is happening?_____

_____

_____

How would your compassionate self feel? _____

_____

_____

What would your compassionate self care about? What would they be motivated to do? _____

_____

_____

What would your compassionate self do? _____

_____

_____

How do you think it might turn out? _____

_____

_____

Enacting compassionate alternatives

Trigger situation: _____

_____

_____

My response: _____

_____

_____

_____

How did things turn out? _____

_____

_____

What was helpful? What did you do well? _____

_____

_____

Did any obstacles come up? If so, what were they? _____

_____

_____

What would you (as your compassionate self) want to improve on in your next effort? What might help

you with that?_____

_____

_____

_____

_____

Acknowledgements

I'd like to dedicate this book to my wife, Lisa, and my son, Dylan, who have been lovingly beside me during my journey writing this book and beyond. They've had a ringside seat for my own struggles with anger and irritability and have never wavered in their love and support. It means the world.

I also want to thank everyone who made this book possible. First and foremost, I owe a great debt of gratitude to Paul Gilbert, who gave compassion-focused therapy to the world. Much appreciation goes also to all at Little, Brown who contributed to the development and refinement of the book, in particular Andrew McAleer, Amanda Keats and Lynn Brown.

Finally, many thanks to my colleagues at Eastern Washington University and in the international CFT community, whose support formed the fertile soil that has supported my growth.

Index

References to figures appear in *italic* type; those in **bold** type refer to tables.